Technology Transfer
and Public Policy

Technology Transfer and Public Policy

EDITED BY
YONG S. LEE

QUORUM BOOKS
Westport, Connecticut • London

Library of Congress Cataloging-in-Publication Data

Technology transfer and public policy / edited by Yong S. Lee.
　　　p.　cm.
　　Includes bibliographical references and index.
　　ISBN 1–56720–084–2 (alk. paper)
　　1. Technology transfer—Economic aspects—Case studies.
　2. Economic policy—Case studies.　I. Lee, Yong S.
　HC79.T4T4584　1997
　338.9'26—dc21　　　　97–1699

British Library Cataloguing in Publication Data is available.

Library of Congress Catalog Card Number: 97–1699
ISBN: 1–56720–084–2

First published in 1997

Quorum Books, 88 Post Road West, Westport, CT 06881
An imprint of Greenwood Publishing Group, Inc.

Printed in the United States of America

The paper used in this book complies with the
Permanent Paper Standard issued by the National
Information Standards Organization (Z39.48–1984).

10 9 8 7 6 5 4 3 2 1

To Dawn, my wife,
and Shawn, my son,
who help me understand and appreciate
life, art, and science.

Contents

Figures and Tables

Preface

This book is about the collaborative interactions occurring among research universities, federal laboratories, and industry in the United States. Collaborative interactions are a relatively recent phenomenon, legislatively authorized in 1980, and represent a new paradigm of political economy designed to foster knowledge/technology transfer among various sectors of the economy. The central objective of this collaborative regime is to create competitive advantage in the global marketplace.

Social institutions, however, do not change their cultural orientation quickly just because government inaugurates a new policy. Furthermore, public policy is a social experiment that evolves over time through trial and error and, of course, with no guarantee for its continuity. Needless to say, uncertainties abound in this experimentation.

It is of interest to the students of organizations to inquire how these institutions with different missions, objectives, and cultures are adapting to and structurally coupling with one another in the new collaborative environment. Of equal interest to decision makers in government and industry are what incentives are needed for universities, government laboratories, and firms to collaborate with one another, and, realistically, what kinds of conflicts, paradoxes, and dilemmas may be expected with collaborative interactions. Negotiations for research collaboration and intellectual property also are fraught with misperceptions, suspicions, and even outright distrust. It is of practical importance that the sources of these misperceptions are identified clearly. The practitioners who must work in the trenches are interested in what works and what does not, what is important and what is not, what is simple and what is complex.

Owing to a variety of legislative initiatives and funding made available at the national and state levels, the past decade in the United States has seen a growth of experience with government-university-industry collaboration. This book attempts to document part of this experience and highlights the insights that are believed to be of practical value. To that end it contains a rich body of survey research, stories, and policy scenarios. To offer a larger perspective the book also includes the experiences of several other countries and regions, including the United Kingdom, Canada, Germany, France, Japan, South Korea, and West Africa.

This book grew out of the symposium "Technology Transfer and Public Policy: Preparing for the 21st Century," which was held at Iowa State University in the fall of 1993. The symposium, attended by more than 300 participants from universities, government, and industry, discussed and debated the progress and prospects of various technology transfer initiatives that emerged from the wake of competitiveness pressures throughout the 1980s. The competitiveness pressures became intensified with the end of the Cold War. Several papers presented in the symposium were later published in *Policy Studies Journal* in the summer of 1994. The present volume expands on the symposium by incorporating a significant amount of new empirical and case studies. The volume also provides a policy framework that connects various collaborative interactions which are occurring in the national system of innovation.

The book begins with the premise that technological innovation has become a central element in global economic competition, yet no nation or business firm is self-sufficient in scientific and technological resources. Increasingly, technological innovation requires cross-disciplinary, cross-cultural, and even multilateral efforts and an investment of resources that often exceeds the means available to a single firm. This makes it imperative for the market economy to modify the old concept of competition based on a division of labor and to find a new way of collaboration in the midst of competition. This presents many practical difficulties, not insurmountable but requiring unimaginable diplomacy and patience. In the end, however—after trials and errors—patterns emerge that give a sense of order and a measure of predictability. With optimism, this book presents the stories of collaborative interactions and the lessons they impart.

In preparing for this volume I am grateful to Professor Stuart Nagel of the Policy Studies Organization, who encouraged me to expand the 1993 symposium into a comprehensive text for a larger policy discourse. I am also thankful to the authors of the 1993 symposium, who carefully revisited their earlier findings and brought their manuscripts up to date for this publication. Special acknowledgment also goes to Ames Laboratory and the Institute of Physical Research and Technology at Iowa State University, and Pioneer Hi-Bred International, which provided generous funding for the 1993 symposium. The symposium served as a departure for the present volume. I am indebted to the late Professor Don Hadwiger, the former editor of *Policy Studies Journal*, for his invaluable assistance throughout the process of planning for the symposium. The studies presented in the present volume have been supported by many different foundations and government agencies. The contributors to this volume extend gratitude to their funders individually in their respective chapters. Finally, my appreciation goes to my editorial assistant, Jennifer Bryne, who has done all the chores of editorial work with dedication and enthusiasm. The views expressed in this book are those of the authors alone. In the end, however, I take responsibility for any errors.

PART I

Introduction

CHAPTER 1

Technology Transfer and Economic Development: A Framework for Policy Analysis

YONG S. LEE

When adolescents enter the world of adulthood, they find yesterday's worries and games largely irrelevant as they are faced with new life priorities. Similarly, with the end of the Cold War and the rapid advancement into the age of global economy, the nations of the world find it necessary to focus on the nitty-gritty yet complex issues of interdependence, economic growth, and competitiveness that, in the past, were often overshadowed by the larger issues of war and peace. Not surprisingly, they find that the quest for economic growth and competitiveness is a challenge that is far more complicated and uncertain than anything imagined before. The new challenge seems as though it defines a new playing field and a new set of game rules for competition. But above all, the new challenge demands a "shift of mind" in perspective, in Peter Senge's phrase (1990), from local to global, from sequential to parallel, from competition to collaboration, from linearity to nonlinearity, and from order to chaos.

A central narrative in the global economy, upon which this book focuses, is that, as Porter (1990) argues persuasively, economic development and competitiveness are determined not by the abundance of natural resources but by the rate of technological innovation. Moreover, the rate of innovation is determined not only by the amount of research and development (R&D) invested to create technology but also by *the capacity to pool and transfer* the scientific and technological resources that are historically compartmentalized in the arbitrary social and international division of labor (e.g., public versus private, military versus civilian, business versus education, organizations versus organizations, and nation-states versus nations-states).

As technological innovation is becoming increasingly multidisciplinary, multilateral, and costly and while market competition is intensified, industrial firms and nation-states find it no longer possible to be "self-sufficient" in technological innovation. Increasingly, the needed scientific and technological (S&T) resources, they find, are "out there" in other boundaries: other firms, other sectors, and other nations. Rationality, therefore, dictates that they strategically "outsource" these S&T resources. The term "outsourcing" now has entered the new lexicon and become the business equivalent of survival in the global marketplace. Of course, the case for outsourcing cannot be overstated, because no external source can actually substitute for in-house R&D capabilities (Fusfeld, 1994). Yet, the corporate imperative to pool externally available resources engenders a new economic order that nation-states now must address.

But creating the capacity to pool and transfer is no small task. To pool, to transfer, and to create, the old cherished boundaries must be torn down, old habits and assumptions unlearned, new incentives invented, new partnerships forged, and new patterns of interaction established.

During the past decade—actually, well before the collapse of the Cold War— many nations, especially the nations in the European Union and the United States, have taken the first step by experimenting with various collaborative technology transfer alternatives. While it is still too early to make a qualified assessment of these efforts, the experiments begin to shed some valuable insights as to what works and what does not, what is important and what is not, what is simple and what is complex. In the United States, for instance, technology licensing from university to industry was a concept central to the Bayh-Dole Act of 1980. However, experience indicates that the negotiation and management of university-based technologies are far more complicated than generally assumed, making university-industrial collaboration not an easy partnership. A closer look at institutional motivations for collaboration shows that the players, whether they are business firms or universities, are far more idiosyncratic than generally imagined.

The purpose of this book is to document these insights, as we believe they are useful for future policy and management discourse. In this book we present these insights via case studies, survey research, and policy narratives. To maintain a broader policy dialogue we also present studies that document various ways in which different governments have intervened in the market and "picked winners and fixed losers," while attempting to speed up their social rate of innovation. In the main, however, the emphasis is on U.S. experience, and the policy experiments presented in the book focus on interactions between universities and industry and between federal laboratories and industry. Our aim is not to describe the characteristics of the emerging technology transfer structure but rather to peer into what looks like an elusive "black box" in the transfer process: public-private and sectoral interactions.

TECHNOLOGY TRANSFER AND RELATED TERMINOLOGY

Since several ideas are used interchangeably in the discussion of technology transfer, it is useful to list them here and clarify their usage. The first point to be made is that the term "technology transfer," as we use it in this book, is a catch-all phrase that should not be interpreted literally. When legislative debate occurred on the Bayh-Dole and Stevenson-Wydler Technology Innovation Bills, the term "technology transfer" was meant largely to emphasize the ideas of "transformation" and "utilization." Over time, it gathered a broader meaning in policy discourse. Probably, the broadest usage of the phrase now is one that is proffered by the National Science Board (NSB): "Technology transfer can cover a wide spectrum of activities, running the gamut from the exchange of ideas between visiting researchers to contractually structured research collaborations involving the joint use of facilities and equipment" (NSB, 1996, p. 4-18).

In practical terms, what is "transferred" includes a wide range of intellectual properties, including new knowledge and understanding, patents, designs, prototypes, hardware, software, trade secrets, processes, technical skills, and management skills. Yet, a common thread through all is the human factor. When people are trained and transferred (or exchanged), they bring with them the knowledge and know-how that are central to technological innovation. In this connection, as Lederman (1994) argued, technology transfer is very much a "body contact sport." As such, he insisted, conversations, consultations, and coaching become far more important than publishing and circulating papers.

The term "transfer" itself also should be read broadly—although the *American Heritage Dictionary* defines it as "to convey or shift from one person or place to another." Even though this "linear" definition depicts much of what happens in technology licensing, training seminars, and turnkey projects, in practice, technology transfer projects increasingly take the "nonlinear" form, in which different resources from different organizations are pooled together to create new technology. With an emphasis placed on cooperation, Bozeman, Papadakis, and Coker (1995) preferred to substitute the phrase "cooperative technology paradigm" for technology transfer. With the passage of the Small Business Innovation Development Act (1982), the federal government increasingly began to use the phrase "cooperative technology programs" when referring to public-private initiatives for the development and use of technology.

The story of the next-generation Boeing 777, currently under construction, is a splendid example of this type of pooling. Persuaded by the airlines, as the Council on Competitiveness reported (1996), in October 1990 Boeing embarked on the design of a new airplane class, Model 777, and a whole family of aircraft based on the original 777 model to fill the market niche between Model 767 and Model 747. To integrate design and sales strategy Boeing officials, from the very beginning, brought in personnel from British Airways, All Nippon Airways, Japan Airlines, and United Airlines to participate in a full-time, on-site advisory capacity during every step of the 777's design and production. The result was:

Their participation substantially altered the design of the plane. Responding to airlines' call for maximum flexibility to allow for potential changes in consumer demand, Boeing designed the 777 so the airlines could reconfigure the cabin rapidly. The 777's two-engine capability (versus four engines for the 747) made the 777 more fuel-efficient and easier to maintain, thereby reducing the airlines' costs. Similarly, the "service-ready, on time" mandate met airline demands for greater reliability. At the airlines' suggestion, Boeing also introduced a wide range of adjustments, including wider fuselage-to-engine distance, a readjustment in the fuel data unit, and the standardization of many features considered optional on other aircraft. In all, the airlines got Boeing to take action on roughly 1,250 items they identified. (*Council on Competitiveness*, 1996, p. 4)

If the word "transfer" is pushed to its literal meaning, we can say that ideas are conveyed (transferred) from one person or place to another. But this is too generic to be useful. Therefore, until a more agreeable terminology is discovered, in this book we use the term "transfer" interchangeably with "cooperation" and "collaboration"—insofar as the purpose is to "transform" scientific advances to practical applications and "diffuse" their adoption. Thus, unless otherwise defined, the phrase "technology transfer" incorporates the ideas of diffusion, knowledge transfer, know-how transfer, research and development collaboration, technology cooperation, and technology collaboration.

The methods of transfer and collaboration are diverse, and the choice of a particular medium varies depending on the nature of intellectual property rights concerning the particular knowledge, technology, and know-how. If, for example, a particular knowledge (e.g., how to make widgets) is considered a "public good" and remains in the public domain, everyone has equal access—provided that each satisfies some basic qualifications. However, when that particular knowledge acquires a privileged status as "(private) intellectual property," it enjoys legal protection, allowing the knowledge supplier to collect rent in the form of user fees or royalties. The examples are patents and trade secrets, in which case licensing (exclusive or nonexclusive) becomes the main avenue for their transferability. Frequently, especially in recent years, companies (domestic or international) merge or create jointly owned companies for reasons of technological cooperation. Between licensing and merging there is a range of transfer mechanisms: consulting, technical assistance, contract research, colloquia, forums, affiliates, affiliate centers, consortia, partnerships, alliances, research parks, and science towns.

THE R&D ESTABLISHMENT IN THE UNITED STATES

A rationale for developing technology transfer policy is to create an infrastructure in which various components in the national innovation system can be linked and allowed to interact, exchange, and cooperate in pursuit of innovation. Who are the major players in the United States that are to be linked for this purpose? Figure 1.1 depicts the major R&D players at the national level that the federal government wishes to link in pursuit of technology transfer: federal laboratories, research universities, and private firms. In 1996, the U.S. R&D establishment spent approximately $184.3 billion for research and development,

Figure 1.1
The Technology Transfer System in the United States

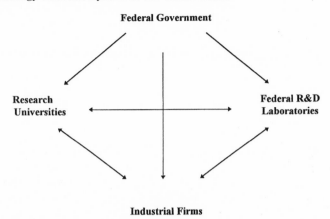

Note: The single-headed arrows indicate the flow of R&D revenues and policy directions, and the double-headed arrows indicate R&D collaboration.

or 2.48 percent of the gross domestic product. This amount represented approximately 44 percent of the R&D investment total of the OECD (Organization for Economic Cooperation and Development) countries. At the sub-national level, the participants are larger in number with a diversity of needs (see Chapter 3 for details). Participants at this level include nonprofit institutions and the 50 states and their municipalities.

In the United States, the federal government is the single largest R&D revenue supplier. In 1995, for example, it provided 35.5 percent ($60.7 billion) of the total national R&D expenditures ($171 billion). Of this, the federal government spent $20.3 billion (33.4%) for industry, $13 billion (21.4%) for universities, $8 billion for FFRDCs (federally funded R&D centers or federal laboratories) (13.2%), $0.9 billion (1.6%) for nonprofit R&D institutions, and $16.7 billion (27.5%) for its own intramural research (NSB, 1996, p. 4-6).

Equally important to the power of its purse, the federal government has authority at its disposal to shape the national technology transfer process. In the reservoir are the authority to reallocate intellectual property rights, provide R&D tax incentives, tighten or relax antitrust laws, and tinker with trade policy. Historically, too, the federal government has directly participated in agricultural and industrial innovation and diffusion. The establishment of land-grant universities, agricultural extension stations, the military industrial base, and the National Aeronautics and Space Administration are the exemplars. More recently, in the 1970s and 1980s, the federal government has taken initiatives to establish Engineering Research Centers under the auspices of the National Science Foundation (NSF) aimed at facilitating close university-industry collaboration. To help the U.S. semiconductor industry regain competitiveness in the global marketplace, the federal government established another partnership with industry, thereby creating the SEMATECH Corporation. Furthermore, in 1988 Congress mandated the NIST (National Institute of Standards and Technology) to establish regional manufacturing technology centers as a way to accelerate technology transfer from universities and federal labs to industry.

The major R&D performers in Figure 1.1 include approximately 200 research-intensive universities, approximately 700 federal laboratories, and American industry. The research-intensive universities, largely a product of the postwar vision expressed in Bush's (1945) *Science—The Endless Frontier*, perform over 95 percent of all university research. In 1995, universities and colleges spent a total of $21.6 billion on R&D and performed approximately 50 percent of all basic research of the nation. The sources of this support included the federal government ($13 billion or 60.2%), internal institutional sources ($3.9 billion or 18.1%), states ($1.6 billion or 7.4%), industry ($1.5 billion or 6.9%), and other charitable organizations ($1.6 billion or 7.4%) (NSB, 1996, Appendix table 5-2).

Universities operate a countless number of in-house research laboratories, institutes, and centers. Since the late 1970s, however, largely in response to the urging of the federal and state governments, they have also established over 1,000 university-industry research centers (UIRCs) aimed at increasing university-industry research collaboration (Cohen, Florida, & Goe, 1994). In addition, many research universities and their associations operate FFRDCs. In 1995, the federal expenditure for these university-operated labs was estimated at $5.3 billion. Note that the federal expenditure for industry-administered FFRDCs in 1995 was about $1.8 billion. Since, mission-wise, these university-operated FFRDCs are separable from universities, Figure 1.1 includes them as part of federal R&D laboratories.

The federal R&D laboratories consist of more than 700 research laboratories with an expenditure of $24.7 billion in 1995, $16.7 billion (67.6%) of which represented intramural research and, as discussed, $8 billion (32.4%) as support for FFRDCs. There are currently 40 FFRDCs, some of which are also designated as "national laboratories," and they are federally owned and funded but operated by universities, industrial firms, or nonprofit institutions. While universities operate nineteen FFRDCs, industrial firms operate six, and nonprofit institutions operate fifteen.

University-operated FFRDCs are prestigious and generally large. Some of the better-known FFRDCs include Argonne National Laboratories, operated by the University of Chicago with an expenditure of $274 million; Brookhaven National Laboratories, by the association of nine northeastern universities with an expenditure of $213 million; Jet Propulsion Lab, by Cal Tech with an expenditure of $741 million; Lincoln Laboratory, by MIT with an expenditure of $292 million; and Lawrence Berkeley, Lawrence Livermore, and Los Alamos National Laboratories, by the University of California with a combined expenditure of $1.51 billion (NSB, 1996, Appendix table 4-26).

Industry operates nine FFRDCs (also called GOCOs [Government-Owned Contractor-Operated labs]), which had an expenditure of $1.8 billion in 1995. Large GOCOs include Oak Ridge National Laboratories, operated by Martin Marietta with an expenditure of $319 million; Sandia National Laboratories, by AT&T with an expenditure of $888 million; and NCI Frederic Cancer R&D Center, with an expenditure of $107 million.

Nonprofit institutions also operate fifteen FFRDCs. The four largest, with expenditures between $100 and $200 million, are Aerospace Corporation, C31 Federal Contract Research Center, National Renewable Energy Research Laboratory, and Pacific Northwest Laboratories. Although FFRDCs are mission-oriented laboratories, they represent a large reservoir of scientific and technological resources, both basic and applied, that are potentially translatable to industrial applications.

A century ago, as Fusfeld (1994) writes, American industry had zero self-sufficiency in industrial research. In 1995, American companies spent an estimated $99.3 billion of their own on research and development and an additional $20.3 billion in federal funds. Furthermore, industry spent $1.8 billion for the FFRDCs they operated. The number of industrial labs in the United States is currently estimated at over 16,000 (Bozeman and Crow, 1990). Large industrial labs are owned by members of the Industrial Research Institute, a trade union that represents 280 large corporations. These corporations perform roughly 70 percent of all industrial research. In addition to these in-house laboratories, American industry is assisted by many independent R&D laboratories. Among the large, well-known independent labs are SRI International, Battelle Memorial Institute, Arthur D. Little Company, and Southwest Research Institute. Another element in the U.S. industrial R&D infrastructure for technological innovation is foreign R&D investment. In 1993, foreign-owned companies in the United States, numbering about 225, spent roughly $14.6 billion for research and development (NSB, 1996, p. 4-46). Public-private consortia also represent another component of the industrial R&D infrastructure. Examples of this type are the SEMATECH Corporation, Microelectronic Research Centers, and NSF-sponsored Engineering Research Centers.

Now that the players in the U.S. R&D establishment have been identified, the next question is: How does the U.S. government attempt to link these players and create a technology transfer regime? The following section addresses this question. The central premise of the technology transfer regime is the assumption that when all the players are linked together and interact, the grand total will be much greater than the arithmetic sum of its parts.

EVOLUTION OF THE U.S. TECHNOLOGY TRANSFER POLICY

Table 1.1 lists the major federal initiatives on technology transfer from 1980 to 1993. Relevant portions of these statutes are included in the appendixes. The

Table 1.1
Federal Technology Transfer Initiatives: 1980–1993

Year	Legislative/Executive Initiatives	Highlights
1980	Bayh-Dole Act (PL 96-517)	Permitted universities, nonprofit firms, & small businesses to own title to inventions from research funded by the federal government so they may license these inventions to industry for commercialization
1980	Stevenson-Wydler Technology Innovation Act (PL 96-480)	Mandated federal labs to take an active role in technical cooperation with industry by establishing at each laboratory an Office of Research and Technology Application (ORTA).
1982	Small Business Innovation Development Act (PL 97-219)	Required federal agencies to provide special funds for small business R&D within the scope of their agency mission.
1984	National Cooperative Research Act (PL 98-462)	Encouraged firms to enter into joint precompetitive R&D ventures without fear of antitrust laws and eliminated the treble damages standard of antitrust laws in litigation arising therefrom.

10

Year	Act	Description
1986	Federal Technology Transfer Act (PL 99-502)	Empowered government-owned government-operated labs (GOGOs) directly to enter into cooperative R&D agreements (CRADA) with firms and established the Federal Laboratory Consortium (FLC) for Technology Transfer.
1987	Executive Orders 12591 and 12618	Further articulated the Federal Technology Transfer Act for administrative purposes.
1988	Omnibus Trade and Competitiveness Act PL 100-418	Designated the National Institute of Science and Technology (NIST) as lead agency to establish and administer Manufacturing Technology Centers (MTC).
1989	National Competitiveness Technology Transfer Act (PL 101-189)	Extended the CRADA authority to all government-owned contractor-operated federal labs (GOCOs).
1993	Defense Authorization Act (PL 103-160)	Directed the Advanced Research Projects Agency (ARPA) to promote dual-use technology via technology reinvestment.

1980 Stevenson-Wydler Technology Innovation Act, enacted into law when it appeared that industrial innovation in the United States was faltering, was the first major legislation that sought to create a framework for building linkages between generators of knowledge (universities and federal laboratories) and users of knowledge (industry and state and local governments) (see Appendix A).

The basic rationale for this "forward-looking" legislation was based on the recognition that technological innovation was central to the process by which an economy grows and renews itself and on the belief that the U.S. economy was slipping in its rate of technological innovation. Despite this recognition, many new scientific discoveries and advances made at universities and government federal laboratories were untapped for industrial innovation, and there was a lack of a national policy concerning technology transfer in the federal government (United States Congress, 1980b).

As a first step, the 96th Congress proposed a multifaceted approach designed to facilitate "cooperation among academia, federal laboratories, labor, and industry, in such forms as technology transfer, personnel exchange, joint research projects, and others" (United States Congress, 1980b). The approach included, among others, (1) the establishment of Centers for Industrial Technology affiliated with universities and other nonprofit institutions; (2) the mandate for federal agencies and their laboratories to transfer federally owned or originated technology to the private sector, for which the act set aside 0.5 percent of the agencies' research budgets; (3) the endowment of a National Technology Medal to be awarded to individuals or companies who deserve special recognition by reason of their outstanding contributions to the promotion of technology; and (4) the exchange of scientific and technological personnel among academia, industry, and federal laboratories.

During the last decade, the Stevenson-Wydler Act has been amended many times. While university-industry collaboration continued to progress satisfactorily, federal laboratories failed to make progress because they were without authority at the laboratory level to enter into cooperative development arrangements with industry. An amendment was made to the Stevenson-Wydler Act in 1986 under the Federal Technology Transfer Act, which allowed federal laboratories (only government-owned government-operated laboratories [GOGOs]) to enter directly into Cooperative Research and Development Agreements (CRADAs) with industrial firms. The Federal Technology Transfer Act also established a Federal Laboratory Consortium for Technology Transfer to function as a networking organization. In 1989, with yet another amendment (the National Competitiveness Technology Transfer Act), the CRADA provision was extended to contractor-operated federal laboratories (GOCOs).

In 1980, in the midst of debate over the Stevenson-Wydler Act, the 96th Congress enacted another major piece of legislation into law, the Bayh-Dole Act, amending the patent and trademark laws (see Appendix B). The act, considered a "Magna Carta" to universities, nonprofit research institutions, and small businesses, reallocated ownership of all patent rights in federally funded research from the federal government to any nonprofit research institution or small-business contractors. For large businesses, the act provided exclusive licenses for specific uses intended for commercialization. The rationale for this legislation was recognition of the fact that "the roots of the 1980 recession [were] in a longer term economic malaise which [arose] out of a failure of American industry to keep pace with the increased productivity of foreign competitors" and that "the slowing of productivity improvement during the past few years [paralleled] the discouraging decline in the rate of investment in plants and equipment" (United States Congress, 1980a). Arguing that the means of improving productivity was inherent in the creation of new technologies, the proponents of the Bayh-Dole Bill were successful in creating a new incentive system for universities, nonprofit institutions, and small businesses. Granting patent rights to their federally funded research made it easier for contractors to expedite the commercialization of research. Dissenters pointed out that the bill violated "a basic provision of the unwritten contract between the citizens of this country and their government; namely, that what the government acquires through the expenditures of its citizens' taxes, the government owns" (United States Congress, 1980a).

The Small Business Innovation Development Act of 1982, which came after years of legislative hearings and debate, applies a strategy somewhat different from that of the Bayh-Dole Act and the Stevenson-Wydler Act. Whereas these two acts apply the idea of "pushing" technology to market, the Small Business Innovation Development Act applies the idea of "market-pull" of technology. The legislation mandates all federal agencies whose research budget exceeds $100 million to establish the so-called Small Business Innovation Research (SBIR) programs and set aside a certain percentage of their research budget, initially 1.25 percent, for SBIR projects. The rationale underlying the SBIR program was that small business is the principal source of significant innovations. Under the SBIR authority, which is in effect until the year 2000, these federal agencies are to solicit research proposals from small business firms and make awards using two specific criteria: to meet each agency's research need and to demonstrate commercial potential. Ultimately, the grantee is expected to bring innovation to market with private sector investment.

In 1984, the 98th Congress turned their attention to the need for "precompetitive" R&D collaboration among firms (an issue related to monopolies and antitrust laws) and enacted the National Cooperative Research Act. The general perception of Congress, as witnessed by many private testimonies, was that the extant federal and state antitrust laws were "unclear" about precompetitive, joint R&D ventures among firms. As a result, the "treble damage standard" of antitrust laws created a practical effect of dissuading firms, rightly or wrongly, from entering into joint R&D ventures. The increasingly competitive environment of the global economy made it necessary for Congress to address this ambiguity. As rationale, the 98th Congress declared:

The international competitiveness of U.S. firms in both mature and emerging industries depends on their ability to remain at the frontiers of technological development. Equally important, the security of the United States vitally depends on the ability of U.S. firms to maintain their technological edge. Research and development is critical to the success of these efforts.

In many industries, however, the research and development necessary to maintain competitiveness has become increasingly costly and risky—indeed, often prohibitively so. In addition, limits on the available pool of skilled scientific and technical personnel may preclude any single company from gathering the talent needed to make an R&D project successful.

In recent years, many of our trading partners have recognized the need for collaborative R&D efforts. Having seen the potential for tremendous economies that could be achieved through such efforts, firms in other countries have formed numerous R&D projects, often with government encouragement. (United States Congress, 1984, p. 3105)

Recognizing that the antitrust laws as they are commonly interpreted (or misinterpreted) constitute a barrier to joint R&D ventures, the National Cooperative Research Act "clarified" the ambiguity by eliminating the treble damage standard of antitrust litigation for "joint R&D ventures" and limiting liability to actual damages and attorneys' fees. To maintain the integrity of antitrust laws, Congress limited the elimination of treble damages "narrowly" to particular "pre-competitive" joint R&D ventures (see Appendix C). The act defined a "joint R&D venture" to mean "theoretical analysis, exploration or experimentation, or the extension of basic scientific knowledge into practical application, including prototype development." A joint R&D venture, that is, R&D collaboration between two or more separate firms, may include, for example, "the establishment of research facilities, the collection and exchange of research information, the conduct of research on a proprietary basis, the prosecution of patent applications, and the granting of licenses."

To maintain the integrity of "competition" under antitrust laws the act explicitly excluded three types of activities: (1) joint production or marketing; (2) exchange of information among competitors relating to costs, sales, profitability, or prices that are not deemed "reasonably required to conduct the research and development that is the object of such program"; and (3) any restriction on other R&D activities, including the sale, licensing or sharing of inventions, that are not developed through the joint R&D ventures. For these exclusion areas and other "gray" zones, however, the act instructs courts to use a "liberal" standard of reasonableness while determining antitrust violations. What this means is that "courts must realistically analyze the competitive effects of any challenged joint R&D program. If a joint R&D program has no anticompetitive effects, or if any such effects are outweighed by its *procompetitive* effects, then it should not be deemed to violate the antitrust laws" (italics added).

In addition to these four pillars of legislation, which have given birth to the collaborative transfer system, the decade has seen a multitude of legislation tinkering with administrative structures pursuant to technology transfer. In the

1988 Omnibus Trade and Competitiveness Act, for example, Congress mandated the newly renamed National Institute of Standards and Technology to build a national infrastructure for manufacturing technology transfer. With "new wine in the old bottle," the NIST was then charged with the responsibility to build and administer regional Manufacturing Technology Centers that would work with industry, state governments, and R&D institutions (federal labs, universities, nonprofit institutions, and state economic development programs). As the Cold War suddenly came to an end, Congress also began to focus on the Department of Defense's Advanced Research Projects Agency to find ways to integrate civil-military technologies (the Defense Authorization Act for FY 1991). With the passage of the FY 1993 Defense Authorization Act, Congress renamed (actually reverted to the original name) the Defense Department's Defense Advanced Research Projects Agency (DARPA) as ARPA by dropping "Defense" and charged the agency with the additional mission of promoting dual-use technology.

The federal government has not been alone in its technology transfer efforts. State interest in economic development has been extensive (Paget, 1990). In recent years, state spending on applied science and technology programs has been rapidly on the increase. In 1988, for example, state spending for research and development reached $1.2 billion, a 62 percent increase over the 1977 total (Carnegie Commission, 1992). And unlike the federal government, state programs strategically focus on the specific goals of technology-driven economic development (Carnegie Commission, 1992). State activities emphasize the development of technology offices, information/networking, technology/research centers, research parks, and incubator programs. Aware of a funding gap in precommercialization research, many states also have moved to create seed/venture capital, precommercialization research grants, and equity/royalty investment programs. They have also begun to implement technical/managerial assistance and training programs for high technology firms (Phelps & Brockman, 1992).

In a nutshell, during the past sixteen years Congress has built a rudimentary structure for the collaborative technology transfer paradigm. The declaration of intent, however, is not the same as policy implementation. Nor can it predict policy outcomes. Policy evolves through trial and error and often nonlinearly. Meanwhile, the policy analyst examines what assumptions are empirically valid and what are not, what expectations are realistic and what are not, what troubles, and what compounds. Our interest in this volume is to bear witness to the dynamics of interaction among the institutions of innovation—first cross-nationally and then within the United States.

AN OVERVIEW OF THE BOOK

As we look at the complex dynamics of technological innovation and transfer, many issues and questions require examination. Chapters 2 through 5 look at technology transfer as a subset of broader science and technology policy and highlight differing strategies among nations. In Chapter 2, Lederman provides comparative data on science and technology (S&T) policies among several leading industrialized countries, including France, Germany, Japan, the United Kingdom, and the United States. In this chapter Lederman examines the strategic roles the governments of these nations have played in directing, coordinating, and financing S&T efforts and the consequences that appear to follow from these approaches. The comparison of S&T strategies among nations leads the author to conclude that, comparatively speaking, the U.S. R&D system and organization are at the pluralistic, less centralized, and more market-oriented end of the spectrum, whereas the French system and organization are at the more centralized, planned, and strategically targeted end of the spectrum. The United Kingdom, the former Federal Republic of Germany, and Japan are somewhere in between, depending on who is looking at what part of the system.

In Chapter 3 Johnson and Teske offer a detailed and critical examination of U.S. science and technology policy. The authors challenge the popular theme, as presented by Lederman, that unlike most other nations that pursue industrial policy, the United States has pursued S&T policy that is pluralistic and largely ad hoc in nature. Based on a broad historical review of U.S. involvement in the market, the authors conclude, "Contrary to perspectives that the United States has always been a laissez-faire, totally market-based economy, the federal government has long been involved with aiding businesses and, more recently, with technology-based industrial policy."

Inasmuch as international technology transfer is recognized as a key element in the nation's economic growth and competitiveness, it is a balancing act. For newly industrialized countries, technology transfer (importation) from advanced nations represents a critical element that helps close the technology gap in a relatively short period of time. If international technology transfer is not managed with caution, however, the host nation may run the risk of inviting foreign dominance in key sectoral areas. On the other hand, the technology-supplier nations, by transferring key technologies to other nations too liberally, may run the risk of giving away valuable resources, thereby creating new and formidable competitors in the global marketplace. How do nations deal with international technology transfer? What strategies do these nations use to import and export key technologies? In Chapter 4, Hahm and Plein offer a case study of South Korea (a nation that in 1996 became a member of the Organization of Economic Cooperation and Development) and, to a limited extent, Taiwan.

When applied strategically to increase the national capacity, as shown in the case of South Korea, technology transfer can be a potent instrument of economic development. A sharp contrast is illustrated by Bingen and Simpson in Chapter 5, which focuses on a less-developed country that has been unsuccessful in making capacity transfer possible—capacity transfer that "assures the broad diffusion of ideas and the craft of agricultural science." The authors provide a detailed and critical analysis of the Mali government, which has attempted without success the transfer of the SG 2000 agricultural extension strategy. The failure of technology transfer in Mali is traced to the top-down bureaucratic implementation of new technology that neither gave due consideration to the traditional indigenous technology nor induced broader citizen participation.

Chapters 6 through 13 are devoted to the U.S. experience of domestic technology transfer. Chapters 6 through 9 provide data and case studies examining the patterns of interaction between universities and industrial firms. Chapters 10 through 14 focus on interaction between federal laboratories and industrial firms.

Since the Stevenson-Wydler Act and the Bayh-Dole Act, research universities in the United States have been expected, and under pressure at times, to generate more public benefits from their research (i.e., contribute to economic development) by working closely with industry on technological innovation. In Chapter 6, Matkin looks at the University of California system as a point of departure and demonstrates how the funding gap extant on campuses drives the research university to collude between two powerful public policy agendas. One agenda is to maintain the university's traditional independence, carrying out its roles of teaching and research untainted by the lures and demands of the marketplace. The other is to become more active in economic development activities, including the development of intellectual property and the establishment of companies in order to exploit university research. UC's story, argues the author, offers parallels with the experiences of other universities and illustrates an emerging pattern in the responses of higher education to the new pressures to become economically relevant.

In Chapter 7, Lee and Gaertner present a large-scale technology commercialization experiment carried out at Iowa State University, initially made possible by support from the U.S. Department of Commerce. Because the funding gap was not an issue because of federal support, ISU has largely been able to avoid the vexing problems of conflict of interest that occurred in the UC system. Instead, the ISU experiment has focused on the dynamics/complexity found in the process of transforming academic research into industrially palatable near-market/generic technologies. The authors show that technology transfer from university to industry is not a linear process; it is a myth that universities transfer their research (patents) out the door to industrial firms. In reality, university transfer is an interactive, iterative process in which firms (users) interact with academic researchers in every step of the innovation process. Furthermore, focused applied research is a protracted innovation process often leading to many more technological spin-offs and inventions that also require additional focused applied research.

Why do some academics engage in technology transfer activities while others do not? In Chapter 8, Rahm provides survey data that distinguish two types of academics, with different characteristics: *university-bound researchers* and *spanning researchers*. Compared to university-bound researchers, according to Rahm, spanning researchers tend to initiate communication with firms personally; and they are more inclined to have informal links to firms, more likely to hold patents, and more likely to come from universities that have in place firm-friendly curricular offerings as well as institutional firm-friendly programs and organizations.

Clearly, in the United States expectation is strong that the research universities play a significant role in the national system of innovation, including close collaboration with industry on technological innovation. While no one really challenges this expectation in principle, serious debate continues over the level at which this collaboration might occur—for example, generic technology versus technology development, and one-to-one interaction between academic scientist and industrial scientist versus institutional interaction through technology licensing. Critics point out the dangers of shifting emphasis in the university from the great utilitarian purposes (e.g., the welfare and betterment of all humankind) to economic development and competitiveness. Others fear that the efforts to foster privatization of research can actually slow down the rate of technological innovation. At this point, one wonders, how do U.S. academics in general view the idea of university-industry collaboration on technological innovation and transfer? What role, if any, do they believe that they should or should not play in university-industry collaborations, and why? In Chapter 9, Lee addresses these questions and provides the results of his survey on university faculty. Not surprisingly, the data show a pluralism of views that characterize the contemporary U.S. academic climate. Support is strong when university-industry collaboration is interpreted as contributing to economic development, but it wanes when transfer implies a privatization of research. Lee finds, the more "public" the purpose of university-industry collaboration, the stronger the support; conversely, the more "proprietary" the nature of transfer, the greater the opposition. Furthermore, to the extent that a general support exists on the ground of economic development, funding pressures appear to play an important role in their consideration.

Turning our attention to federal laboratory–industry interaction, Berman, in Chapter 10, looks at CRADAs (Cooperative Research and Development Agreements) between the two sectors. Emerging from the 1980 Stevenson-Wydler Technology Innovation Act and articulated in the 1986 Federal Technology Transfer Act, CRADAs represent a central piece in the federal technology transfer strategy. A CRADA is a legal agreement between a federal laboratory and a firm to share personnel, equipment, funding, and intellectual property while transforming federally developed research results into commercially applicable technologies. How does the process actually work? Does the strategy work as expected, or does it present difficulties and complications? Who benefits? Addressing these questions, Berman concludes, "While improvements have been made in the CRADA process, negotiations of CRADAs are still often slow and certain legal and organizational barriers remain which impede the use of CRADAs."

In Chapter 11, Bozeman conceptualizes federal laboratory–industry collaboration as a "cooperative technology paradigm." "The intellectual property dictum 'if it belongs to everyone, it belongs to no one' began to take hold,'' Bozeman writes, "as the government labs increasingly moved from a sole focus on public domain to a mandated role as a technology development partner to industry.'' Does the paradigm work? Do the federal labs accept this partnership role as part of their mission? How broadly do federal labs participate in technology transfer activities? Are these activities successful, creating a significant impact? How are perceptions of effectiveness related to various organizational artifacts, including structure, motive, and strategy? Bozeman addresses these questions with a national survey of federal laboratories. While Bozeman finds that technology transfer activity is ubiquitous in government laboratories and that about half the labs view it as an important mission, its effectiveness, as perceived by lab personnel, bears little empirical relationship to lab missions or organizational structures. The important determinants for effectiveness are strategy variables, such as membership in research consortia and person-to-person contact.

Federal technology transfer policy took another turn with the end of the Cold War. A rational response to the end of the Cold War was for the Department of Defense to embark on a program of converging civil-military technologies for dual use. Civil-military integration, in concept, requires a scale-back of the old defense industrial base, in which the Department of Defense would rely on some combination of civilian and defense industrial bases for national security needs. As mentioned earlier, as a signal importance to the dual-use strategy, in 1993, Congress renamed the Defense Advanced Research Projects Agency (DARPA) simply as the Advanced Research Projects Agency (ARPA) by dropping "Defense." Congress also earmarked funds for conversion programs. But in practice, given all the complicated "milspecs" (military specifications) and military standards, is dual use really a workable concept? Where dual use is not practically feasible without also changing the milspecs and other procurement practices—and yet industry is nonetheless forced to implement it—what behavioral consequences are likely to result? In Chapter 12, Brandt offers a critical analysis of dual-use policy with the focus on the defense industrial base. Brandt expects that the contractors encountering difficulties with conversion pressure will seek consolidation, divestitures, mergers, and acquisitions. As a consequence, "the defense industrial base that remains will be smaller, more consolidated, and made up of contractors actively wanting to stay in the defense market.''

In Chapter 13, Roessner and Wise look at national laboratories and universities from an industry perspective. "As technologies grow in complexity," argue the authors, "companies often target their internal research resources on core competencies and utilize outside sources for supporting knowledge or technology.'' What evidence is there that companies do so? Where, if at all, do firms turn when they look for such external assets? Roessner and Wise report the result of their survey of members of the Industrial Research Institute (IRI), approximately 270 large, research-intensive companies. Basing their answers on replies from technology transfer managers in large manufacturing firms, the authors report that larger firms with large R&D budgets tend to ascribe greater significance to external sources than do smaller ones. These firms also rank universities as the most significant external source of knowledge, followed by United States–based firms and then by foreign firms. "Although federal labs have become more visible," the authors write, "they are still relatively unimportant compared to competitors, suppliers, customer firms, and universities as sources of external technology and knowledge."

In conclusion, Chapter 14 provides a summary of major findings presented in this book, including empirical propositions, insights, and caveats.

PART II

Cross-National Case Studies

CHAPTER 2

U.S. Science and Technology Policy in Cross-National Perspective

LEONARD L. LEDERMAN

INTRODUCTION

Technology and science are commonly accepted in the world's leading trading countries as being major contributors to economic and social progress. The purpose of this chapter is to highlight the similarities and differences among four selected countries (France, the Federal Republic of Germany, Japan, and the United Kingdom), the European Union (EU), and the United States. Each country has its own tradition of technology organization and its own historical, political, and economic setting. Each has used different means for determining national technological priorities and strategies and for allocating financial and human resources, with different results. Each of these countries now faces a variety of pressures to modify its system in response to an increasingly competitive and interdependent environment.

The approach used in comparing the civilian technology policies and strategies is that of an objective analyst, who analyzes what countries do rather than what they say and avoids being either spokesman or apologist. Actions taken and decisions implemented, especially in the allocation of resources, are often more revealing of strategies than are formal statements. Practice and actions are more important than preaching and can be used to analyze the policies, priorities, and strategies of countries that have little by way of overt general policy statements as well as those that have formalized national policies and plans.

MAJOR DIFFERENCES IN PRIORITIES AND STRUCTURE

Several important overall differences between the United States and the other four countries should be highlighted before looking at the individual countries.

There has been much discussion, and some literature, attempting to classify the science and technology (S&T) systems in different countries. For present purposes, it may be enough to say that there is general agreement that the United States research and development (R&D) system and organization are at the pluralistic, less centralized, and market-oriented end of the spectrum; the French system and organization are at the more centralized, planned, and strategically targeted end of the spectrum; and the UK, the FRG, and Japan are somewhere in between, depending on who is looking at what part of the system (Lederman, 1987; Martin & Irvine, 1989).

These other countries each achieved a consensus some time ago that the central government has a clear responsibility to support S&T to serve civilian industrial needs. This includes supporting S&T to develop new and improved products, processes, and services, especially in areas of increasing international competition. This proactive policy is due in part to their smaller size; smaller domestic markets; constrained financial, natural, and human resources; high proportion of gross national product (GNP) devoted to exports; and the aftermath of World War II.

In the United States, no such consensus exists; debate continues about such a strategy, with differing views in the industrial, political, and educational communities. Without such a consensus, much of the United States debate centers on organizational changes rather than on achieving a consensus on basic policies, priorities, and mechanisms. There have been proposals to establish a Department of Science and Technology (by the Presidential Commission on Industrial Competitiveness), a Department of Industry and Technology, a Technology Foundation, a National Applied Science Administration, a National Civilian Technology Agency or Department (a civilian DARPA), and others. However, a reasonable case can be made that the absence of a more proactive federal stance with regard to civilian commercial technology is, in itself, a policy decision, especially given the numerous executive and congressional reviews under both Republican and Democratic leadership during the past two decades.

By contrast, each of the other countries has a specific ministry or department in the national government charged with the responsibility of furthering industrial S&T interests. The United States government has no such organization, although the 1988 Omnibus Trade Act gives the Department of Commerce some additional responsibilities in this area; and the technology policy document issued by the Office of Science and Technology Policy late in President George Bush's administration moved part of the way toward a more proactive policy.

On February 22, 1993, President Bill Clinton and Vice President Al Gore issued a 36-page policy document and plan entitled *Technology for America's Economic Growth: A New Direction to Build Economic Strength*. The document sets forth three overall goals:

1. Long-term growth that creates jobs and protects the environment;
2. Making government more efficient and more responsive; and
3. World leadership in basic science, mathematics, and engineering.

The Clinton-Gore document includes the following key points: (1) Develop a national network of manufacturing extension centers to help small and medium-sized businesses gain access to technology. (2) Invest in applied R&D in fields such as advanced manufacturing, aerospace, biotechnology, and advanced materials. (3) Increase partnerships between industry and the national laboratories. (4) Develop a partnership with the American auto industry to enable the development of a "clean car," creating jobs and protecting the environment. (5) Expand the Commerce Department's Advanced Technology Program to provide matching grants for industry-led R&D consortia. (6) Develop a National Information Infrastructure and "information superhighways," including (a) support for the Higher-Performance Computing and Communications Initiative that is developing new technologies for our most powerful computers—supercomputers able to process enormous quantities of information rapidly—and for a national high-speed network (information superhighway) to make this high-performance computing more accessible and (b) development of new applications for high-performance computing and networking in health care, lifelong learning, and manufacturing. (7) Improve the environment for private-sector investment and innovation by (a) making the incremental research and experimentation tax credit permanent, (b) reducing capital gains for long-term investments in small businesses, and (c) reforming antitrust laws to permit joint production ventures. (8) Ensure greater government efficiency and responsiveness by (a) the federal government using technology to cut its costs, improve energy efficiency, and improve the quality and timeliness of service and (b) the government working with industry to develop technologies (software, computer, and communications equipment) that increase the productivity of learning in schools, homes, and workplaces. (9) Enhance the management of U.S. technology policy by (a) high-level leadership and coordination by the vice president, the Office of Science and Technology Policy, and the National Economic Council; (b) developing a true partnership among the federal government and industry, labor, academia, and the states; and (c) regular evaluation of programs, to determine whether they should remain part of the national investment in technology.

In each of the other countries, there is greater emphasis than in the United States on focusing or strategically targeting national S&T efforts on areas believed to be important for future economic development. These areas include electronics, computers, informatics, biotechnology, materials, robotics, and manufacturing technologies. Support in such areas for academic research and education and for industrial R&D and commercial activities is considered strategic, and increasingly government and private resources are being provided. Since each of these countries is targeting many of the same technological areas, overcapacity could result that would make recoupment of public and private investment difficult and could put further strains on international technological competition and trade (Lederman, 1985, 1987; Lederman, Lehming, & Bond, 1986; Martin & Irvine, 1989; Organization for Economic Cooperation and Development, 1988).

Except for the United States and Japan, the higher education of students in these countries is supported by the central government as a social overhead. All qualified students have a right to higher education—often in the field and institution of their choice, if space is available—with low or no tuition costs and often with stipends. In Japan, support is provided in the form of no-interest loans repaid over a period of 13–20 years after graduation, graduate student fellowships, and graduate research awards. It is important to note, however, that a smaller proportion of the college-age population in the European countries participates in higher education than in the United States and Japan. Research and education are less often coupled in the other countries than in the United States and the FRG, with education having more of a pedagogical and less of a research orientation (Lederman, 1985, 1987, 1989; Lederman, Lehming, & Bond, 1986). Relationships between academia and industry have tended to be weaker in the other countries than in the United States. Historic distrust and disinterest have existed, with academia feeling that research of industrial interest is less desirable and industry feeling that academia could contribute little to its needs. Recently, this distrust and disinterest have lessened, and numerous bridges are being built, in part as a result of government policies and incentives (Lederman, 1987, 1989; Lederman, Lehming, & Bond, 1986).

Historically, engineers have been accorded higher status in Japan, the FRG, and France than in the United States or the UK. This is shown in part by higher prestige, proportionally more degrees, and a greater proportion of engineers in top industrial, academic, and government positions (Embassy of France, 1989).

The mobility of faculty members and industrial and government scientists and engineers is relatively low in the other countries as compared to the United States. It is not unusual in these other countries for faculty members and R&D personnel in other sectors to spend all or most of their careers in one organization. Greater effort and central government incentives have been applied recently to encourage more mobility between sectors and movement to strategically important S&T areas in order to improve knowledge, know-how, and technology transfer (Lederman, 1987; Lederman, Lehming, & Bond, 1986; Organization for Economic Cooperation and Development, 1988).

The other countries place much greater emphasis than the United States does on formal international cooperation in S&T, both bilateral and multilateral. A considerably higher proportion of their central government funds supports such cooperation than in the United States. A much higher proportion of their graduate students and postdoctoral researchers do their work in other countries (often in the United States) and significantly greater effort is made to keep up with progress and literature from other countries (Lederman, 1985, 1987; Lederman, Lehming, & Bond, 1986).

In contrast with the United States, the other countries regularly assess and/or evaluate the effectiveness and results of S&T efforts. For example, on December 23, 1985, the French government passed a law that requires the Ministry in charge of S&T "to present a yearly assessment to Parliament of the 'strategic choices' of national science and technology policy, presenting the position of France in international competition in comparison with major foreign countries.'' In the UK, the S&T Assessment Office of the Chief Scientific Advisor was established to help departments, research councils, and the University Grants Committee assess the results of their R&D expenditures. In addition, the Royal Society and the Royal Academy of Engineering in 1986 established the Science and Engineering Policy Unit to provide assessments and advice. In the FRG, the Research and Technology Ministry has a technology assessment group that compares West German S&T with that of other leading countries (Lederman, 1989). In Japan, assessment of S&T progress is a continual part of the consensus mechanisms used to establish goals and objectives. This includes the Prime Minister's S&T Council and the large DELPHI study conducted periodically to assess the views of scientists and engineers from a broad range of government, university, and industrial organizations. The National Institute for S&T Policy is designed, in part, to perform such assessments (Institute for Future Technology, 1988).

SPECIFIC COUNTRY INFORMATION

The sections below provide a brief summary of the central government policies, organization, strategies, and special programs for civilian industrial technology in each of the other nations and the EU.

France operates the most centralized and planned system of these countries. The government provides a higher proportion (51%) of total national S&T funding than in the other countries. The Ministry of Research and Technology is responsible for the coherence of the national S&T policy and for the major part of federal R&D funding. Other important ministries in the field are Telecommunications and Space, Industry, and Higher Education. Public S&T is performed in agencies that carry out government policies and priorities in scientific research, space, atomic energy, technology transfer and innovation, health and medicine, oceans and fisheries, and energy conservation and renewable energy.

A top priority is the promotion, development, and increase in industrial S&T. In the 1990s, government industrial S&T funding is expected to increase by 30 percent, which is a larger increase than other S&T funding objectives. In order to increase the relatively low proportion of R&D financed by industry, the government has introduced a series of direct and indirect incentives. Specific national programs include aeronautics, telecommunications, biotechnology, production technology, electronics, new materials, nuclear and other energy technology, and space (Embassy of France, 1989; Ministere de la Recherche et de la Technologie, 1986, 1988).

The government of the Federal Republic of Germany believes that in a free-market economy the primary responsibility for civilian technology rests with industry and relies heavily on the private sector, which is responsible for the majority of S&T funding (over 60%). Nevertheless, certain areas like Airbus are heavily subsidized. A wide spectrum of industrial technologies benefits from government S&T funding, both directly and through various European programs. Further strengthening of private-sector initiatives was assisted by tax incentives as a part of the 1990 tax reforms, the current venture capital pool, and government procurement.

The Ministry of Science and Technology is the main federal organization, accounting for almost 70 percent of the federal government's support for civilian R&D. About 40 percent of the federal government's R&D expenditures is devoted to the category "promotion of market-oriented technology." Included in this category are nuclear and other energy sources, information processing, electronics, microelectronics, production engineering, materials, supersonic aviation, biotechnology, and ground transportation. The Economics Ministry provides additional funding to promote market-oriented technology development (Bundesministerium fur Forschung und Technologie, 1988; Federal Ministry for Research and Technology, 1988; National Science Foundation, 1986).

Japan's most fundamental S&T strategy mechanism is the setting of national policy through an emerging consensus judgment. The most important formal coordinating body is the Council for Science and Technology in the prime minister's office, composed of ministers, senior educators, industrial managers, scientists, and engineers. Special councils are formed periodically to assess progress in different fields and to recommend priorities. Government agencies, including the Ministry for International Trade and Industry (MITI) and the Science and Technology Agency (STA), operate research institutes that plan and conduct work in close cooperation with industry. STA also performs important coordinating and advisory services in the national government. Each agency acts independently, and STA and MITI employ an array of advisory councils and industry associations to ensure that government-conducted and government-sponsored research will be consonant with private-sector S&T interests.

Noteworthy among STA-supported programs is Exploratory Research for Advanced Technologies. It supports teams from industry, academia, and government that are led by key individuals in programs of interdisciplinary breakthrough R&D. MITI has an elaborate system in support of industrial S&T, carried out in its own laboratories and through active promotion of privately supported research institutes. The focus is on performing nonproprietary R&D in certain product areas (e.g., semiconductors and new synthetics) and focused R&D initiatives. MITI's National Project System focuses R&D in national priority areas. The programs are carried out primarily with industry participation, and costs are shared by industry and government. Industry provides a higher proportion of total national S&T funding (about 70%) in Japan than in any of the other countries. In fact, industry provides 98 percent of the R&D performed in industry, and the government only 2 percent.

The government actively encourages private S&T by a system of financing and tax incentives. Included are favorable interest rates (e.g., from the Japan Development Bank), contracts for commercialization of innovations, capital investments, and conditional, interest-free loans. Tax incentives provide special tax credits for incremental R&D above previous levels, R&D performed by small and medium-size firms, and the cost of depreciable assets for R&D in basic technologies (e.g., new materials, biotechnology, or high-performance robotics). Special programs include information technology, computers, semiconductors, new synthetics, new materials, robotics, energy and resources, the "human frontier," and the Key Technology Centers (Agency of Industrial Science and Technology, 1988; Anderson, 1984; Gamota & Frieman, 1988; Institute for Future Technology, 1988; National Science Foundation, 1988a; National Technical Information Service, 1989).

The UK has no strong central policy or coordinating body for S&T. The Cabinet Chief Scientific Advisor and staff in the Cabinet Office are much like the White House Office of Science and Technology Policy in the United States. The Advisory Council on Science and Technology advises the prime minister and provides a central focus for consideration of S&T priorities and opportunities. The general thrust of government policy in support of civilian technology is to support basic technology and cooperation between and transfers from universities and industry and to provide other assistance. The government has announced its intent to increase civilian R&D and to reduce military R&D.

The Department of Trade and Industry (DTI) is the main government department concerned with industrial applied research and technology, but other organizations also have major functions. DTI's Requirements Board identifies and recommends support of R&D important to industrial needs, as do similar advisory bodies in the other government departments. The LINK program, which cuts across a number of departments, funds up to one-half the cost of developing technologies in areas such as molecular electronics, eukaryotic genetic engineering, nanotechnology, and biotransformations. Other specific programs include manufacturing and information technology (Alvey and its successor, IT88), optoelectronics, advanced materials, biotechnology, aeronautics, microelectronics, and CAD-CAM. The British Technology Group, a quasi-governmental and private investor body, which the UK government is attempting to sell, identifies and promotes innovations with industrial applications and supports some R&D (Cabinet Office, series; Cabinet Office Advisory Council for Applied Research and Development, 1986; Central Office of Information, 1989; "Innovation, Using Technology," 1988; "Research and Development in the United Kingdom in 1986," 1988).

EUROPEAN COOPERATION

To complete this summary, mention should be made of some of the special European cooperative S&T efforts that are growing in scope and size. It should be pointed out that while EU cooperative S&T efforts are notable and expanding, they so far have been relatively small. One observer estimates that "the entire budget of the European Union is less than that of, say, two major ministries in

just one of the 12 member states; and of this, R&D gets only 3.1 percent"
("Science in Europe," 1989).

The largest of the EU programs (about $400 million per year) is the European
Strategic Programme for Information Technologies, focusing on microelectronics, information-processing systems, computer-aided manufacturing systems,
and artificial intelligence. Next in size is the use of Basic Research in Industrial
Technology and the development of advanced materials. A third element of the
EU Framework Programme is designed to facilitate a compatible advanced telecommunications system.

The Framework Programme for 1990–1994 had the following allocations:
Information and Communications Technologies, about $2.665 billion; Industrial
and Materials Technologies, about $1.066 billion; Environment, about $662 million; Life Science, about $889 million; Energy, about $977 million; and Human
Capital and Mobility, about $621 million. The total level of support is about
$6.840 billion over five years.

A number of the European countries are cooperating outside of the EU framework. The most significant effort is the EUREKA program, which extends European basic and precompetitive S&T into areas "closer to the marketing of
technological products" (Commission of the European Communities, 1987,
p. 67). These activities are jointly supported by the West European governments
and industry. One example is the microelectronics cooperative program—the
Joint European Submicron Silicon Initiative—which has attracted considerable
support from the EU countries. EUREKA's total cost from 1985 to 1990 was
about $4 billion, of which about 40 percent came from the French government
and industry (Commission of the European Communities, 1987, 1988; Lederman, 1987; McLoughlin, 1989; "Science in Europe," 1989; "Science and Technology in Europe," 1988).

It should be noted that this chapter focuses on industrial civilian technologies
for the nongovernment marketplace. The EU and the various countries frequently have large nuclear, space, and other technology programs in addition to
those discussed.

DATA ON NATIONAL S&T EFFORTS AND OUTPUTS

One of the best ways of describing and comparing national S&T strategies,
priorities, and results is to examine data on financial and human resources and
outputs. Ideally, we want current and comparable measures of S&T, but comparable data on inputs exist only for R&D, which is somewhat narrower and
does not cover the follow-on technology investments (e.g., engineering design
and manufacturing). (Readers who wish the detailed data, sources, and technical
notes for this section should see National Science Foundation [1991].)

Table 2.1 shows indicators of the science and engineering effort relative to
the size of each country. Total R&D as a percentage of gross national product
(GNP) is similar in magnitude, ranging from 2.0 percent for the UK to 3.0

Table 2.1
Indicators of the Science and Engineering Effort Related to Country Size

Indicator	US	Japan	FRG	France	UK
GNP (billions of constant 1992 dollars)	4118	1446	722	645	681
R&D, 1989	111	46	21	15	13
R&D/GNP ratio	2.7%	3.0%	2.9%	2.3%	2.0%
Nondefense R&D/GNP ratio	1.9%	3.0%	2.8%	1.8%	1.6%
R&D Scientists and Engineers (thousands)	949	442	166	109	101
R&D Scientists and Engineers per 10,000 Labor Force	77	69	54	45	36
Nonacademic Engineers per 10,000 Labor Force	188	187	182	113	137

Note: Data are for a year in the 1987–1989 period, depending upon country and item.

percent for Japan (and 2.7% for the United States). For nondefense R&D as a percentage of GNP, the range is greater, from 1.6 percent for the UK to 2.9 percent for Japan (and 1.9% for the United States). In the United States, 66 percent of government R&D funding is for defense; in contrast, in Japan only 4.8 percent of government R&D funding is for defense (as of 1988).

The United States and Japan have the highest number of R&D scientists and engineers per 10,000 persons in the labor force, 77 and 69 respectively, followed by the FRG, France, and the UK at the low end, with rates varying from 54 down to 36. In absolute size of GNP, R&D funding, and the number of R&D scientists and engineers, the United States is larger than the total of the other countries combined.

Figure 2.1 shows the distribution of R&D expenditures by the source of the funds. The relative contributions of government and industry to R&D funding and performance vary significantly by country, reflecting differences in their industrial structures, government policies, and patterns of government defense-related R&D spending. Japan and the FRG have the largest shares of industrial R&D funding (72% and 65%, respectively); France has the smallest (43%), and

Figure 2.1
Distribution of R&D Expenditures by Source of Funds: 1988

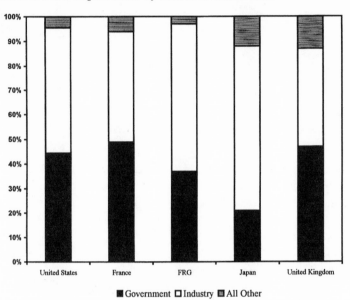

■ Government □ Industry ▤ All Other

the UK and the United States are the next smallest (each at 51%). Conversely, France has the largest share of government R&D funding (51%); the comparable figure for the United States is 47 percent. The UK has a somewhat anomalous distribution of R&D funds by source, receiving 37 percent from government, 51 percent from industry, and 11 percent from other sources. This distribution largely reflects the relatively higher proportion of R&D funds that the UK receives from abroad (Cabinet Office, series). The Clinton administration announced its intention to change the defense-civilian balance from 60–40 percent to 50–50 percent over the next several years.

Comparing output of degrees in the natural sciences and in engineering for each of the countries, the United States grants almost twice as many first university science and engineering degrees as Japan and almost eight times as many as the FRG. In 1988, the United States awarded 197,000 first degrees in natural science and engineering, compared with a total of 182,000 degrees for the other four countries combined. However, in 1988, a much lower share of U.S. university graduates received first degrees in engineering (7%) than in France (26%), Japan (20%), the FRG (14%), or the UK (13%).

Japan, whose population is about half that of the United States, graduated 76,362 engineers in 1988—about the same number as the United States (70,400).

At the doctoral level, the United States graduates more than 2.5 times the number of engineers as does Japan, and more than three times the number in the FRG and the UK. However, over one-half of the engineering doctorates granted in the United States are to foreign citizens, and only about 50 percent of all Ph.D. recipients remain in the United States. In France, almost 60 percent of all doctoral degrees granted are in the natural sciences and engineering, compared to 44 percent in the United States. Almost 17 percent of doctoral degrees in Japan are in engineering, and almost 13 percent in the United States, compared with 17 percent in the UK, less than 8 percent in the FRG, and 4 percent in France.

Figure 2.2 displays the shares of U.S. patents in which inventors from these countries have received the largest number of patents in the 1975–1988 period. Bio-affecting drugs is the patent class in which most FRG, French, and UK inventions are patented in the United States. The largest number of Japanese-origin U.S. patents are in the area of internal combustion engines. Japanese inventors received 37 percent of all U.S. patents in this class, and 50 percent of all U.S. patents in photography. U.S. inventors have large numbers of patents in the stock materials, electronic computers and data processing systems, surgery, measuring and testing equipment, and bio-affecting drugs patent classes. U.S.-held patents in each of these categories represent at least one-half of all such patents.

Figure 2.3 shows what has happened to the U.S. trade balance in high technology and non–high technology manufactured products from 1970 to 1988. High technology is defined here using the Department of Commerce DOC-3 definition, which includes the R&D intensity of supplier intermediate and capital goods industry as well as final products. The United States had a high-technology trade balance of $8.1 billion in 1988 and $2.7 billion in 1987, after experiencing its first deficit in this category in 1986. By comparison, the United States had a trade surplus of $26.7 billion in high-technology products in 1980. High-technology goods accounted for 41 percent of all U.S. exports of manufactured products in 1987, up from 34 percent in both 1980 and 1974.

Data on the U.S. high-technology balance of trade indicates that the United States has done reasonably well in exports of such products, but has imported much more from other countries into the United States (National Science Foundation, 1988b). The data on balance of trade in high technology, by region, indicates that between 1980 and 1987 the U.S. balance with the EU and Canada was positive and growing more positive; in contrast, with Japan and the East Asian newly industrialized countries it was negative and growing more negative (Figure 2.4). In 1988, Japanese products accounted for 35 percent of all U.S. high-technology imports, and the $22 billion U.S. high-technology trade deficit with Japan is almost six times that of 1980. The U.S. high-technology trade balance with Europe and Canada has increased from 1980 to 1988.

Figure 2.5 displays 1965–1987 world export shares of technology-intensive products from 24 reporting countries on exports to and imports from each of nearly 200 partner countries. Technology-intensive products are defined as those for which R&D exceeds 2.36 percent of value added (DOC-2 definition). Japan

Figure 2.2
Shares of U.S. Patent Classes in which Inventors from Selected Countries Have
the Largest Number of Patents: 1975–1988

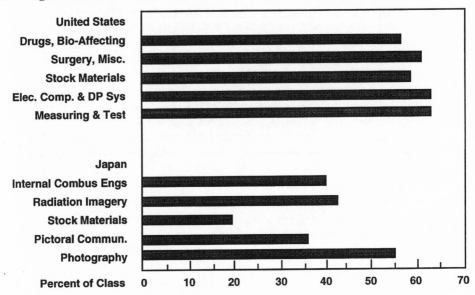

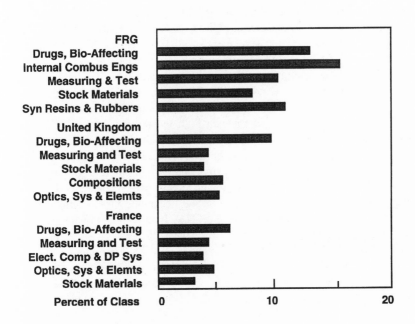

Figure 2.3
U.S. Trade Balance in High-Technology and Non–High-Technology Manufactured Products

(Billions of Dollars)

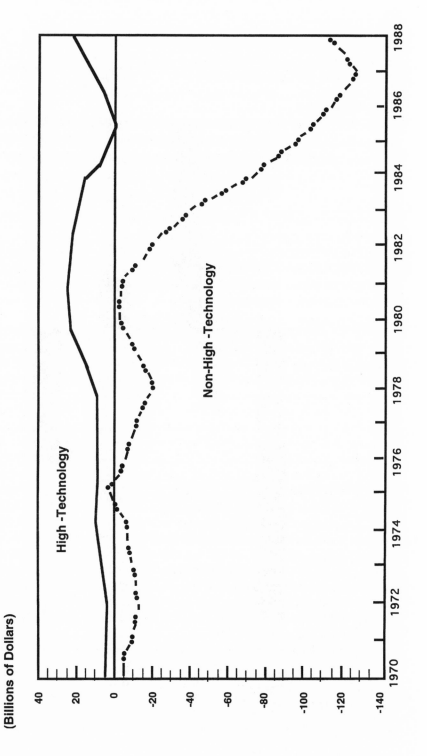

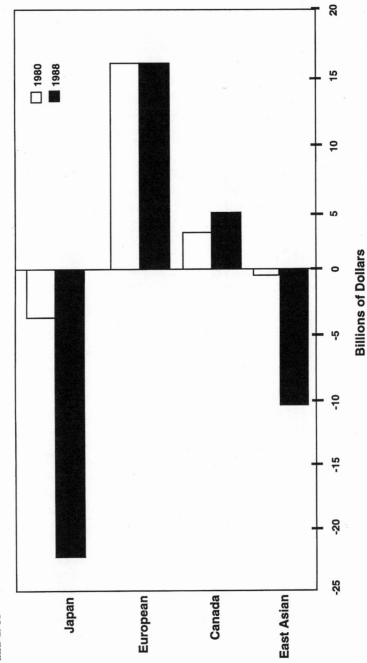

Figure 2.4
U.S. Trade Balance in High-Technology Manufactured Products by Selected Countries and Regions: 1980 and 1988

Figure 2.5
World Export Shares of Technology-Intensive Products: 1965–1987

Percent

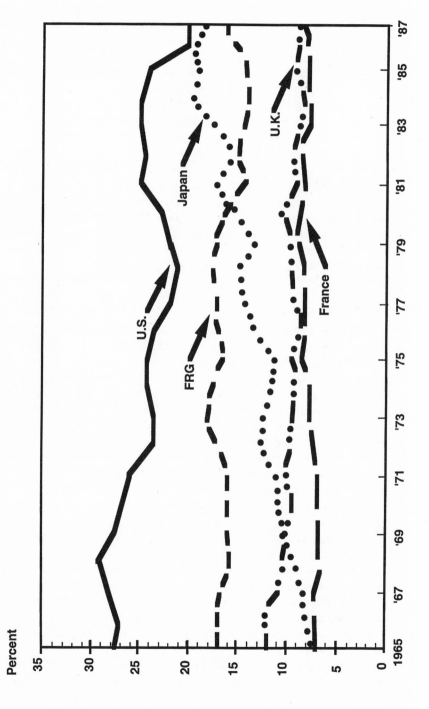

is the only one of these countries that has steadily increased its share of technology-intensive exports from 1965 to 1987; however, Japan has experienced a decline in this percentage recently. The Japanese share of such world exports nearly doubled between 1970 and 1987; in 1987, it was about equal to that of the United States—19%, versus 21%. After recovering from a low of 21% in 1978, the U.S. world export share of technology-intensive products remained stable between 24% and 25% from 1981–1985. However, the U.S. share declined significantly from 1985–1986, dropping from 24% to 21%. This was largely because of increased exports from countries other than the four discussed here.

Figure 2.6 shows world export shares of technology-intensive products by selected product field in 1987 (DOC-2 definition). The United States dominates in aircraft and parts, and leads in office and computing machines. In addition, the United States leads in agricultural chemicals and engines and turbines (not shown in Figure 2.6), as well as equipment. The FRG leads in elastic materials and synthetics, and electrical machinery and equipment. Japan dominates in radio and TV equipment and communications equipment, and also leads in professional and scientific instruments.

OPTIONS

Before concluding, we should ask what options this cross-national comparison suggests. However, before addressing this question, the following cautions should be noted. The elements of a system for supporting and conducting S&T are interrelated with each other and with the broader national context. Individual elements should fit into the overall national context and are not necessarily transferable from one country to another. While one country is looking at the policies and strategies of other countries with a view to what can be learned and possibly applied, the other countries are doing the same. A number of changes have been introduced that could move the countries closer together in their policies and strategies. However, their organization and resource allocations remain very different. Finally, the advantages and disadvantages of optional policies and strategies are not clear. There is little objective assessment information revealing what works better or worse, under what circumstances, and why. The positive and negative consequences of a particular option frequently depend on how it is implemented.

With these cautions in mind, it is useful nonetheless to consider some options in light of changing objectives and needs. This can be useful, even if it serves the purpose of reinforcing commitment to current policies and strategies, with or without some modifications. The following list of questions is offered for consideration, based upon the "Major Differences in Priorities and Structure" discussed earlier.

1. First, and foremost, should the United States move further toward greater government support for nonproprietary S&T of use to industry, especially in

Figure 2.6
World Export Shares of Technology-Intensive Products by Product Field: 1987

Percent

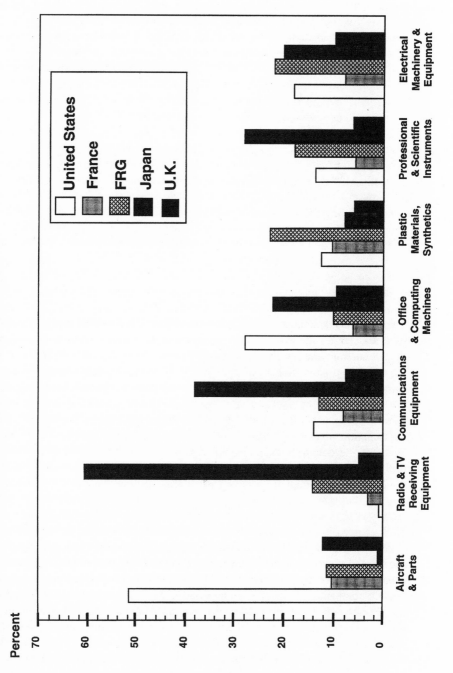

areas of increasing international technological competitiveness? Each of the other countries accepts this as part of the responsibility of the central government and has employed both direct and indirect mechanisms to discharge it. In the United States, no such consensus exists, and debate continues about the advantages and disadvantages of such a strategy, with differences of view in the political, academic, and industrial communities. Proposals by the Clinton administration would move further in this direction. While a consensus seems to be forming that the U.S. government should be more proactive, there are strong differences on how and in what ways to be proactive.

2. Is it desirable to focus graduate support on fields where demand is growing strongly and is greater than supply? For the United States, there is also the question of whether it should shift toward more direct support for graduate students. Most U.S. science and engineering graduate students receiving financial assistance from the federal government are supported as part of project grants to faculty; in contrast, most graduate students in the European countries are supported by low or no tuition costs, fellowships, and often stipends.

3. Should the United States engage in more cooperative activities with other countries, especially where the costs of facilities and equipment are high? As discussed above, each of the other countries allocates proportionately more resources to such cooperative ventures than does the United States. With regard to international cooperation, there are some indications that participation by United States scientists and engineers may not be as high as it was in earlier periods. The advantages and disadvantages of the various forms of cooperation (e.g., bilateral, multilateral, sharing of decisionmaking, and the location of facilities) in particular fields of S&T need to be considered carefully.

4. Should the United States move toward greater centralization or coordination of government S&T activities and needs? This question has been raised frequently in the United States. Of course, centralization is not synonymous with coordination or quality, and no good evidence can be drawn from the experiences of the countries examined to support the greater efficacy of more centralized versus more pluralistic systems. These countries run the gamut in this regard, and several countries have shifted along the spectrum in both directions.

CONCLUSION

This chapter demonstrates that there are many similarities and differences in the S&T policies, strategies, priorities, and practices among these countries— especially differences between the United States and other countries. In analyzing the comparative advantages and disadvantages, it appears as if some of the advantages, when carried to an extreme, can become liabilities. For example, the U.S. reliance on pluralistic, shorter-term project support contributes to greater flexibility, mobility, and market orientation. It also results in less stability, less proportionate investment in infrastructure, and less general support for graduate students than exist in other countries. Such advantages and disadvantages tend to be reversed in most of the other countries, which tend to provide longer-term programmatic support, principally from a single agency or ministry. It is not surprising that some of the more important recent changes appear to be designed to lessen the disadvantages, while maintaining the advantages. In this way, the countries can learn from each other; and they can adopt or adapt that which serves their individual country needs, while seeking to preserve their unique advantages.

NOTE

This chapter is based upon an ongoing assessment of the science and technology policies, priorities, and programs of the United States and other countries. The author gratefully acknowledges the assistance of staff members at NSF and other U.S. government agencies; the science and technology counselors of foreign embassies in Washington, DC; U.S. science and technology counselors overseas; officials in the ministries of science, technology, industry, and education responsible for S&T; staff in the OECD and EU; and individuals in academic and industrial S&T in each of the countries. A special acknowledgment goes to Jennifer Bond, Program Director, Science and Engineering Indicators, Division of Science Resources Studies, NSF. The analysis presented in this chapter is that of the author and should not be interpreted as reflecting the views of NSF, the U.S. government, or the individuals who provided information, review, or comments.

CHAPTER 3

Toward an American Industrial Technology Policy

RENÉE J. JOHNSON AND PAUL TESKE

INTRODUCTION

The question of whether the government should pursue an industrial technology policy is highly controversial in the United States. The American value of encouraging free economic markets seems at odds with an explicit government policy of favoring some industries and technologies over others. ''Picking winners'' and ''fixing losers,'' as industrial policy is often characterized (Graham, 1992), does not fit the American ethos of reliance on free-market competition. Wilson (1990) argues: ''There is widespread agreement that the USA and Britain are much less likely to have coherent industrial policies than Japan and France. This is partly a matter of ideology.''

In the past fifteen years, particularly as Japan and other international competitors have made significant inroads into markets previously dominated by American firms, policymakers have faced increasing pressure to pursue industrial policy programs modeled on those in these competitor nations. Ezra Vogel (1982) and Johnson (1982) argue that much of Japanese economic success can be traced to the industrial policies of Japan's Ministry of International Trade and Industry (MITI). Those opposed to having an American industrial policy have disputed this interpretation and emphasized other factors such as culture and managerial innovation (Hayes & Wheelwright, 1984; Ouchi, 1981; Trezise, 1983). Nonetheless, discussions attributing Japan's success to MITI provided a large push in the American debate about industrial policy.

In this chapter, we address the issue of industrial technology policy. There are many kinds of industrial policies (Graham, 1992; Johnson, 1984; Wilks & Wright, 1987; Wilson, 1990). Lehne (1993) notes that there are two definitions: a broad one that includes everything government does to affect industries and a narrow one that focuses on direct sectoral programs. We argue that America has long had and continues to have an implicit policy in the broad sense and is now moving toward developing an explicit policy in the narrow sense.

The recent emphasis on converting the American industrial base away from defense and toward civilian markets has accelerated this trend but has not been its primary cause. Other nations' catching up with American productivity levels and the consequent international trade implications are the driving force. While U.S. industrial programs do not go nearly as far as many in other nations, in large part because of the continued faith in free markets and reliance on private firms to provide infrastructure services, many of these programs have explicitly borrowed ideas from successful models in other countries as well as historical models from the United States.

In addition to ideological concerns, there are cultural and institutional factors that may tend to subvert wholesale industrial policy in the United States. As Wilson (1990, p. 60) argues: "Those countries which have operated the stronger forms of industrial policy . . . were characterized by weak elected politicians or attenuated party competition and a strong permanent bureaucracy . . . in contrast, in the USA, political competition is considerable, elected politicians are strong, and the permanent bureaucracy is weak. Picking winners and losers would be an impossible politically charged task."

By industrial technology policy, we mean an explicit set of government programs designed to encourage the development of new technologies, new products that use these technologies, and the deployment of technologies into other industrial processes. The latter emphasis is often called technology transfer. What makes some of these new programs explicit, then, is that they inherently involve targeting funding for the specific industries that government officials believe have the potential to be economically competitive in the future. Generally, these programs have focused on manufacturing technologies, which Cohen and Zysman (1987) have argued are far more important, even in a postindustrial economy, than many policymakers recognize. As Graham (1992, p. 22) notes: "Little of the Industrial Policy debate touched upon services, though one day that will surely change."

BEHIND AN AMERICAN INDUSTRIAL TECHNOLOGY POLICY

Graham (1992) provides a comprehensive discussion of the development of the idea and the politics of the debate in the 1980s, when industrial policy was alternately perceived as a right-wing or a left-wing idea. The term "industrial policy" itself has become much discredited in America; in 1984, Lee Iacocca argued: "the first thing we do is get a new name for it . . . never call anything industrial policy" (Graham, 1992).

However, while industrial policy has become more salient as the American position in international trade has faded, informed observers recognize that the issue is not totally new. Issues related to a government-sponsored industrial technology policy go back to the very founding of this nation. While industrial policy adherents have been argued to include both "preservationists," who favor shoring up declining industry, and "modernizers," who advocate modernization and labor-force retraining, the latter group has largely won the battle, as the former group's goals have been discredited (Norton, 1986). Competitiveness is the goal that industrial policy advocates have rallied around, at least since the mid-1980s (Graham, 1992).

In the past, our implicit industrial policy has largely been based on the use of technology in defense. Particularly since World War II, American policy-makers have recognized that the best defense and the least labor-intensive defense needs to employ state-of-the-art technology that can stay at least one step ahead of possible opponents. The federal government, then, has subsidized basic scientific research and development (R&D), as well as procurement of specific military weapons systems that develop and employ advanced technologies. Most of the businesses in the military contracting sphere are tied to government in a very close relationship that has very little to do with competitive economic markets.

Another element of a federal industrial policy has been federal support for research and development (R&D) beyond defense purposes. This has included support for the National Aeronautics and Space Administration (NASA), agri-cultural technologies, new energy sources, health research through the National Institutes of Health, small-business innovation, and basic and applied research in universities or in university/industry consortia through the National Science Foundation (NSF). The federal government has also used its tax policy and antitrust powers to promote elements of industrial policy.

Senator Ernest Hollings, a critical politician supporting industrial technology programs, observed: "We've got an industrial policy, but it's about the sorriest you've ever seen." (Graham, 1992). More than a decade ago, the Urban Institute argued that there were already 265 federal programs targeted to industrial sectors, operated by over 25 agencies and costing over 10 percent of the American gross national product, with loan guarantees the most rapidly growing segment (Levinson, 1982). In the past, however, these programs were not very well coordinated and arguably did not compose a broad-based industrial technology policy.

Furthermore, the federal government is not the only important institutional actor that shapes American policy toward industry. Since the founding of this nation, the states (or at least some states) have been more innovative in most areas of industrial technology policy than the federal government. While the federal government has become much more involved in industrial policy activities since World War II, state activism has certainly exceeded that of the federal government over the past decade. Today, there are literally hundreds of state and local activities that aid business development and expansion.

HISTORICAL FOUNDATIONS OF FEDERAL INDUSTRIAL TECHNOLOGY POLICY

Contrary to perspectives that the United States has always been a laissez-faire, totally market-based economy, the federal government has long been involved with aiding businesses and, more recently, with technology-based industrial policy. Over time, this involvement has taken on several different dimensions.

From the earliest founding of the republic, the federal government has assisted with basic infrastructure development for commerce. The provision of postal services, government land grants, and protection for the construction of canals, roadways, and later railroads are prominent examples (Goodrich, 1960; Hounshell, 1984; Scheiber, 1987). In 1838, Congress made every rail route a mail route to promote this promising new technology. To further develop the nation's transportation infrastructure, the Pacific Railway Act of 1862 gave railroads subsidies of credit and public land to complete the transcontinental link from Omaha to Sacramento. In the area of communications, Congress subsidized Samuel Morse to develop his experimental telegraph line.

In a broader sense, the federal government was prominently involved in promoting commerce through the establishment and protection of property rights (Mowery & Rosenberg, 1989; North, 1990). An entire new school of political economy and law/economics has focused on the important role played by the explication, delineation, and enforcement of property rights and contracts in economic development. Without these activities, private-sector actors might expend valuable resources battling over property rights issues rather than developing new technologies and making transactions.

Another critical element of federal industrial policy since the 1890 Sherman Antitrust Act has been antitrust policies to promote competition (McCraw, 1984). Furthermore, when market structures did not allow competition, starting with the Interstate Commerce Act in 1887, the federal government began to regulate the prices and other activities of private-sector firms.

For more than a century, the federal government has played an important role in supporting basic research and development as well as more applied research and associated technology transfer and training. The justification for a government role in R&D relates to the aspects of knowledge as a public good that will be underprovided by the market as competitors try to "free ride" off one another. Baily and Chakrabarti (1988) argue that the overall return to society from basic R&D is about twice that of the private return to the actual researchers and developers. The federal government's first major endeavor in this area came with the Land-Grant College Act of 1862, which provided land and financial support for the establishment of a university in each state dedicated to agricultural and mechanical studies. The Hatch Experimental Station Act of 1887 took this idea one step further, by providing federal grants to the states for the establishment of agricultural experiment stations and research.

World War I provided the impetus for much more intensive government involvement in private business by shifting the American economy from predominantly agricultural to predominantly industrial. Given the necessity for large-scale war planning and industrial coordination, President Woodrow Wilson established the War Planning Board and temporarily nationalized some infrastructural industries for the war effort.

Next, the Great Depression pushed President Franklin Roosevelt to step up government efforts to aid the private economy. His New Deal programs, including the great "alphabet soup" agencies of the NRA, RFC, WPA, TVA, and the like, set the foundation for a more active government role in peacetime. The federal government became involved with massive infrastructure investments. These programs were essentially designed to put people to work and get businesses moving again via worker-training programs, loans to businesses, and other direct efforts.

World War II also helped to clarify the increasingly critical role of technology in military affairs. From new methods of identification (radar and sonar), communication (microwave radio signals), and weapons of mass destruction (the atomic bomb), war became more technologically sophisticated. The federal government recognized that to develop these technologies thoroughly, it needed federal laboratories filled with the best scientists (Mowery & Rosenberg, 1989).

After World War II, Congress established the National Science Foundation (NSF) to fund basic academic research at universities. The Soviet launching of Sputnik in 1957 challenged the superiority of American research in space and aeronautics. Congress responded by expanding technology education in the 1958 National Defense Education Act, by establishing the Defense Advanced Research Projects Administration (DARPA), and then by establishing NASA, the National Aeronautics and Space Administration.

The next major post–World War II catalyst for federal research efforts came after the oil-supply problems created by the 1973 Arab oil embargo. In 1977, Congress established the Department of Energy, a major role of which was to support research into alternative energy resources and improve the utilization and conservation of existing supplies.

This brief historical sketch outlines a few major efforts of the federal government over time in its important role in laying a legal framework for business expansion, in providing various forms of infrastructure, including intellectual infrastructure, and in funding and developing new technologies, especially in wartime and in the past 50 years. Note that most of these programs are still in effect. More recently, several other programs have been added to this foundation, completing a true industrial technology policy.

TECHNOLOGY POLICY PROGRAM EMPHASES

Ergas (1987) cited two basic kinds of science and technology programs that governments can use to advance industrial policy: "One pushes out the technological frontier and develops leading edge industries, the other concentrates on diffusing technology that has already been developed'' (Baily & Chakrabarti, 1988). With its defense emphasis in the past, the United States has stressed the first approach, but it increasingly is recognizing the need for the second. This broad division can be made more specific. Feller (1992) argues that U.S. state programs can be divided into four main emphases: (1) Research Infrastructure/ Human Capital; (2) Generic/Precompetitive Research; (3) Spin-Off/Product Development; and (4) Technical Assistance/Manufacturing Modernization. The first two emphases are closer to Ergas's notion of "technology push."

In addition to these different programmatic emphases, industrial technology programs might be developed along several other dimensions. As we show below, the combined federal and state American industrial technology programs have elements from virtually all of these categories, truly making them "full-service" policies.

Funding is probably most important. Industrial technology programs can be funded in many ways—completely by government, completely by business (with relaxation of government rules, for example), or through a combination. Most American policies use a combination, with federal funds matching private and, often, state and local funding. Policymakers assume, probably accurately, that requiring some matching efforts from private businesses will mean that the businesses will only utilize programs that they are willing to invest in themselves.

Another defining element of these programs relates to their target business firms. Some industrial policy strategies, including some interpretations of Japanese successes, involve the development of a few large firms with the capacity to be strong global competitors. However, some American policymakers view large firms as able to take care of themselves in terms of locating and adopting (if not actually inventing) technologies and focus more on the needs of smaller and medium-sized firms in deploying existing technologies. Similarly, some R&D programs focus not so much on existing firms of any size but on start-up firms that are just an idea in an entrepreneur's mind.

Given American history, another key element is the target application. Most American advanced technology efforts have been geared first to the military. Flamm (1987) illustrates this development process for the computer. Advanced Research Projects Administration (ARPA) funding of semiconductor research, high-definition television (HDTV), and other emerging technologies suggest that the emphasis on defense applications is still extremely important in federal programs. Typically, the defense applications come first, and civilian spin-offs are developed later. Sometimes the spin-off projects are successful, as in the computer industry; but sometimes they are not, as with nuclear power plants. Another alternative, often referred to as dual-use projects, is to target and develop civilian applications before or at the same time as defense applications.

Another defining element is related to the dominant approach of the specific programs. For example, a program can focus on the development of basic research or on infrastructure. This would make ideas or infrastructure accessible and usable across nearly all business sectors. The National Science Foundation (NSF) and various state programs' higher education research infrastructure and information highway initiatives aim to develop a twenty-first-century information infrastructure that will move data as effectively as the interstate highway system allowed physical goods to move in the latter half of this century. An alternative approach, one closely identified with European-style industrial policy, involves sector-specific programs that focus on a single industry or a single application or on clusters of firms, such as those in traditional heavy manufacturing or in high-technology firms. Historically, American technology policy has avoided this approach, but that is changing. ARPA targets sectors, the National Institute of Standards and Technology's (NIST) Manufacturing Extension Partnership (MEP) targets specific sectors, many different state programs target specific sectors, and the federal laboratories are being asked to target specific sectors.

Another important dimension of these programs is their institutional approach. In the past, some government technology programs were provided in a passive fashion; government officials waited for firms with problems to seek out their assistance or advice. Increasingly, programs are becoming aggressive in selling their services to firms, sometimes "shopping around" new technologies in an outreach function.

Finally, the geographic approach of the program can be important. Some programs, such as agricultural extension programs, are geographically extensive, with many small centers physically close to their clients. This makes it easier for firms to take advantage of the service. The alternative is to have concentrated, often university-based, programs that are physically close to very large pockets of scientific expertise. This allows more contact and interaction among more experts in one place, but not as close physically to widespread firms. To some extent this dimension parallels the issues of basic R&D, likely to be located at a few concentrated university centers, versus technology transfer to widespread firms located in widely dispersed locales.

A full-fledged industrial technology policy is comprehensive and includes a range of programs that cover virtually all of these dimensions. We shall illustrate below that in America we have indeed moved toward a full-service industrial technology policy.

CURRENT FEDERAL PROGRAMS

As befits the largest national economy in the world, Americans spend more on research and development than anyone else. The United States accounts for approximately 44 percent of the industrial world's R&D investment total. The current U.S. R&D expenditure from government, industry and universities totals $171 billion, which represents approximately 2.4 percent of GDP. This percentage is quite similar to that of Japan (2.7%) and Germany (2.5%) (National Science Board [NSB], 1996).

The focus of U.S. R&D, however, is quite different from that of most of these competitor nations. The nondefense R&D/GDP ratios of both Japan (2.69%) and Germany (2.40%) considerably exceeded that of the United States (2.05%) in 1993 and have done so for years (NSB, 1996). However, the United States' growing commitment to nondefense R&D can be observed in the change in its R&D/GDP ratio from 1.77 percent in 1981 to 2.05 percent in 1993 (which represents a constant 1987-dollar expenditure increase from $68.2 billion in 1981 to $105.6 billion in 1993). This shift is indicative of the recent policy focus on economic competitiveness and the need for greater commercialization of research initiatives.

Research and development in the United States is a large category that encompasses a range of activities, from basic scientific research, most often performed in university laboratories, to precommercial research in industrial laboratories, to the final development of a product for market, more likely to be the province of firms closer to their markets. When we examine the breakdown of American R&D, we find, not surprisingly given market incentives, that most of it is toward the more applied end of the spectrum: In 1995, $101.7 billion was spent on development, $39.3 billion on applied R&D, and $29.1 billion on basic research (or 59%, 23%, and 17% of total R&D, respectively) (NSB, 1996). The budgetary emphasis on development research indicates that the United States is indeed committed to science and technology efforts that will increase the likelihood of technology transfer.

With the reduction of Cold War threats in the late 1980s and 1990s, many have argued that the federal government's technological emphasis on defense has been too narrow and that, at a minimum, broader national security concerns ought to include the health and international competitiveness of American industry. The Defense Advanced Research Projects Agency, or DARPA, became the focus of many industrial policy debates in the 1980s. Many argue that this increasingly visible agency, relatively small within the huge Pentagon establishment, should turn more of its attention from high-technology weapons research to civilian applications. While the Department of Defense has had many technological pushes outside of ARPA (DiFilippo, 1990), such as SDI, or "Star Wars" in the 1980s, and also funds basic research through programs like the Office of Naval Research, ARPA has played a critical role in many important technologies since World War II.

Advanced Research Projects Administration

This agency was created in 1958 (originally as ARPA, later changed to DARPA, now again called ARPA) to advance technology. ARPA has no laboratories of its own, and its staff has never exceeded 160 scientists. Yet, with a relatively modest budget (currently about $1.5 billion), ARPA has exerted extraordinary influence over technology development for more than three decades, in part because its funds are employed in a flexible fashion. *Barron's* called ARPA "by far the biggest venture capital fund in the world" ("The Government's Guiding Hand," 1991, p. 36). Former ARPA director Robert Cooper noted: "ARPA probably has the largest unrestricted pot of money in the government or even in industry [for development contracts]. That's where its power lies."

ARPA can be given significant credit for the development of the American computer industry, which remains at the forefront of the world (Flamm, 1987), as well as major advances in artificial intelligence, composite materials, digital gallium arsenide circuits, and even the PC mouse. In telecommunications, former ARPA director Bob Kahn pushed for the development of the technology of "packet switching" and ARPANET in the 1960s, which led to the Defense Data Network. ARPANET also led directly to today's rapidly growing Internet system, which is transforming communications and data networks.

As the debate about its role continued in the 1980s, ARPA played an even more expansive role, by funding up to $100 million per year of Sematech, the Semiconductor Industry Research Consortium (see below), and the National Center for Manufacturing Science, which does research on advanced machine tools, and by providing nearly $30 million for research into high-definition television (HDTV). In 1989, Congress encouraged ARPA to go even further and become a full-fledged venture capital operation by authorizing $25 million for *equity* investments in firms developing promising technologies.

In a 1991 report, the Carnegie Commission on Science, Technology, and Government argued that DARPA should be transformed into a National ARPA, with a single national technological focus, rather than the dual-use focus on military first with civilian spin-offs. Many believe ARPA has done an excellent job given its mandate and should expand that mandate to the civilian sector. Edward David, former Bell Labs executive and science advisor to President Nixon, asserts that "among all the outfits that dispense public money, this one has produced the most." Many believe this is true because ARPA has attracted top specialists and has not been micromanaged by superiors in the Pentagon or in Congress. Some see ARPA as a positive example of smart people in government being able to pick winners successfully—not in every case, but with as much or more success as investors in the market.

President Clinton seems to have taken the Carnegie Commission's recommendation seriously in renaming the agency ARPA and giving it the central managing role of his Technology Reinvestment Project (TRP). The TRP was launched in March of 1993 to "stimulate the transition to a growing, integrated, national industrial capability" (Clinton & Gore, 1993). TRP funds are available for three key areas: technology development, to create new technologies with the potential for commercialization within five years; technology deployment, to disseminate existing technology for near-term commercial and defense products and to support improved use of technologies in small businesses, and manufacturing education and training, to strengthen engineering and workforce capabilities necessary for a competitive industrial base (Clinton & Gore, 1993). With ARPA taking the lead in the coordination and integration of the government's various technology transfer efforts, the United States' industrial technology policy is much more explicit than it has been in the past.

National Aeronautics and Space Administration

The National Aeronautics and Space Administration (NASA) was formed in 1958, after Sputnik, but its precursor, the National Advisory Committee for Aeronautics (NACA), had been established in 1915. While NASA focused mainly on defense and space applications, private-sector commercial considerations soon became important as well. AT&T asked NASA to launch Telstar, the first important communications satellite, which got NASA involved in satellite-launching activities. Advanced technology spurred by NASA led to commercial ventures like COMSAT and INTELSAT in the international communications field. The miniaturization of electronics associated with NASA's space efforts led to commercial applications like long-duration pacemakers, miniature diagnostic transmitters, and other important medical technologies.

After successfully putting humans on the moon and particularly after the 1986 *Challenger* disaster, the central role of NASA has been much less clear. In 1992, to expand NASA's role in technology commercialization, Administrator Dan Goldin established the Office of Advanced Concepts and Technology (OACT) as a flexible, customer-driven organization that will try to stimulate significant commercial applications. OACT provides a point of contact for university and industrial researchers, bridges the gap to commercial applications both in space and on earth, and aids in technology transfer.

National Science Foundation

Congress established the National Science Foundation (NSF) in 1950 to fund basic research in the United States. Most of NSF's funding to universities has been on a programmatic basis, to individual applicants from the various academic disciplines in universities. In the 1960s, however, NSF began to also pursue a larger mission of capacity building at universities, with a more significant role for industry to come later as well.

One of NSF's recent initiatives is the Engineering Research Center program (ERC). The ERC program was established in 1984 with the goal of "developing fundamental knowledge in engineering fields that will enhance international competitiveness of U.S. industry and prepare engineers to contribute through better engineering practice" (General Accounting Office [GAO], 1988, p. 2). Since 1984, 21 NSF-sponsored ERCs have been developed nationwide. NSF announced on May 23, 1996, that it would be investing another $48 million to open four new ERCs at the University of Southern California, the Massachusetts Institute of Technology, the University of Michigan, and the University of Washington. The foci of these centers range from semiconductor manufacturing to particle science and technology to emerging cardiovascular technologies to biotechnology process engineering.

The industrial policy focus of the ERC program is twofold: to influence the coordination of research and development between industry and academia and to create a new generation of engineering students amenable to strong influences from the industrial sector on research, design, and manufacturing.

The central criteria NSF uses in awarding center grants are research quality, contribution to international competitiveness, and engineering education (GAO, 1988, p. 3). One concern NSF has had is whether it should identify and seek proposals in specific research areas considered most important in furthering U.S. economic competitiveness. Beginning with the 1988 program announcement, specific research areas were listed based on NSF's assessment of their economic potential. Such targeting most certainly constitutes industrial policy activity. In fact, the National Research Council (NRC) recommended in 1988 that NSF continue and expand its specification of key technological areas. They argue that "In a program whose ultimate goal is enhancing competitiveness, specifying areas in advance could keep the focus on competitiveness because these areas would be determined by an assessment of what areas potentially have the greatest economic impact" (GAO, 1988, p. 21).

Another of NSF's six foci for funding a proposed ERC site is its capability for and commitment to industrial involvement and technology transfer (GAO, 1988, p. 16). While many of the industries participating in the ERC program contributed to university research before the ERC program was established, industrial sponsors nonetheless believe that interaction between university and industry personnel has increased since their establishment (GAO, 1988, p. 3).

A spin-off of the ERC program has been NSF's Industry/University Cooperative Research Centers (I/UCRCs). These are centers that encourage highly leveraged industry/university cooperation by focusing on fundamental research recommended by their industrial advisory boards. Each center is established to conduct research that is of interest to both industry and the university, with a provision that industry take over full support of the center within five years.

NSF has also been involved with the development of supercomputers with which to provide scholars access to the technology through the National Advanced Scientific Computing Centers. While NSF largely funds basic research, in 1977 it established a Small Business Innovation Research Program on the more applied side, to help smaller business (500 or fewer employees) gain access to technology.

Small Business Administration

Following NSF's lead, the Small Business Administration (SBA) funds an Innovation Research program that supports high-risk business R&D for commercialization. Each of eleven federal agencies with extramural R&D budgets exceeding $100 million are involved. The program involves three phases. In phase one, feasibility studies are funded at up to $100,000. If a proposal reaches phase two, an award of up to $750,000 for development can be made. In the final phase, phase three, either private funding or outside government funding must also be obtained to commercialize the product developed in phases one and two. In 1994, the program funded 4,000 projects totaling more than $700 million. Since 1983, these agencies collectively have awarded more than $3.2 billion to support about 25,000 small-business research projects.

In 1993, the SBA launched a new three-year pilot program called the Small Business Technology Transfer Program (STTR). The STTR Program distributes awards for cooperative research and development conducted jointly by a small business and a nonprofit research institution. Like the Small Business Innovation Research program (SBIR), the STTR also has three phases: a start-up phase, a development phase, and the final phase in which the research is to become commercialized. The final phase does not involve any STTR funding; it is the responsibility of the small business to find a source of funding for commercialization. The SBA makes STTR awards to those projects it deems most qualified, most innovative, and most likely to have market potential. The SBA recognizes its role, as part of the federal government, in helping to select and support certain small business that might enrich economic development and technology transfer initiatives for the future.

National Institute of Standards and Technology

Under a Republican president and without much fanfare, the seeds of a broader civilian-based industrial technology policy were planted in Congress's 1988 Omnibus Trade and Competitiveness Act. This changed the Department of Commerce's Bureau of Standards to the National Institute of Standards and Technology (NIST). It also created the Advanced Technology Program and suggested that NIST play a leading role in guiding industrial productivity. NIST operates laboratories with 2,500 staff scientists and research budgets over $283 million. The bulk of NIST's research projects are oriented toward high technology and setting common standards.

The 1988 law made NIST the center of civilian-based business assistance programs in technology. It led to two programs that form the core of NIST's efforts to date. The first, as mentioned above, is the Advanced Technology Program (ATP), which provides seed funding to companies doing generic technology research aimed at commercial viability. The ATP program started with modest funding of $10 million to fund research "up to the stage where technical uncertainties are sufficiently reduced to permit preliminary assessment of commercial potential, and prior to development of application-specific commercial prototypes. Generic technology means concepts, components or processes, or scientific investigations that potentially could be applied to a broad range of products or processes" (National Institute of Standards & Technology, 1992).

While the ATP program was initially targeted for elimination by the Republican Congress in 1995, President Clinton continually vetoed such legislation, stating that "the bill [H.R. 2076] constitutes a short-sighted assault on the Commerce Department's technology programs that work effectively with business to expand our economy, help Americans compete in the global marketplace and create high-quality jobs" (National Institute of Standards & Technology, 1996). Ultimately, 1996 funding levels for the ATP were set at $221 million, representing significant growth from its 1988 funding levels.

The second program, called the Manufacturing Extension Project (MEP), coordinates regional Manufacturing Extension Centers (MECs), previously called Manufacturing Technology Centers, with the aim to develop technology transfer activities in traditional manufacturing firms. The regional centers are not federal agencies; they are not-for-profit organizations created with local, state, and federal matching funds. Since the MEP program began, 60 regional centers have been created to help manufacturers improve their productivity and competitiveness through the transfer of appropriate modern technology. The program target is the approximately 70 percent of all small and medium-sized manufacturing companies that is reported to be "unable, unwilling, or unprepared to adopt technologies and practices that would enhance their competitiveness" (Manufacturing Technologies Centers Report, 1992). The target is estimated at more than 350,000 American manufacturing firms with fewer than 500 employees. In 1992, NIST set a target for expansion to 30 MECs and 100 new field offices to supplement the MECs. The program has grown more quickly and broadly than even NIST expected. Currently, there are 60 MECs and approximately 250 field offices participating in the MEP program.

Federal R&D Laboratories

The federal government has established 726 of its own laboratories for a wide range of research with total budgets of more than $25 billion. In recent years, these laboratories have been under pressure to become more involved in research related to civilian industrial applications. In 1986, Congress created Cooperative Research and Development Agreements (CRADAs) under the Federal Technology Transfer Act of 1986, to allow flexibility in intellectual property arrangements and in resource sharing by the industry and federal-lab partners. The number of cooperative R&D agreements between the laboratories and industry increased from 17 in FY 1989 to 196 in FY 1992. Still, overall, in 1993 less than 5 percent of the spending on federal laboratories went toward joint projects with the private civilian sector (Andrews, 1993). However, Congress passed the National Technology Transfer and Advancement Act of 1995, which further liberated the ability of industry and the federal laboratories to engage in cooperative research and development, suggesting that CRADAs are likely to expand in the future.

Other Activities

While funding R&D is a major role for government in industrial policy, it is not the only important role. Government choices about procurement have great impact on technology development, not only in defense but also in areas like telecommunications and computers. Another important activity includes training workers to use advanced technology. This comprises funding for technology education at all levels of schooling, specific worker training or retraining programs, and/or import-readjustment retraining programs.

Tax credits are another way the federal government influences expenditures on R&D. To increase private-sector R&D, the Congress provided a tax credit in 1981. Since then, this program has been renewed seven times, most recently on December 31, 1996. Between 1981 and 1994, more than $24 billion was provided to industrial R&D through these indirect tax expenditures (NSB, 1996). However, measurements of the program's success have varied widely. While some contend that it has had only marginal impact on industry's R&D spending, others in technological growth areas report that they substantially rely on the tax credit for innovation (Office of Technology Assessment, 1995).

Since 1890, with the passage of the Sherman Antitrust Act, the federal government antitrust regulations have acted to limit the sharing of research and technology among firms in the same industry as a way to promote competition and to prevent cartels. With competitor nations showing a successful and different model of joint industry/government research, especially the large and threatening 1981 Japanese "Fifth Generation" computer research effort, the federal government began to relax the rules against cooperative R&D with the 1984 National Cooperative Research Act. The antitrust rules related to shared research were relaxed and placed on a "rule of reason" basis. The Reagan Administration, despite misgivings about industrial policy, pushed for the establishment of Sematech in 1987. The goal was "to improve the equipment, materials, and techniques involved in the manufacturing process, as opposed to improving the design of semiconductor devices themselves" (Smith, 1990). After seven years and nearly $1.4 billion in expenditures (including $100 million annually from ARPA and funding from private industry), Sematech has helped the U.S. market share of the $10 billion world market grow from 37 percent to 46 percent ("Uncle Sam's Helping Hand," 1994; Hafner, 1993). Sematech has become a success story to many advocates of more active government involvement in technology development.

Summary

While the dollars involved in some of these programs are not large and while some expect private industry or the states to make the programs sustainable in the long run, the funds are growing, and many elements of a federal industrial technology policy are already in place. In examining specific programs, history is clear that exogenous events such as military or economic competition have very often stimulated the federal response. It is also clear that these programs are not just temporary transitions in the defense conversion area. Many were started well before the breakdown of the Soviet Union. As global economic competition becomes intensified, federal programs will likely continue and expand. Policymakers seem to be more comfortable with these approaches. As David Vogel (1989) notes: "What is significant about these initiatives [Sematech and other efforts] is not that they occurred. . . . It is rather that they evoked virtually no political opposition. Thanks in part to Japan's MITI, fifteen years after Congress had refused to appropriate funds to construct a supersonic transport, the American electorate appeared to have shed much of its hostility toward government support of high technology."

CLINTON'S PROPOSED TECHNOLOGY PLAN

While he does not use the term, for the political reasons noted above, President Clinton is far more interested than were his Republican predecessors in developing an industrial technology policy. Despite the fact that his ultimate policies get reshaped by Congress, his administration has emphasized risk sharing with private firms and working with industry consortia rather than individual firms.

The Clinton plans have been influenced greatly by four recent reports on technology and government policy: the 1991 report of the Council on Competitiveness, *Gaining New Ground: Technology Policies for America's Future*, which examined nine U.S. industrial sectors and argued for a greater federal government role in R&D, a greater role for federal laboratories in technology transfer, and more cooperation among firms; the 1992 Competitiveness Policy Council *First Annual Report to the President and Congress: Building a Competitive America*, which argued for federal government attention to technology issues as well as savings and investment, education and training, and trade policy; the 1992 National Academy of Sciences report *The Government Role in Civilian Technology: Building a New Alliance*, which called for a $5 billion Civilian Technology Corporation, shielded from political micromanagement, that would support precommercial R&D and make commercial applications develop more rapidly; and the 1994 report *Science in the National Interest*, the first presidential statement on science since 1979, which argued that long-term investments in basic science such as mathematics, physics, chemistry, and biology provide the seeds for important advances in engineering, technology, and medicine that will keep the U.S. economy competitive in the future and ultimately provide national security.

Building on some of these ideas, President Clinton presented his initiative, called *Technology for America's Economic Growth: A New Direction to Build Economic Strength* (Clinton & Gore, 1993). The specific elements of the initiative most relevant to technology transfer include investment in a national information infrastructure, accelerated investment in advanced manufacturing technologies, and improving the technology available for education and training. Vice President Gore has been given the main responsibility for implementing the programs in the initiative, along with the Federal Coordinating Council for Science, Engineering, and Technology (FCCSET) and the Office of Science and Technology Policy.

President Clinton faced opposition to these programs from the Congress that was elected in 1994. Congress's focus on research and development is more traditional in that they support R&D funding for defense-related projects and would like to decrease funding for nondefense R&D. In the spring of 1995, Republicans proposed to eliminate the Department of Commerce and, with it, NIST and the ATP. However, the Commerce Department managed to survive because of the popularity of many of its programs and strong executive support. President Clinton requested $835.5 million for the department's Technology Administration for fiscal year 1997.

One clear emphasis of the Clinton program is to shift government's role in research and development away from defense and more toward the civilian sector. Indicative of this shift is the decrease in the percentage of federal R&D funding going to national defense from 59 percent in 1992 to 53 percent in 1996 (NSB, 1996). Another characteristic of this shift is the continued easing of restrictions on joint R&D efforts between the public and private sector as demonstrated in the National Department of Defense Authorization Acts for 1993, 1994, and 1995 and the passage of the National Technology Transfer and Advancement Act of 1995. Each of these acts streamlined procedures for technology transfer to small civilian businesses and extended the potential uses of CRADAs. The number of active CRADAs between federal laboratories and private industry increased from 108 in 1987 to approximately 975 in 1991 (NSB, 1996).

As the Clinton plan notes, the federal government is not the only public-sector institution active in industrial technology policy. The American economy, after all, is the sum of the fifty state economies. And most of the states have long been active in economic development and are increasingly shifting their emphasis to industrial technology policy. Given the intense competition between the states for jobs, they have strong incentives to play in this game.

STATE INDUSTRIAL TECHNOLOGY PROGRAMS

While the current array of federal programs is very important to business development, states have also played an important role historically. In recent years, state efforts have often been more aggressive than those at the federal level.

Historically, the states were critical players in the provision of infrastructure (canals and roadways) and other early economic development efforts (Hansen, 1990; Scheiber, 1987). After World War II, many state economic development policies, particularly in the Southeast, took on elements of "smokestack chasing." Low taxes, cheap labor, areas with weak unions, few environmental protection laws, and firm-specific deals were offered to get manufacturing firms to move their plants from the North to the South. While these programs did help boost the economies of some southern states, for the nation as a whole they were essentially zero-sum. Eisinger (1988) has documented how some states shifted their industrial policy strategies in the late 1970s and 1980s from smokestack chasing to developing new firms—that is, from supply-based to demand-based programs. These states moved toward an industrial technology policy, with an emphasis on nurturing new small businesses. All 50 states have adopted initiatives to support and facilitate public-private cooperation to develop and apply new technologies. States spent a total of $385 million on federal/state cooperative technology programs in 1994, 22 percent more than in the previous year (Coburn, 1995).

State Cases

Several states have been particularly active in implementing technology-based economic development programs (Feller, 1992; Fosler, 1988; Holusha, 1993b; Osborne, 1988; Schmandt & Wilson, 1987; Shapira, 1990). Feller (1992) argues that there are basically four models that state programs offer: (1) research infrastructure/human capital programs, perhaps best exemplified by the Advanced Technology Programs in Texas, as well as university-based initiatives in Massachusetts and Florida; (2) generic/precompetitive research, best illustrated by New Jersey's Advanced Technology Centers, as well programs in Ohio and New York; (3) spin-off/product development, in which Pennsylvania's Ben Franklin Partnership has been most active, and (4) technical assistance/manufacturing modernization, in which Michigan, Georgia, Ohio, and Pennsylvania have been most active.

Related to the fourth category, according to the National Governors Association, twelve states currently provide services from field representatives who, like the agricultural extension agents, call on manufacturing firms to offer assistance. These states include Pennsylvania, Georgia, Indiana, Iowa, Maryland, New Jersey, New York, North Carolina, Ohio, South Carolina, Tennessee, and Virginia (Holusha, 1993a). Most of the extension services in the dozen or so states that have them do not explicitly target certain industrial sectors, although concentrations of firms in different areas makes for implicit targeting of efforts (Shapira, 1990).

Overall, the states offer a wide variety of different models of technology development. With time and experience, there has been some convergence; several states have centers for advanced technology at major universities, some small outreach programs, and some incubators to spin off and assist the development of new businesses and products. Many of the same "critical technologies," such as biotechnology, fiber optics, advanced materials, and telematics, are all being researched in many of these states. The state programs are also increasing active liaisons to federal small-business and NIST programs, helping their businesses apply for grants and sometimes helping combine them into joint venture applications. States may be learning from each other that a wide variety of programs aimed at different points in the research and development and production cycles are useful.

CONCLUSIONS

The United States is moving toward a comprehensive industrial technology policy to position its key industries relative to international competitors. "Competitiveness" rather than "industrial policy" has become the more accepted term in political discourse. Some of the recent programs emphasize defense conversion as a technology strategy, but the transition from the Cold War emphasis is not driving the trend, although it has helped accelerate it. Because the term "industrial policy" has become laden with such negative connotations relative to the American myth of a free-market approach to technology development and technology transfer, policymakers often underplay the extent to which federal and state programs are growing in funding and in impact.

In the past, federal activity was largely uncoordinated and did not have civilian applications as a major goal. Under the Clinton administration, programs are more centrally coordinated in the White House and NIST plays a critical role in coordinating agency efforts. Defense is no longer the primary emphasis of American technology policy.

There are already a considerable number of linkages between the technology programs in the most innovative states and the current federal programs. As a former governor, Clinton recognizes the important role the states can play, and his initiative is geared to working with the states, for example, in the Manufacturing Extension Partnership program. Pragmatically, he seems to realize that there are not enough resources to build federal programs from scratch without help from the states, but he also seems to want to work with the states in these areas. Lewis Branscomb of Harvard (1992) argues: "Federal-state collaboration with long-term budget commitments can help stabilize the budget rollercoaster that most state manufacturing programs experience."

While the states have sometimes acted as innovative experimental models, they are concerned only with their own competitive advantage versus other states and nations, and not with American competitiveness more generally. Looking across the states, there is some duplication arising in research and in other technology programs. For example, Sternberg (1992) argues that more than twenty collaborative university centers for research into photonics were established in the United States between 1980 and 1991. As the 1992 Annual Report of NIST's Visiting Committee on Advanced Technology notes: "Currently there are many state and local competitiveness initiatives and programs that together constitute a substantial effort, but coordination of these activities is lacking."

As the federal government moves toward establishing a national industrial technology policy, coordination will become more critical. Indeed, coordination of a growing number of individual programs aimed at small businesses, specific technologies, specific industrial sectors, labor force retraining, and infrastructure development may actually come to define the extent to which America develops an explicit industrial technology policy.

CHAPTER 4

Technology Transfer Strategies and Economic Development in South Korea

SUNG DEUK HAHM AND CHRISTOPHER PLEIN

INTRODUCTION

The emergence of a global economy has been signaled by many in circles of policymaking and study (Graham, 1992; Krugman, 1994; Young, 1988). A common theme running through such discussion is that in order to be an effective player on the world stage, nation-states require a thorough knowledge of policy options at home and policy actions abroad. In this regard, policy issues relating to technology transfer are increasingly cast in the context of state management of trade and technology development for international competitiveness.

The role of the state in managing international technology transfer presents a set of important questions for development and exploration. Chief among these are (1) What sort of "policy tools" are available for use? (2) What sort of environmental constraints do other states and the nature of technology place on the implementation of these policy tools? These questions can begin to be addressed through the study of the experiences of specific states. This study evaluates the Korean experience in technology transfer from 1962 through 1992. We explore distribution patterns of technology transfer in key industrial sectors and evaluate the role of Korean government policy in managing that distribution. We give particular attention to two policy tools: (1) direct investment policy and (2) technology licensing policy. We consider the Korean experience in the context of two major foreign players in its economy—the United States and Japan—and we discuss the limits of state policy discretion imposed by the character of technology and the actions of foreign actors. We also briefly explore the Korean experience in the context of other newly industrialized countries' experiences. We close with a brief summary and offer some exploratory thoughts on the implications of Korean technology transfer strategies for other newly industrialized countries.

TECHNOLOGY TRANSFER CONCERNS IN NEWLY INDUSTRIALIZED COUNTRIES

Technology transfer is recognized as a major determinant in the fortunes of newly industrialized countries to foster economic development. There is also a growing realization that technology transfer also is an important component of the economic fortunes of those countries that export it. Regardless of export or import objectives, technology transfer is shaped in large part by associated policy strategies. For a newly industrialized state, fostering technology transfer is a balancing act. Technology importation can help industries accumulate technology in a short period of time; but, by the same measure, those industries can expose themselves to foreign dominance in key industrial sectors. Technology transfer is also a balancing act for those states seeking to share technology with newly industrialized states. Transfer strategies can encourage the development of foreign markets, integrated development processes, and trade alliances. By transferring technology, however, the state runs the risk of giving away valuable resources, creating new competitors, and losing position in the global market. Indeed, such transfer of technology from newly industrialized countries (NICs) to developing countries poses greater risks than that of technology transfer from technologically advanced countries to NICs. This is because technological gaps between NICs and developing countries are much smaller. Given such opportunities and dangers, the path that the state seeks to pursue through its policy becomes critical to the outcomes of technology transfer. Whether a state can pursue a consistent strategy over time or make corrections or anticipate adjustments are substantial questions facing those seeking both to export and to import technologies.

The idea that a developing state can consciously direct the course of technology development runs counter to the arguments of those who hold that economic development is more dependent on technological trends and the decisions of actors from abroad (for a discussion, see Lall, 1993). The dependence approach holds that technology transfer, particularly foreign investments, can lead to rapid economic growth in developing nations. But it also warns of the dangers of dominance, especially as manifested in foreign control of domestic markets, the absence of domestic production ownership, and exploitation of host country resources (see O'Donnell, 1973; Evans, 1979). This approach assumes the dominant influence of the "donor" country or firms over the developing "host" country.

Recent research on the developmental experiences of newly industrialized economies suggests that this assumption may not hold true (see, for example, Chou, 1988; Mardon, 1990, Lall, 1993). For example, Chou (1988) and Mardon (1990) argue that a host country's policy toward technology transfer is more important than the characteristics of technology from donors. Indeed, foreign investments in Korea have been minimal and have not been the primary source of economic growth. Additionally, domestic markets have not been strongly dominated by foreign firms or multinational corporations. Numerous scholars have identified Korea as a clear illustration of the independence of the state to set its course of development (see Amsden, 1989; Deyo, 1987; Haggard & Moon, 1990; Hahm & Plein, 1994; Mardon, 1990; Wade, 1992). But as recent events suggest, the success of the state in setting the course of development through policy tools aimed at manipulating technology and monetary inflows may not be so clear-cut.

The middle ground here, an argument that is developed in the following sections, is that the ability of state policy to control the direction of technology transfer will vary over time. Important variables in the ability to influence the type of technology transfer include (1) the capacity of the state to exercise control over domestic markets, (2) the capacity of a state to absorb new technologies, (3) the prerogatives of the state to obtain certain technologies, and (4) the nature of the technology itself.

Without the ability to exert influence over domestic markets and capital, the capacity of the state to guide technology acquisition will be limited. Thus, in those states with relatively strong governmental institutions, such as Korea, there have been coordinated policy initiatives aimed at technology transfer. States need to be strong to carry out this function because they must be able to exercise the power to allocate resources to preferred sectors in order to achieve technology gains. This ability to pick "winners and losers" in industrial policy decisions is seen by many as the hallmark of the strong state (see Amsden, 1989; Bernard & Ravenhill, 1995). In this regard, Korea is a standout example, as the government has sustained efforts to acquire technology since the 1960s (see Hahm & Plein, 1995a). In those states where governmental institutions are rather weak, we would expect the ability to influence technology transfer to be minimal. Yet, the relative power of the state vis-à-vis capital and markets is not static, a point that is perhaps too often overlooked by developmental state theorists (see Hahm & Plein, 1995b). Governments of those states in advanced stages of development face challenges in controlling markets that may be outstripping state influence. Thus, in the case of Korea, the maturation of large firms in the marketplace means that they can choose their own courses of development somewhat independent of the state. This crisis of the postdevelopmental state is manifested in a sense of uncertainty as to what the role and content of future government policy should be. In the face of the tides of social and economic liberalization, this is precisely the challenge that Korea is now facing. It may well also be the fate of other NICs in the near future.

The capacity of the state to absorb new technologies is a function of many variables. In one sense, the original factor endowments of a country will play a role in the capacity to absorb new foreign technologies. Thus, natural resource bases will help to influence the type and scope of foreign technology transfers.

Existing transportation and infrastructure networks and social institutions will influence the pace of absorption. Human resources, in terms of labor pools and markets, will also have a role to play in influencing technology adoption (see World Bank, 1993). But the state also has the capacity to influence absorption prospects through various policy initiatives. Thus, for example, the ability of the state to encourage, if not force, high savings rates among the populace will increase the available pool of capital to invest in domestic infrastructure in order to attract foreign technology. This was certainly the case of postwar development in Japan and has been a factor in the economic development successes of Korea and Taiwan. Or, the state can make investments in human capital through education, job training, and the development of research and development centers, as has been the case of Korea (Hahm & Plein, 1995a).

A third factor to consider is the prerogative of the state to acquire certain types of technology. Traditionally, technology has been seen as a means to the particular ends of industrial policy. In strong-state economies, such as Korea, industrial policy is targeted at priority sectors for development. Thus, to develop basic industry, such as textiles and apparel, it becomes important to acquire technology "off the shelf." This may take the simple form of acquiring from foreign suppliers new equipment that has the desired technology "embedded" in it (World Bank, 1993, p. 318). Or, as we shall see, the wholesale acquisition of equipment and processes associated with a technology may be achieved by encouraging foreign direct investment. Recently, technological capacity has begun to be seen as an end in itself in states such as Korea (Hahm & Plein, 1995a). Technology licensing arrangements and the establishment of research and development capabilities are two methods of increasing technological capacity (World Bank, 1993, pp. 318–320).

But what the state wants and what it can have may be two different things. This is a fourth factor that we need to bear in mind in exploring technology transfer to NICs. In one instance, a state may acquire a new technology only to learn that it is not applicable to domestic needs, capacities, or uses. A more vexing problem, perhaps, for the state is the situation where acquisition of new technology is denied on the terms preferred by the state. This is becoming an issue for NICs encountering difficulties in obtaining "knowledge intensive" technologies. The World Bank (1993, p. 319) observes that "Particularly in R&D-intensive sectors such as chemicals, machinery, and electronics, firms are increasingly unwilling to license technology; they believe royalties provide an inadequate return for actions that may impair their own long-term competitiveness." As we will see later, Korea has reacted to this situation by signaling an increasing willingness to allow foreign direct-investment arrangements to acquire these technologies. As we argue, this represents, to a degree, a reversal in Korean policy practices.

The experiences of NICs, especially in Asia and particularly with Korea, illustrate that the state has the ability to influence the flow and nature of technology transferred to it from foreign sources. Korea has been able to influence the course of technology transfer through a mix of policy instruments that have been applied to realize economic, industrial, and technology policy aims. In particular, the regulation of foreign direct investment and technology licensing have been particularly useful in shaping the flow of technology from more developed countries, such as Japan and the United States. As we will discuss, the Korean experience reveals that patterns of technology transfer cannot be explained simply by concentrating on what has been transferred from donor countries, such as the United States and Japan. Rather, attention should be focused on the host country and on the policy strategies that appear to shape its patterns of technology transfer. In short, the question turns from the economics of *what* to the policies of *how* technology transfer is accomplished.

THE KOREAN EXPERIENCE IN TECHNOLOGY TRANSFER

A brief historical review of the Korean economy helps put Korean industrial development into perspective. A small and overpopulated country, Korea is poorly endowed with natural resources. However, one well-recognized attribute is its relatively skilled and devoted workforce. Despite extraordinary constraints, Korean economic planners have surmounted many challenges. For the problem of a small domestic market, they pursued international export markets; for lack of product technology, they borrowed foreign technologies; and for the problem of natural resource shortages, they imported with the foreign exchange they earned from industrial exports (Collins, 1990; Westphal, 1990). Since the early 1960s, Korea has been transforming itself from a predominantly agricultural economy to an industrialized economy (for a detailed discussion of industrial transformation, see Choi, 1986).

The Korean experience reveals the links between industrial planning and technology transfer strategy (Chin, 1986; Choi, 1986). Through the use of five-year economic development plans, Korea has sought to shape foreign investment and technology transfer patterns. The first and second Five-Year Economic and Social Development Plans (FYESDPs), from 1962 through 1971, marked the take-off stage for industrialization in Korea. As Korea was almost completely dependent on developed nations in the area of production facilities and technologies, primary emphasis was placed on the importation of technologies for application in industrial production processes. Priority was given to fostering strategic import substitution industries, such as energy and building materials, while focusing on the development of export-oriented light industries.

In the 1970s and early 1980s, Korea entered its growth stage. With the third and fourth FYESDPs (1972–1981), emphasis was placed on building an industrial foundation by fostering a select group of industries, including machinery, metals, chemicals, shipbuilding, and electronics. Serious efforts were made to enhance imported technologies and to upgrade domestic capabilities to absorb these technologies. By the 1980s, Korea's strategy for technological development began to bear fruit. Independent capacity for development in light industry was achieved, and Korea reached a level of minimal dependence on foreign technology in heavy and chemical industries. With the fifth and sixth FYESDPs (1982–1991), the development of strategic industries was targeted, with focus given to developing indigenous technologies and acquiring new, knowledge-intensive industries.

Common throughout the Korean developmental experience has been the use of state policies to control patterns and distribution of foreign technology transfer. Technology transfer primarily has taken two channels, and the Korean government has sought to influence these channels through related policy tools. One has been direct investment, which, as the name implies, involves the direct participation of foreign firms in domestic sectors of the economy. The second has been technology licensing, which involves arrangements for a country to pay royalties to utilize technologies developed by foreign firms.[1]

Direct Investment

Over the course of the past two decades, Korea's government policy on direct investments has seen dramatic swings to adjust to new market realities and new domestic capabilities. For example, reflecting the need to acquire technological know-how quickly and to spur industrial development, Korea pursued a liberal policy on direct investment during the 1960s. Any form of bona fide foreign capital, including fully owned subsidiaries, was courted by offering extensive incentives.[2] By the 1970s, this situation had changed. The government reversed policy on direct investment and tightened control. This reflected the Korean government's view that industrial development had reached a point of domestic "absorbing capability" to assimilate relatively mature technologies. The prevailing viewpoint during this time was that continued direct investment would constrain autonomous industrial development. The 1980s saw another change as the government gradually reversed restrictions and substantially relaxed direct investment guidelines to adjust to changes in the global marketplace. Afraid that Korea might become a competitor, foreign sources were reluctant to grant licenses for high technologies, particularly those of a knowledge-intensive nature. As a result, the Korean government turned to direct investment schemes to attract the transfer of more advanced technologies.

After the adoption of the first FYESDP in 1962, direct investments increased in Korea. Between 1962 and the end of January 1993 there were 2,258 direct investments from Japan, amounting to a total of approximately $4.18 billion, and 960 direct investments from the United States, amounting to approximately $2.9 billion. Direct investments from Japan and the United States together account for 80 percent of all foreign direct investments and 70 percent of the dollar total (Korean Economic Planning Board, 1993). These patterns clearly show that Japan and the United States are the two major investors in Korean manufacturing industries.

Patterns in direct investment illustrate the acceleration of investment since the

Table 4.1

Distribution Pattern of Direct Investments from Japan and the United States in Korean Manufacturing Industries: 1962–January 31, 1993

Direct Investments from Japan

No. of cases (%)

Industries	Low-Technology	High-Technology	Sub-Total
Labor-Intensive	603 (31%)	416 (22%)	1,019 (53%)
Capital-Intensive	269 (14%)	635 (33%)	904 (47%)
Sub-Total	872 (45%)	1,051 (55%)	1,923 (100%)

(Note: Service industries and others account for another 335 direct investments; therefore, the total of all Japanese direct investments is 2,258.)

Direct Investments from the U.S.

No. of cases (%)

Industries	Low-Technology	High-Technology	Sub-Total
Labor-Intensive	179 (28%)	133 (20%)	312 (48%)
Capital-Intensive	55 (8%)	283 (44%)	338 (52%)
Sub-Total	234 (36%)	416 (64%)	650 (100%)

(Note: Service industries and others account for another 310 direct investments; therefore, the total of all United States direct investments is 960.)

Source: Korean Economic Planning Board (1993).

1970s. During the 1961–1971 period, annual direct investments averaged only 40 cases per year. By the 1972–1981 period this rate dramatically increased to 112. During the 1982–1991 period this rate rose to about 225 cases per year. The overall trend seems to have followed the rapid development of the Korean economy. A positive investment climate in the 1980s and the loosening of restrictions on direct investment in 1984 no doubt contributed to this accelerated pattern (Yu, 1986). Despite this growth, however, between 1962 and 1984 the share of direct investments in Korea as a portion of total foreign capital inflow remained low, averaging approximately 5 percent of the total capital inflow (Korean Economic Planning Board, 1985).[3]

The distribution pattern of these direct investments among four industry groups is reported in Table 4.1.[4] As of January 31, 1993, direct investments from Japan in Korean manufacturing have been concentrated in capital-intensive, high-technology industries (33%). Direct investments from the United States also have been concentrated in capital-intensive, high-technology industries (44%), but to a stronger extent. Furthermore, when we group direct investments between low-technology and high-technology industries, we find no particular differences in the distribution pattern of direct investments between Japan and the United States. Direct investments from both countries are concentrated in high-technology industries, with this pattern slightly stronger for the United States.

These patterns can be seen as providing evidence of the rapid structural transformation of Korean industrialization, thereby increasing demand for high technologies. These results contrast with earlier studies that argue that direct investments from Japan were concentrated in low-technology industries while direct investments from the United States were concentrated in high-technology industries in Korea (Kojima, 1973, 1977, 1985; Lee, 1980). These results also do not support the frequently voiced contention that direct investments from both Japan and the United States had been concentrated in labor-intensive, high-technology Korean manufacturing industries during the period of 1973 to 1979 (see Lee, 1984).[5]

Cumulative data for the 1962–January 31, 1993, period do not inform us whether or not there was any change in the type of direct investment during that period. By the early 1970s, Korea was well on its way toward rapid industrialization, characterized by a transition from labor-intensive, low-technology industries to labor or capital-intensive, high-technology industries such as heavy and chemical industries (Lee, 1984). Moreover, from the early 1980s, Korean technology development focused on new knowledge-intensive industries, including biotechnology, computers, semiconductors, and telecommunications. This suggests that in the early 1970s and 1980s changes occurred in the patterns of direct investments from Japan and the United States.

To test this argument, we have divided the era into three periods (1962–1972, 1973–1978, and 1979–January 31, 1993) and have looked at the distribution pattern of direct investments from Japan and the United States for these three periods (see Hahm & Plein, 1994, for detail). During the first period direct investments from both Japan (48%) and the United States (39%) were concentrated in labor-intensive, low-technology industries. During this time, multinational firms in both Japan and the United States looked to Korea as a source of cheap labor for manufacturing and assembly production (Westphal, Kim, & Dahlman, 1985).

During the period of 1973–1978 direct investments from Japan (57%) and the United States (41%) were concentrated in labor-intensive, high-technology industries. These investments were highly concentrated in high-technology industries, although direct investments from the United States were more concentrated in capital-intensive, high-technology industries than were the direct investments from Japan. These results also reflect, in part, a strategy of Korea's government to initiate policies aimed at facilitating the development of a domestic high-technology industrial base.

However, during the period of 1979–January 31, 1993, direct investments from both Japan (38%) and the United States (45%) again were concentrated in capital-intensive, high-technology industries, but this pattern was more dominant among American investment divisions. In sum, this analysis reveals that differences existed in patterns of direct investments from Japan and the United States only during a period between 1962 and 1972. However, after 1972 these differences were less pronounced. Since 1979, direct investments from both Japan and the United States have concentrated in capital-intensive, high-technology industries. These trends reflect, in part, changes in Korean policy aimed at nurturing and sustaining what was becoming a relatively sophisticated technology base.

The analysis of these time periods shows no substantial difference between Japan and the United States in patterns of direct investment in Korean manufacturing industries. More important, Korea's policy decisions and its industrial and economic conditions appear to have played a powerful role in determining patterns of direct investment. In particular, these patterns may be seen as the result of a policy emphasis on selective restriction of direct investment.[6]

Technology Licensing

Technology licensings (TLs) were initiated in 1962. At first, Korean policy was quite restrictive. Through the mid-1960s, Korea's TL policy was notable for its restrictions on royalty ceilings and on the duration of licensing arrangements. In the early years of industrialization, acquisition of advanced technology was not viewed as critical to economic development. Rather, emphasis was placed on securing basic and intermediate technologies available off the shelf to aid in such established industries as plywood, shoes, and textiles. These technologies could be more easily acquired through mechanisms other than TLs. With a more secure footing in developing an industrial base and with increased demand for relatively advanced technologies, such as consumer electronics, the 1970s saw a significant change in Korean TL policy (Kim & Dahlman, 1992). Restrictions on TLs were relaxed in 1970 and 1978 (Kim, 1986; Westphal, Kim, & Dahlman, 1985; Yu, 1986). The policy was further relaxed in 1984 by procedural changes in TL arrangements, which shifted emphasis from an approval system to a reporting system (Korean Ministry of Science and Technology, 1986). Rather than seeking the blessing of the state, private interests could engage in TL as long as they abided by reporting procedures. The obvious consequence was to liberalize the process.

The total number of TLs, as of February 28, 1993, amounted to 8,147 cases with a royalty payment of $7.1 billion. The period of 1987–February 28, 1993, accounts for over 50 percent of all such cases. Similarly, royalty payments rose dramatically in the 1980s and early 1990s. The last 1987–1993 period accounts for 75 percent of cumulative royalty payments ($5.3 billion).[7] As in the case of direct investment, the major players in technology licensing have been Japan

Table 4.2
Distribution Pattern of Technology Licensings from Japan and the United States
in Korean Manufacturing Industries: 1962–February 28, 1993

Technology Licensings from Japan
No. of cases (%)

Industries	Low-Technology	High-Technology	Sub-Total
Labor-Intensive	156 (4%)	1,424 (37%)	1,580 (41%)
Capital-Intensive	391 (10%)	1,910 (49%)	2,301 (59%)
Sub-Total	547 (14%)	3,334 (86%)	3,881 (100%)

(Note: Other industries account for an additional 203 licensings; therefore, the total number of licensings from Japan is 4,084.)

Technology Licensings from the U.S.
No. of cases (%)

Industries	Low-Technology	High-Technology	Sub-Total
Labor-Intensive	125 (6%)	486 (24%)	611 (30%)
Capital-Intensive	132 (7%)	1,297 (63%)	1,429 (70%)
Sub-Total	257 (13%)	1,783 (87%)	2,040 (100%)

(Note: Other industries account for an additional 139 licensings; therefore, the total number of licensings from the United States is 2,179.)

Source: Korean Ministry of Finance (1993).

and the United States. From 1962 to February 28, 1993, the number of TLs from Japan was 4,084, with the amount of royalty payments over $2.2 billion. During this period, the number of TLs from the United States was 2,179, with royalty payments amounting to over $3.4 billion. The total number of TLs from Japan and the United States and the total amount of royalty payments to those two countries are 6,263 (87% of TLs from all countries) and $5.632 billion (80% of total royalty payments). This shows clearly that Japan and the United States are the predominant sources of TLs for Korean industry.

Table 4.2 shows the distribution of technology licensings as of February 28, 1993. TLs from Japan in Korean manufacturing industries tend to concentrate in capital-intensive, high-technology industries (49%). TLs from the United States also concentrate in capital-intensive, high-technology industries (63%), but to a greater extent. When we group TLs into low-technology and high-technology industries, we find no discernible differences in the distribution pattern of TLs between Japan and the United States, as both countries strongly focus on high-technology industries.

TLs from both Japan and the United States are concentrated in capital-intensive industries, with this tendency more pronounced for American direct investment. These results contrast sharply with previous research that argued that the United States transfers new and sophisticated technology generally characterized as capital-intensive, whereas Japan transfers mature and standardized technology that is mostly labor-intensive (see Kojima, 1977).

Again, cumulative values for the entire 1962–1993 period do not show whether there was any change in the type of technology licensing. Technology licensings from Japan and the United States clearly are concentrated in high-technology industries throughout the entire period. Again, these results reflect the rapid transformation of Korean industrialization and the consequent increasing demand for high technologies. These results also can be seen as a consequence of Korean government policy regarding the use of TLs for the development of high-technology industries.

THE EXPERIENCE OF OTHER NICs

The Korean experience may exemplify a situation in which the state controls the flow of foreign direct investment and technology licensing. As we have discussed, the Korean experience also, ironically, shows the *limits* of state influence. To be sure, the Korean experience is not much different from other NICs that were controlling in-flows of investment and technology for the purposes of state-directed economic development policy objectives. If differences exist at all, they reflect the convergence of different historical and cultural experiences and different resource endowments.

Among Asia's NICs, Korea and Taiwan stand at the apex of success and have stimulated much comparative study (see Kang, 1995). The way we see it, there are important similarities as well as differences between the Korean and Taiwanese experiences. Perhaps the most important similarity between the two nations has to do with the fact that both countries made a heavy use of direct investment and technology licensing as tools for economic development. Taiwan's regulation of direct investment and technology licensing has close parallels with the Korean experience. During Taiwan's initial industrialization phase—from the late 1950s through the early 1970s—direct investment became a key element in developing a manufacturing base (World Bank, 1993, pp. 132-133). Since then, Taiwan has placed greater restrictions on direct investment while encouraging technology licensing (World Bank, 1993, p. 21). As has Korea, Taiwan has recently embarked on the road to a high-technology base.

The most distinctive difference between Taiwan and Korea relates to firm ownership patterns. Among NICs, Taiwan appears to show a greater level of state ownership of enterprises. This contrasts sharply with Korea, where direct state ownership of firms is very limited (Kang, 1995, p. 569). Further, many privately held companies in Taiwan are small-scale, family-oriented firms (Fallows, 1994; Kang, 1995; World Bank, 1993). This also contrasts sharply with Korea, in which large business conglomerates, called "chaebol," dominate in the Korean economic structure.

The emphasis on mixing direct investment and technology licensing in Korea and Taiwan stands in contrast to the practices of other NICs in East Asia. Hong Kong and Singapore appear to encourage direct investment as the primary tool for industrialization (World Bank, 1993, p. 21). Other newly industrializing states in Asia, such as Indonesia, Malaysia, and Thailand, also seem to follow this pattern. Fallows (1994, pp. 263–269) warns that these countries are running the risk of overly exposing themselves to external dominance, especially by large Japanese firms. This warning cannot be taken lightly; as Bernard and Ravenhill (1995) have observed, there is a growing trend that Japan and, to a lesser extent, Korea and Taiwan are utilizing developing Asian economies as a platform for export-based production. In these trade triangles, more advanced Northeast Asian countries supply technologies and manufacturing arrangements to less-developed Asian countries, from which to export finished products to the United States, Western Europe, and other foreign markets. Because these arrangements are often structured through direct investment projects, profits flow back to those providing the means of manufacture and technology.

The economic and political desirability of such arrangements is subject to interpretation. Bernard and Ravenhill (1995) argue that such arrangements may lead to regional tensions, primarily between Asian NICs and Japan. It is also argued that these arrangements put the United States at a competitive disadvantage (Fallows, 1994). The World Bank (1993), on the other hand, looks favorably on direct investment as a tool of economic development in developing nations. Such arrangements are seen as providing the spark for broader development, since foreign investment provides a multiplier effect that creates support for other industries, including the service sector.

In the end, the ability of NICs to draw lessons from the successes and failures of more economically and technologically advanced states is a critical threshold in achieving economic and societal objectives. The World Bank, known for its neoclassicist views, acknowledges that government intervention in Northeast Asia "resulted in higher and more equal growth than otherwise would have occurred." And yet, it also makes a point that similar efforts in developing countries elsewhere have not been successful (World Bank, 1993, p. 6). Nonetheless, the World Bank suggests that the experiences of Southeast Asian economies with minimal government intervention may be a better model of development (World Bank, 1993, p. 7).

CONCLUSION

This chapter has examined how Korea, a recipient of technologies from advanced countries, has incorporated those new technologies and developed its industrial economy. The Korean experience reveals how the state can use various policy tools to shape patterns of technology transfer through direct investment and technology licensing. Of these two, technology licensing arrangements have played the dominant role in Korean technology transfer policy strategies. However, our findings reveal that there is more to state control of technology transfer than policy options. While such policy instruments as technology licensing and direct investment controls provide discretion, the limits of state influence are constrained by the dynamics and imperatives of changing technologies. This in itself is an important lesson for all (especially other NICs) to keep in mind in regard to international technology transfer.

For example, in the first stage of industrialization in Korea, particularly the 1962–1972 period, the prerogatives of technology donors affected distribution patterns in Korean manufacturing industries. Since then, Korean policy toward technology transfer has emerged as an influential determinant of that distribution. In the 1970s, the transformation of the Korean economy became apparent. In response, the Korean government shifted emphasis to sustaining more growth through policies designed to establish an industrial base in which domestic, rather than foreign, players prevailed. Notable changes in technology transfer policy strategy included encouraging technology licensing arrangements, in order to acquire more sophisticated production resources, and tempering foreign dominance through joint venture requirements. As the 1980s progressed, Korea continued to liberalize direct investment and technology licensing arrangements to encourage further development of capital-intensive, high-technology industries.

However, the advent of new, knowledge-intensive technologies in the late 1980s forced Korea to reconsider its technology transfer strategies. Having now achieved a standard of industrial sophistication, the acquisition of knowledge, processes, techniques, and skills, rather than the machinery of production, is the driving force in contemporary technology transfer policy. However, in a highly competitive global marketplace, high-technology leaders are not as willing to license new technologies. In short, today's nascent entrants into high-technology markets are seen as tomorrow's fierce competitors. As a result, Korea is now entertaining direct investment as a means of attracting such new advanced technologies as genetic engineering, semiconductors, and telecommunications.

In a world economy where increasingly a premium is placed on technological sophistication as a key to international competitiveness, the role of the state in shaping patterns of technology transfer becomes a critical element in economic policy planning. Experiences such as those of Korea and Taiwan help to shed light on this complex subject. As NICs consider prospects for the future, policymakers and analysts will do well to investigate the variety of policy tools and experiences that shape patterns and implications of technology transfer.

NOTES

This chapter draws on a paper presented at Iowa State University (which was published as Hahm, Plein, & Florida, 1994) and on a paper presented at Georgetown University (which was noted as Hahm & Plein, 1994). Sung Deuk Hahm gratefully acknowledges the summer research support of the Georgetown Graduate School of Arts and Sciences.

1. Measurements focusing on direct investments and technology licensings capture only a portion of the overall activity involved in technology transfer. Other measures include technical collaboration through training and education and the importation of "embodied" technology-intensive goods.

2. In order to encourage foreign direct investment and minimize regulatory obstacles, the Korean government implemented the Foreign Investment Encouragement Law in 1960. Provisions of the law include such incentives as a five-year tax holiday, duty-free status for imported machinery and raw materials used as manufacturing capital, and protection against foreign property being expropriated by the state (Yang, 1972, p. 244). In 1966, incentives under the Foreign Investment Encouragement Law were strengthened with the passage of the Foreign Capital Inducement Law. The same year, the Office of Investment Promotion was created to respond to the information needs and inquiries of foreign investors (Yang, 1972, p. 245).

3. In this regard, Mardon (1990) and Pack and Westphal (1986) argue that direct investments have played a minor role in Korean development and have been much less important than in other developing countries because Korea has emphasized external borrowing rather than direct investments. Direct investment participation was rejected in the sectors that were deemed strategic and sensitive through government intervention. Instead, the major source of technology for large firms has been technology licensings. In terms of number of cases, these arrangements account for almost half of formal technology importation.

4. We classify industries into the four industry groups in accordance with their level of technology and production factor intensity: labor-intensive, low-technology industries; labor-intensive, high-technology industries; capital-intensive, low-technology industries; and capital-intensive, high-technology industries. Following Lee (1984), we used Hufbauer's (1970) estimates of factor- and skill-intensities of goods.

The labor-intensive, low-technology industries are food, tobacco, textiles, wearing apparel, leather and leather products, footwear, wood and wood cork products, furniture and fixtures, rubber products, plastic products, fabricated metal products (except machinery and equipment), and other manufacturing. The labor-intensive, high-technology industries are printing; publishing and allied industries; machinery; electrical machinery; apparatus, appliances, and supplies; transport equipment; and professional and scientific equipment. The capital-intensive, low-technology industries are beverage, paper and paper products, pottery, china and earthenware, glass and glass products, other nonmetallic mineral products, and basic iron and steel products. The capital-intensive, high-technology industries are industrial chemicals, other chemical products, petroleum products, and basic nonferrous metal products.

5. Some differences do appear, however, when investments are divided only between labor-intensive and capital-intensive industries. In particular, Japanese direct investments are somewhat more concentrated than United States direct investments in labor-intensive industries. This may reflect the difference in factor endowments between the two countries (Dunning, 1988; Lee, 1984; Mason, Kim, Perkins, Kim, & Cole, 1980). In the case of Japan, up until the late 1970s labor-intensive practices characterized various manufacturing industrial sectors, whereas United States manufacturing has been characterized by capital-intensive practices.

6. Similar findings have been advanced before (see Mardon, 1990). Korea does not

seem to be alone in this ability to influence the course of foreign technology transfer. Our findings in the Korean experience are consistent with the conclusion of Chou's (1988) analysis in Taiwan.

7. The number of TL cases jumped from 33 in the First FYESDP (1962–1966) to 434 a decade later (1972–1976), to 2,078 (1982–1986), and to 3,471 in the 1987–1991 period (Korean Ministry of Finance, 1993). Patterns in TL arrangements reflect the steady transformation of the Korean economy. From 1961 through 1966, the first FYESDP, the annual average of TLs was only 7 cases per year. However, it increased dramatically, to 57 per year, during the second FYESDP of 1967–1971, to 87 per year during the 1972–1976 third FYESDP period, to 245 per year during the 1977–1981 fourth FYESDP period, to 416 per year during the 1982–1986 fifth FYESDP period; during the 1987–1991 sixth FYESDP period, it rose to about 694 cases per year. The liberalization policy regarding TLs has had considerable influence on this increase (Yu, 1986).

CHAPTER 5

Technology Transfer
and Agricultural Development
in West Africa

R. JAMES BINGEN AND BRENT SIMPSON

INTRODUCTION

For over 70 years, the successful international transfer of improved technology
has been largely responsible for many of the success stories in agricultural development throughout sub-Saharan Africa. From the spread of oil palm and rice
hybrids developed in Zaire in the 1930s, through the introduction of improved
cotton varieties in Central and West Africa and maize hybrids in East and Southern Africa in the 1950s and 1960s, to the bio-control of cassava mealy bug in
the 1980s, large numbers of African farmers have benefited from the diffusion
of improved agricultural technology.

Building on this history of technology transfer, the Sasakawa Africa Asso-
ciation/Global 2000 projects have been attempting since 1986 to implement a
"second" green revolution strategy in several East, West, and Southern African
countries. In contrast to the "first generation" green revolution in Asia, these
projects recognize that the agro-ecological, institutional, and economic conditions throughout most of sub-Saharan Africa do not allow for the easy transfer
of standardized technology packages or "quick fixes." Instead, the projects seek
to identify and develop technology, work with farmers, train extension staff, and
help bring about specific policy changes (credit, input supply, land reform, etc.)
that encourage small farmers to adopt improved technology and practices.

For African farmers, Sasakawa Global 2000 (SG 2000) holds out a "dream
of a commercial African agriculture made up mainly of small to intermediate-
sized family farms that use modern science-based technologies" (Dowswell,
1993, p. 99).[1] At a time when many bilateral and multilateral donor agencies
appear to be turning away from agriculture, SG 2000 stands as a highly visible
model that other private foundations, private enterprise, and bilateral agencies

might adopt for their own agricultural development programming in sub-Saharan Africa. Given the potential influence of SG 2000 in setting a standard for technology transfer projects, its underlying assumptions deserve close scrutiny. In particular, a review and examination of the program's key technical and institutional assumptions concerning technology transfer could offer important insights for Africa's policymakers.

Drawing upon the experiences of an agricultural and rural development program in Mali (Office de la Haute Vallée du Niger, OHVN), this chapter suggests that the long-term contribution and sustainability of programs like SG 2000 will depend as much on political, institutional, and organizational factors as on the technology being promoted.[2]

Following a brief description of the SG 2000 program and an overview of rural development policy and strategy in Mali, this chapter reviews selected technology development and transfer issues in the OHVN zone of Mali and draws lessons for SG 2000 as well as for other efforts that look to technology transfer as the key to agricultural development in sub-Saharan Africa.

SASAKAWA GLOBAL 2000: BACKGROUND

Since 1986, SG 2000 projects[3] have been working with the ministries of agriculture and farmers in several sub-Saharan African countries in the hope that "farmers on Africa's best lands [would] use modern research information and higher input levels to produce more food" (Dowswell, 1993, p. 99).[4] The projects hold firmly to the principle that technology—the use of appropriate purchased inputs, including improved seed, fertilizer, and crop protection chemicals—can increase agricultural productivity and thereby help to lift Africa's smallholders out of poverty.

Three operational components define the overall SG 2000 approach: policy and planning support, technology transfer, and input credit and delivery.

Policy and Planning Support

SG 2000 projects usually include three types of policy and planning support. First, one or two internationally recruited advisors work closely with a national planning and coordinating advisory group associated with the agriculture ministry in each country to set project objectives and priorities. Second, the projects provide supplementary budget and logistic support to carry out field operations. And third, each project employs a management information system to monitor all project operations and budgeting and to permit annual financial and material adjustments. These management information systems allow each SG 2000 country project to assure that its funds "are properly used" and to assure "budgetary flexibility" in response to changing project needs and opportunities.

Technology Transfer

With a focus on promoting "intensified food production," SG 2000 projects in sub-Saharan Africa concentrate either on irrigated production or on areas that generally receive more than 700mm of annual rainfall. This highly restrictive orientation derives from an underlying SG 2000 assumption that "agriculture must be intensified on lands that can stand more-intensive cultivation and should be decreased in the more-fragile ecologies" (Dowswell, 1993, p. 99). This narrow approach to an agricultural development strategy for sub-Saharan Africa has become increasingly widespread. In order to attain a measure of sustainable agricultural production in sub-Saharan Africa, for example, Reardon argues that since "available low-input extensive systems will not meet growth needs and under usual circumstances can lead to degradation of marginal lands, the solution [to sustainable agriculture] lies in intensification through use of fertilizer, small-scale irrigation, animal traction, and hybrid seeds" (Reardon, 1995, p. 347; also see Cleaver & Schreiber, 1994).

SG 2000 projects use farmer-managed technology evaluation and training plots (PTP) as the centerpiece of their technology transfer activities.[5] On these quarter- to half-hectare plots, selected farmers agree to follow an SG 2000 technological package (including the use of improved varieties, planting densities, fertilization recommendations, and improved cultivation practices) "for two or three of the most important food crops for which proven and markedly superior technology is available" (Dowswell, 1993, p. 100). The project assures input supply and uses the plots as demonstration and training sites for neighbors and for other participating farmers.

The contribution of these plots in the overall SG 2000 approach depends largely upon farmer training through village-level organized groups that are supported by front-line extension workers. On average, SG 2000 devotes a quarter of its country project resources to assuring that small-scale farmers have the management knowledge needed to take full advantage of the improved inputs. These groups represent a key feature of the SG 2000 program in each country. "By associating in a farmers' organization, small-scale producers have a better chance to succeed in commercial agriculture. Technical and economic information flows more easily through organized farmers' groups and farmers are more likely to gain price advantages through collective action" (Dowswell, 1993, p. 105).

Input Credit and Delivery

It is widely recognized that farmers' access to improved technology presents one of the most difficult problems in technology transfer (Cleaver & Schreiber, 1994). SG 2000 addresses this issue in the short run by giving its front-line extension officers responsibility for input distribution and credit recovery. In the longer term, the program encourages governments to create the conditions necessary to promote greater private investment in input supply and credit. As Dowswell (1993, p. 101) notes, "farmers consistently say that getting the recommended PTP inputs on time, and being trained in using them, are the most attractive and distinguishing features of the SG 2000 field demonstration program."[6]

SG 2000 Lessons for Technology Transfer

Based on its ten years of experience in sub-Saharan Africa, the Sasakawa Global 2000 Agricultural Program has achieved remarkable success in generating yields on its production test plots that are two to three and sometimes four times higher than general smallholder levels (Borlaug & Dowswell, 1996). With this noteworthy record, the SG 2000 suggests that it offers three important lessons related to the transfer of agricultural technology for intensified food production in sub-Saharan Africa. First, improved technology can double and triple yields on most farms when it is available for areas receiving more than 700mm of annual rainfall. Second, small-scale farmers will adopt improved technologies when inputs are provided on time, a market exists for increased production, and economic incentives exist to increase production. Third, agricultural extension services can become effective agents for technological change when provided with adequate transportation, budgets, and a mandate to operate farmer-oriented field testing and demonstrations.

Despite the apparently straightforward attractiveness of such lessons, several embedded assumptions concerning the institutional dimensions of SG 2000 deserve careful scrutiny. Without such inquiry, SG 2000 and similar technology transfer efforts run the risk of ending up on the growing "junk heap" of African agricultural development projects. The OHVN in Mali offers a practical and instructive case upon which to base this inquiry.

The OHVN technology transfer program parallels many of the SG 2000 principles, and it may, in fact, receive SG 2000 support in the near future. Moreover, as the brief review of the OHVN and Mali's rural development policy suggests, SG 2000's lessons are not new, nor is technology transfer a neutral or apolitical activity. As the following review suggests, some of the additional, key lessons for technology transfer must account for the ways in which technology transfer is mediated by various institutional and economic interests, many of which must be understood in their broader political and historical context.[7]

RURAL DEVELOPMENT POLICY IN MALI: AN OVERVIEW

Since political independence in 1960, Mali's leaders have consistently struggled to weave a comprehensive rural development policy from separate government programs designed to achieve food self-sufficiency, generate foreign exchange, and promote broad-based village-level development. Committed to sustaining both the traditional pattern of collective village life and smallholder production, Mali's leaders have regularly promoted governmental programs oriented toward revitalizing the productive forces of the traditional village economy.

Throughout most of the 1960s, the government idealized the rural Malian village as a model of socialist organization and a key institution in building a new Malian socialist society. To improve the delivery of agricultural services and structure the economic participation of villagers in development, the government sought to extend agricultural and cooperative services down to the local or *arrondissement* level through the establishment of Rural Growth Zones (ZER, Zones d'Expansion Rural). In each of these zones, local agricultural agents were to help test and extend new technology, while a Cooperative Service would supply villages with consumer goods and market the agricultural surplus.

By the mid to late 1960s serious flaws in this strategy became obvious. The agricultural service was burdened with an ineffective and cumbersome administrative structure. Most village-level agricultural posts went unfilled; and when agents were in place, they spent more time on administrative duties than in extending technical agricultural advice and services. Moreover, rural cooperatives never effectively served the villages. Consumer goods remained in the cities, and agricultural equipment and supplies were unavailable to farm households.

The only agricultural and rural development success story during this period was found in those areas of the country where the government had given the French parastatal, the CFDT (Compagnie Française pour le Développement des Fibres Textiles), a monopoly for cotton production and (later) marketing. With an improved technical package, based largely on the company's extensive experience in Central Africa, and a guaranteed supply of seed, insecticides, fertilizer, and equipment and marketing for producers, the CFDT increased cotton production fivefold while the rest of Mali's agricultural sector stagnated.

Within four years of the 1968 coup d'état, the Agriculture Service planned to put Malian agriculture back on track through an expansion of the CFDT formula into foreign-financed, rural development *opérations* responsible for administering all commodity-based agricultural services in each of the country's agro-ecological zones (see Bingen, 1985). The OHVN was created as one of these *opérations* in the early 1970s in order to focus on tobacco, rice, and vegetable crop production in the well-watered zone close to the capital city of Bamako in the southwestern part of the country.[8]

As the international markets for Mali's peanuts and cotton began to weaken in the early 1980s, the once successful peanut production *opération* (Opération Arachide et Cultures Vivrières, OACV) folded; the now nationalized CMDT (Compagnie Malienne pour le Développement des Fibres Textiles) cotton program was forced to scale down and concentrate its efforts in the country's most productive cotton production areas. In response, and with assurances of continued U.S. financing into the 1990s, the government expanded the OHVN geographic area of responsibility in order to continue providing rural development services to villagers who had been served previously by the CMDT and the OACV. Not only did this new charge add cotton to the OHVN extension program, it also required the OHVN to work in a large, new, northern, semi-arid agro-ecological zone for which it did not have a package of improved agricultural technology.

In the late 1980s, the government asked the OHVN to restructure its operations in conformance with the provisions of the country's World Bank–supported structural adjustment program. Among other changes, this required the OHVN to undertake policy and organizational changes that would transfer more development responsibilities to the rural population and increase the role of the private sector in rural development. This restructuring involved specific measures to reorganize the OHVN management system and structure; reduce the number of personnel; and transfer commercial activities such as credit, input supply, transport, and marketing to "organized collectivities." By 1992, the OHVN had significantly reduced personnel—largely through the reorganization of the extension program and the transfer of credit, input supply, transport, and marketing responsibilities to Village Associations (VAs), banks, and private suppliers. In addition, the OHVN had cut some operating costs by 10 percent, and private transporters were handling more than 90 percent of cotton and tobacco marketing. Finally, with improved management skills, many VAs were able to negotiate equipment and supply purchases directly with private suppliers; and over 100 VAs had credit agreements with private suppliers and banks.

To summarize, this brief historical review should remind us that SG 2000–type programs and approaches to technology transfer, including those that focus on the timely delivery of agricultural equipment and supplies with reasonable credit terms, are not new to some parts of sub-Saharan Africa.

TECHNOLOGY TRANSFER AND DEVELOPMENT IN THE OHVN

As part of the government's 1988 policy to restructure Mali's rural development organizations, the OHVN adopted an extension strategy that reflects many of the assumptions and features that are central to the SG 2000 program. Frontline extension agents receive regular in-service training on special technologies from subject-matter specialists and are expected to pass on this information to farmers through a fixed schedule of visits with contact farmers and village extension groups. Most of the contact farmers manage demonstration plots to display various technologies in the OHVN program of technical recommendations.

Like the SG 2000 program, the core of the OHVN extension program consists of a package of well-known technological recommendations centered around the use of improved seed varieties, cultivation practices, animal traction, the use of fertilizer and pesticides, and simple natural resource management technologies. The smooth operation of this process and the effectiveness of this technology transfer system in the OHVN—similar to that of SG 2000—depends heavily upon the assumption that research will supply new and improved technology, that inputs will be available in a timely manner,[9] and that the OHVN offers the most important source of technical information and supplies to farmers. Serious technical and organizational questions have been raised concerning both the adaptiveness and availability of the OHVN package of technology. SG 2000 should also consider these questions as it examines its programs and opportunities, especially in West Africa.

Despite a working agreement with the farming systems research unit of the national agricultural research agency to target technical recommendations to different agro-ecological conditions and different economic levels of households, the OHVN technical package continues to be largely unresponsive to the variability in farmers' conditions throughout the zone (Simpson, 1995). Preliminary estimates from a 1992 impact study of maize research indicate adoption rates well below 25 percent for improved maize production technologies. Nearly 70 percent of the OHVN field staff note difficulties in getting farmers to adopt new varieties because of economic constraints (high prices and lack of access to credit) or perceived technical shortcomings compared with current practices.

Moreover, several of the core technical recommendations are in direct conflict with each other. For years, farmers have refused to adopt the technical recommendation to flat plow their fields. Farmers, especially in the semi-arid areas, prefer to practice ridge plowing in order to conserve soil moisture and reduce both wind and water erosion. The flat-plowing recommendation, linked with the OHVN effort to encourage greater mechanization, is necessary for the use of animal-drawn seeders. To operate a seeder, farmers must flat plow their fields and remove the majority of the crop residues to keep the seeders from jamming and skipping. Removal of these residues, however, reduces soil and water conservation capacity and soil fertility. Consequently, the OHVN themes of flat plowing and mechanization reflect serious incompatibilities with its concerns for dealing with soil and water conservation and natural resource management.

Organizationally, field agents report considerable difficulty in working effectively with the village extension groups that play the same role in the OHVN program as the training groups in the SG 2000 program. Membership is limited to men, and attendance tends to be quite erratic. Farmers either do not attend training sessions on a regular basis, or they attend a few meetings and then drop out. Some agents suggest that the static and marginally relevant nature of the technical information that they have to offer farmers in these sessions is one reason that they are unable to attract larger and more regular participation to the group meeting.[10]

At the same time, there is little evidence of effective feedback from farmers to agents or the exchange of farmers' experiences and observations among field agents. In fact, it appears that the OHVN neither expects nor gives any incentive to agents to listen to farmers. Over 45 percent of the field staff report knowledge of a variety or an indigenous practice that is superior to the OHVN technical recommendations. Fewer than 10 percent, however, have ever communicated this information to others in the extension program or to researchers. Moreover, the OHVN monthly staff meetings are not managed to solicit feedback from the field staff. As one mid-level manager commented, "these meetings block the advancement of the OHVN" (see Simpson, 1995).

Finally, the OHVN deals with farmers as if it represents their only "correct" source of the "most advanced" technical information. Descriptions of the SG 2000 program leave the same impression (Borlaug & Dowswell, 1996). In reality, the OHVN may be the largest, but it is not the only technology transfer actor working with farmers. Several other Malian governmental agencies and a large number of domestic and international nongovernmental organizations offer farmers access to information (sometimes conflicting with that given by OHVN agents) and various types of agricultural technology, through a range of independent small-scale projects to complement farmers' activities (see Simpson, 1995, Appendix F).

ISSUES IN TECHNOLOGY TRANSFER

Hayami and Ruttan offer an instructive threefold typology that helps us gain some perspective on key institutional issues raised by the SG 2000 technology transfer program (Hayami & Ruttan, 1985).[11] These authors use the term "material transfer" to cover the most widely accepted notion of technology transfer involving the simple or direct transfer of a specific biological, chemical, or mechanical technology, such as seed, fertilizer, pesticides, and machinery. The bio-control of the cassava mealy bug in sub-Saharan Africa through the release of a parasitic wasp from South America illustrates a modern-day situation of material transfer.

"Design transfer" involves the process through which adaptive research enables the more effective use of imported technology. Many of the International Agricultural Research Centers (IARCs), often in collaboration with national research programs, are heavily engaged in this type of transfer in sub-Saharan Africa. The International Center for Maize and Wheat Improvement (CIMMYT) has played a key role in the development of an improved, high-yielding flint maize variety for use in Malawi; and the International Institute for Tropical Agriculture (IITA) has played a key role in the development of microbial controls for pests, diseases, and weeds to complement bio-control programs. Similarly, adaptive microbial control work at IITA revealed the need for the development of several new technologies.

Finally, "capacity transfer" comprises "the transfer of scientific knowledge and capacity which enable the production of locally adaptable technology. . . . An important element in the process of capacity transfer is the . . . diffusion of the ideas and craft of agricultural science" (Hayami & Ruttan, 1985, p. 261). With Hayami and Ruttan, we argue that the success or sustainability of programs like SG 2000 lies with investments to assure the broadest diffusion of ideas and the craft of agricultural science. We maintain a position, however, that clearly goes beyond Hayami and Ruttan and SG 2000 to broaden the concept of capacity transfer to assure commensurate consideration for local, indigenous scientific knowledge with that circulating in international arenas. Furthermore, we strongly endorse Borlaug and Dowswell's calls for research managers and decisionmakers to bring research closer to farmers' fields and for strengthening agricultural and rural social science education in Africa.[12] But we argue that the successful transfer of technology depends as much upon the knowledge and experiences of women and men farmers who live and farm in highly diverse conditions as it does on the knowledge of scientists and extensionists (see Richards, 1985; Richards, 1989).

Drawing on illustrative evidence from the OHVN in Mali, in this section we argue that the promise of technology transfer in sub-Saharan Africa through programs like SG 2000 will depend upon deliberate steps to incorporate a more complete vision of capacity transfer into what is still fundamentally a material and design transfer approach. Such steps can be taken by looking at three ways in which SG 2000-type programs might become more "capacity-centered" in helping to build a greater measure of flexibility and diversity into the technology development and transfer process.

Getting the Technology Right

The SG 2000 programs in sub-Saharan Africa rely heavily on the introduction of high-input production practices as the motor for increased food production and agricultural development. While rural sociologists and agricultural economists have cautioned against the social implications and economic feasibility of such an approach, current research also raises questions about the sustainability, or long-term viability, of the high-input approach (see Jiggins et al., 1996).

Production agronomists and entomologists have found that various pests contribute overwhelmingly to low yields among both food and cash crops. The development of resistant varieties may offer one solution, but it is widely known that this approach requires a sustained and long-term (10–15 years) investment to bring varieties from the research stations to the farmer's field. Given the growing crisis in most of Africa's research institutions, as well as the continuing disinterest in agricultural research among the donor community, the outlook for such research continuity or an investment commitment appears dim at best. Chemical control represents another option. But, pesticides remain largely unavailable for food crops, raise serious health issues, and/or risk putting farmers on the well-known and destructive "pesticide treadmill." Consequently, programs like SG 2000 may find value in using their production or demonstration plots to showcase farmers' practices for addressing pest problems and to explore alternative integrated pest management solutions (Leisinger, Schmitt, & ISNAR, 1995).

The ongoing research activities of farmers throughout the OHVN zone indicate the presence of a vast reservoir (capacity) upon which to draw in a search for more sustainable technology (Simpson, 1995). Farmers engage in varietal screening (testing), intercropping experiments, and the use of various cultivation practices on an ongoing basis. Similarly, in response to apparently changing climatic conditions, farmers have started to experiment with several agroforestry practices and different methods of fertility management and soil and water control. Building upon this type of experimentation, SG 2000 demonstration plots or PTPs could tap into and benefit significantly from farmers' innovative capacities and the information and material used in their current production practices.

We need to be very clear about one critical issue: This is not a call for, in Borlaug and Dowswell's overstated characterization, a "romanticized" reliance on current farming practices. On the contrary, it reflects the advice and working practices of successful production agronomists around the world, and builds upon Borlaug and Dowswell's own recognition of the "crying need . . . for creative pragmatism in research and extension organisations" (Borlaug & Dowswell, 1996, p. 122). But instead of starting from a "focus on helping farmers," as Borlaug and Dowswell indicate, it starts with the production agronomist's focus on learning from farmers.

In addition to adapting the demonstration plots to accommodate local creativity, it may be useful to examine how they could be integrated into and benefit from the information shared through farmers' existing communication channels. Throughout the OHVN zone—and elsewhere in sub-Saharan Africa—farmers "belong" to several different, overlapping social networks from which they receive and to which they contribute technical information.[13] Both ascribed and achieved roles define channels for the diffusion of new information, while personal ties and friendships also help to facilitate exchanges (Simpson, 1994). Specific locations, such as public spaces and markets, and activities, such as group labor and social events, offer other opportunities to exchange information and ideas.

The contribution of diverse sources of information for farmers has been recognized for some time (see Biggs, 1989) and reminds us that programs like SG 2000 "must seek common cause with the rural community to a much greater extent, in order to achieve a multiplier effect from the wider adoption of a range of less spectacular but hopefully more sustainable techniques" (Leisinger et al., 1995, p. 88).

Investment Portfolios

The SG 2000 effort to limit its technology transfer activities to areas receiving more than 700mm of annual rainfall reflects not only a limited understanding of agricultural potential in much of sub-Saharan Africa but also an oversimplified, technological understanding of the dynamics of African agricultural and rural development (see Farrington, 1995a; Jiggins et al., 1996). Evidence from the OHVN zone in Mali and from elsewhere in sub-Saharan Africa suggests that successful technology transfer with resource- or asset-poor households may depend largely on the capacity of programs like SG 2000 to incorporate agronomic and agro-ecological diversity as well as policy- and household-level economic criteria into the technology design process.

Just over fifteen years ago, CIMMYT introduced the concept of recommendation domains as one way to improve the design of improved technology for specified agro-ecological conditions (CIMMYT, 1980). Given the range of agro-ecological, economic, and logistic conditions that we have learned over the years affects farmers and household decisionmaking, the idea of a household economic portfolio may offer greater value in examining the process of technology transfer. In contrast to the idea of a "recommendation domain" that focuses on agricultural activities, the idea of a "household portfolio" locates agricultural activities within the larger context of a household's economic opportunities and constraints. The idea draws upon a conceptualization of farmers as investors who allocate their scarce human, financial, and physical resources according to perceived short- and long-term low and high risks. It sees rural producers as those who constantly scan the investment horizon to identify the best ways of allocating their resources to protect and improve their standard of living (see Bingen et al., 1994).

Reardon and Vosti's discussion supports this notion. They argue that the search for improved technology must account for how farmers assess the opportunity costs between farm and nonfarm activities as well as the capital/liquidity constraints facing rural households (see Cleaver & Schreiber, 1994; English et al., 1994; and Reardon & Vosti, 1995).

Political Interests

Even before democratization began to sweep across most of sub-Saharan Africa, many observed the importance of democracy and decentralization for local decisionmaking in agriculture (see Mabogunje, 1995). As Gentil noted, extension must be adapted to diverse agricultural environments, to varying ecological conditions, and to differences between farm families and their members. "The most important point to underline is the need to build a sound relationship between farmers, extension workers, and researchers" (Gentil, 1989, p. 28).[14] A closer look at the experience in using village groups in the OHVN zone to promote technology transfer indicates how the interests of various actors—both within villages and between villagers and government development agencies—helps delineate some of the political parameters in the technology transfer process.

The establishment of over 250 village associations (VAs) and extension groups may be one of the most significant contributions in the last ten years to the technology transfer process that is mediated by the OHVN. With functional literacy and management training through the OHVN,[15] the VAs have been largely responsible for mobilizing a flow of significant levels of loan capital from banks, attracting development projects and opportunities from a variety of other public and private agencies, and handling some extension responsibilities (Bingen et al., 1994).

As a model for programs such as SG 2000, the VAs deserve close examination. It is widely recognized that many VAs have been able to accept responsibility for extension and economic activities that were previously controlled by the OHVN. Villagers generally agree that the VAs represent a new and significantly different opportunity from the government's previous cooperative policies and programs. The VAs are not imposed from above—even though the VA organizational structure must conform to government regulations. Each village is left free to exercise the option whether or not to establish a VA, even though a VA is effectively the only way to obtain production and equipment credit from the OHVN development agency.

The VAs represent a significant means for developing "capacity transfer" in the technology transfer process. They offer literacy and management skills training as well as opportunities to make collective investments such as schools, maternities and dispensaries, bridges, dams, grain-storage facilities, and village stores that villagers might otherwise not have undertaken. In other words, the VAs offer one organizational means for moving beyond a simple technical approach to technology transfer[16] and for incorporating villagers' farm and non-farm concerns.

A closer examination of the structure and operation of the VAs reminds us that technology transfer is not a neutral process and that the use of groups like the VAs will not necessarily offer opportunities for diversity and that broad, more equitable responsiveness will be needed to assure everyone's dreams for African agriculture.

Membership is open in principle to all village residents, including women, but some evidence suggests that villagers from minority ethnic groups hold less-than-equal membership.[17] Men from the households of the village founding families generally monopolize and specifically exclude women from all decisionmaking positions and thereby control and set the conditions by which villagers have access to credit and agricultural inputs.[18] Women are specifically disadvantaged. Wives must submit credit requests through their husbands, and group requests from each VA's "women's section" must be negotiated with the men in decisionmaking positions. Limits on the annual line of credit available to each VA mean that the women's requests for loans compete with the requests made for production and equipment loans by the male household heads.

Outside observers commonly (and sometimes romantically) assume that the activities and decisions of such local, village-level organizations would be "open" and "known to all" and thus serve as a means for assuring the broadest access to improved technology. In reality, the VAs are ambiguous structures that continue to rely on the village's customary or traditional organization as the basis for doing business with development agencies and banks (see Hesseling

& LeRoy, 1996). Decisions concerning VA activities are commonly made in the courtyard of the village head, outside the official VA general meetings; and very few of the VAs keep regular written records of their meetings or financial accounts of their economic activities. If records are kept, they tend to be maintained sporadically and/or incorrectly and found scattered throughout various VA officers' homes.[19]

Such ambivalence carries over to positions comparable to that of the "contact farmer" in the SG 2000 program. Most of these individuals are heads of families, and their responsibilities as "contact farmers" often conflict with their familial obligations. Some villages recognize this dilemma and try to find some way to compensate part of the individual's time. Nevertheless, these individuals and the villagers hold conflicting views of a leader's role. Some of these "contact farmers" perceive themselves as being in service to their village; others feel they are equivalent to unpaid (and thereby exploited) frontline extension agents. Villagers hold equally conflicting perceptions. Some feel the farmers represent an effective link to the development agencies, while others feel that the position is used as a way to escape from field work.

In addition to recognizing and dealing with this type of village-level politics, programs like SG 2000 will need to give more explicit recognition to the political implications of their role as an "external" and "new" program. Like SG 2000, many of the 20 to 30 national and international nongovernmental organizations (NGOs) throughout the OHVN zone engage in a wide range of development activities that complement the broader OHVN program. These programs are quite popular among villagers, and many observers argue that they have a comparative advantage over governmental services for working at the grassroots, village level (see Brett, 1993).

Recent experiences with these programs in the OHVN zone, however, raise serious concerns about whether they are launched primarily in response to development fads and the NGO's own predetermined development agenda or in response to village needs. Confronted with opportunities to improve the well-being of their village, many villagers find it difficult to refuse NGO offers of credit, even though they may be unable to meet their counterpart commitment. Villagers commonly find the soft or distributive credit policies of NGO programs very attractive until they confront the need to meet several loan repayments (to the NGOs and the banks) at the same time.[20]

In sum, the village-level institutional framework upon which programs like SG 2000 depend remains tenuous, at best. Village groups and associations represent significant opportunities for technology transfer and development, yet even the most successful reflect significant socioeconomic biases and are unexpectedly fragile groups.

CONCLUSION

After more than two generations of Western European and American efforts to help African governments "get African agriculture moving," it's time to move beyond oversimplified, either-or debates between those who might be labeled as seeking "magic bullets" and those who are criticized for taking "utopian, neo-environmentalist approaches." By focusing on the various relations among the political, technical, and institutional dimensions of technology transfer, this chapter represents one small step in this direction. In conclusion, we suggest three areas for further consideration of the institutional dimensions of technology transfer.

First, we suggest that technology transfer depends as much on organizational capacity as it does on technology. Most organizations currently engaged in technology transfer—whether national agricultural research and extension services or programs like SG 2000—commonly find it difficult to examine openly their policies and procedures through ongoing debate and discussion. As hierarchically organized agencies, built around well-defined roles and patterns of responsibility, they do not encourage employees to think for themselves or to challenge policies and operating standards. By enforcing this type of bureaucratic accountability, organizations ironically provide employees an incentive to protect their positions and defend their roles. Instead of dealing with uncertainty, employees prefer to offer oversimplified versions of problems and to deal with only those problems for which there is a ready solution.

When problems arise in the technology transfer process, the tendency is to "blame" the frontline extension agent or researcher and to call for more training for these individuals. We agree with the need for significantly increased investments in agricultural and rural education in sub-Saharan Africa. But we also call for attention to the organizational dynamics that stifle even the "best and brightest" by replacing innovation and creativity with an almost machine-shop demand to deliver a uniform product or service. This type of organization cannot develop the kinds of diverse and flexible responses that will be required to get African agriculture moving, just as it has long been recognized to stifle the process of technological innovation (Gamser, 1988). As we are discovering with many organizations, even in industrialized countries, the "need has now become the understanding and coordination of variability, complexity, and effectiveness" (Hock, 1995). At issue are the most effective ways to liberate and incorporate the creativity of grassroots producers into the development of new and improved technology.

Second, we suggest the need to look at technology transfer as a political process. Technology transfer is not (and never has been) a politically neutral activity, and it becomes even more politically charged when governmental or nongovernmental agencies seek to work through village-level groups. Work at the grassroots level or with recognized grassroots leaders does not assure the widespread distribution of the benefits of technology transfer. Some groups will benefit some farmers and households, and other groups may benefit others. But, as noted above, given the ambiguous nature of rural organizations throughout much of sub-Saharan Africa, different groups within the same village may benefit the same people and will not necessarily distribute benefits more broadly. Consequently, the democratic structure and dynamics of rural groups and their role in technology transfer for agricultural and rural development cannot be assumed. Farmers and villagers need the opportunities to explore a range of organizational options to accommodate different blends of "traditional" and "modern" organizational norms. At the same time, these local and farm organizations need support that enables them to create a capability to embrace diversity and change.

Third, we suggest that the answer to all types of successful technology transfer (material, design, and capacity) lies in more creative ways of joining public and private resources. Mindful of the interests that are specific to both private and public actors, the identification and adoption of improved agricultural technology will require new partnerships for rural development and new frameworks of institutional collaboration. Instead of sloganeering for privatization and liberalization, it is time to identify appropriate economic incentives and financial guarantees and to design functional networks of combined public and private services that draw upon their separate strengths and enhance their separate capabilities.

Clearly, the creation of a such new and stronger institutional framework must begin with both a bottom-up identification of issues and problems and the establishment of politically powerful farm or rural organizations. Government agencies must assume more responsibility for nurturing these organizations, yet have the capability to step back and aside. We agree that political will and leadership at the top will be critical for Africa's agricultural development, but we suggest that the dream of a new African agriculture will depend upon decisions that recognize the politics of, and seek to incorporate more democratic principles into, the transfer of technology.

NOTES

This chapter is based upon work completed under an agreement between the MSU Department of Resource Development and Development Alternatives, Inc., and pursuant to the conditions of the OHVN Project supported by the United States Agency for International Development (USAID), Bamako, Mali. Any opinions, findings, and conclusions or recommendations expressed in this chapter are those of the authors and do not necessarily reflect the views of USAID or Development Alternatives, Inc., or the Government of Mali.

1. This may not be a "dream," but an illusion (see Tripp, 1993).

2. In the early years of the SG 2000 program in Ghana, Tripp notes, "the most serious flaw . . . was the lack of attention to strengthening local institutions" (see Tripp, 1993; also see Eicher, 1995). For an excellent discussion of many of the assumptions concerning technology in the SG 2000 approach see Jiggins, Reijntjes, and Lightfoot, 1996.

3. For one of the first, critical reviews of SG 2000, see Eicher, 1988.

4. Projects are located in Benin, Ethiopia, Ghana, Nigeria, Tanzania, and Togo; there were projects in Sudan and Zambia.

5. The name given to this plot varies: Production Test Plot, Management Training Plot, or Extension Test Plot.

6. Tripp discusses the problems created by the rapid expansion of the input delivery and credit component during the early phases of the program in Ghana (Tripp, 1993). The dramatically different approaches to the management of input delivery and credit have been the subject of continuing, and often heated, debate between proponents of the SG 2000 and the Training & Visit (T&V) models of technology transfer. For one presentation of this debate, see Farrington, 1995b.

7. For the importance of taking a long-term and multidimensional perspective on development activities in specific areas see English, Tiffen, and Mortimore, 1994.

8. For a more extensive discussion of this background see Simpson, 1995; also see Bingen, Simpson, and Berthé, 1994.

9. In contrast to the SG 2000 program, the OHVN has transferred primary responsibility for agricultural credit, marketing, and input supply out of the hands of its frontline extension staff and to village-level groups who work directly with private input suppliers and banks. The effectiveness of this "privatized system," however, depends upon a significant credit guarantee to the banks that is underwritten by the USAID-financed project (see Bingen et al., 1994).

10. As Belloncle noted in his stinging critique of most extension programs in West Africa, "if African farmers as a whole have not yet adopted the practices recommended to them, the reason is not that they are too complicated; on the contrary, they are too simple to solve farmers' problems" (Belloncle, 1989, p. 39).

11. Since the authors introduce this typology primarily as a means for presenting their historical overview of technology transfer, the categories are used to distinguish among three "phases" of international technology transfer. We adapt this typology to the purposes of our discussion, but we categorically leave aside any reference to a temporal or evolutionary relationship between categories.

12. It is useful to remember that U.S. farmers and agricultural scientists have long debated the relevance of agricultural research at the U.S. land-grant universities (see Bingen, 1995).

13. This is a worldwide phenomenon. In Michigan, for example, we know that a wide variety of farmers and growers have created various types of groups and organizations in order to facilitate the exchange and testing of technical information and practices.

14. For one tentative effort in this direction see Collion, 1995.

15. This training is provided under a contract with CLUSA or, as it is known in the United States, NCBA, the National Cooperative Business Association.

16. See Amanor, 1994.

17. See Gnägi, 1991.

18. Based on a VA's expected marketed production, the banks set ceilings on the amount of credit available for distribution on an annual basis.

19. In other words, as Ferguson has cautioned, even with this "grassroots approach," we need to explicate the ways in which gender, class, and ethnicity influence the processes of problem identification or technology development by individual farmers (see Ferguson, 1994; also see Amanor, 1994).

20. For a discussion of this issue related to early SG 2000 activities in Ghana see Tripp, 1993.

PART III

American University–Industry Interaction

CHAPTER 6

University Technology Transfer and the Problems of Conflict of Interest

GARY W. MATKIN

Like it or not, colleges and universities, particularly research universities, increasingly are being identified as important elements in the economic life of our nation. For some, the prospect of the academy's greater involvement in economic development activities, including the active development of intellectual property and the establishment of companies to exploit university research, seems salutary—part of the natural process by which the academy adapts to the needs of the society that supports it. They therefore desire to increase these activities. Others see such activity as diverting the academy from its appropriate roles and missions, blurring the definition of the institution and taking it into dangerous areas where it may not belong; their agenda is to discourage this kind of behavior.

This chapter uses events at the University of California (UC) between 1989 and 1994 as a case study to illustrate the consequences to the academy of a collision between these two powerful public policy agendas. The university's attempts to establish a separate nonprofit foundation to manage its considerable portfolio of intellectual property and to form a for-profit company to fund development and start-up efforts met with both enthusiastic support and stiff opposition. During the process of the debate, the issues became more sharply defined and lessons to be learned were clarified.

As we will see, California's experience is not uncommon. On the contrary, it illustrates an emerging pattern in the responses of higher-education institutions to the new pressures on them to be more relevant economically. It also permits us to anticipate the consequences for the university, both internal and external, of economic development activities. Lessons drawn from UC's experience thus have general application.

FULL-SERVICE TECHNOLOGY TRANSFER: LURES AND PITFALLS

While the battle between the two policy approaches just described is waged in and around universities, those same universities must deal with day-to-day concerns related to technology transfer activities, often in the absence of policy or clearly understood principles. From the university's point of view, the irreversible trend toward greater involvement between university and commercial interests is driven largely by the prospect of increased revenues. Corporate sponsorship of university research has increased from $70 million in 1972 to over $1.2 billion in 1991. University management of intellectual property has become more aggressive and sophisticated in the last few years, and this has been reflected in an increase in financial returns. At the UC, for instance, royalty income increased from $11.1 million in fiscal 1989–90, to $49.5 million in 1993 and $63.1 million in 1995. This kind of growth leads naturally to a desire, especially on the part of professional technology licensing officers, to expand university efforts into what has been called a full-service technology transfer program. Such a program includes accepting equity in licensing companies in addition to cash royalties, funding the development and expansion of nascent technologies ("funding the gap"), and—the last frontier of university technology transfer efforts—starting up companies to exploit technology developed by the university.

The path toward a full-service technology transfer program, however, has proven to be full of dangers and pitfalls. Several major research universities, including Harvard, Johns Hopkins, the University of Chicago, and Boston University, have taken steps toward implementing the full-service concept and have found that these steps, especially investment in start-up companies, are often costly to the university in terms of both finances and public relations. For example, the president and several members of the board of trustees of Boston University (BU) were investigated for conflict of interest involving the university's investments in start-up companies such as Seragen, Incorporated, which was founded in 1987 to develop some intellectual property owned by BU and received most of its funding from BU until it went public in 1992. John Silber, BU's president, was a director of the company and owned 105,000 shares. He also may have made $386,700 when a Seragen spin-off company, Seradyn, was sold. Several members of the board of trustees were involved in Seragen and the Seradyn transaction and are members, along with BU, of Commonwealth Partners, a venture capital firm.

Similar controversies have marked the efforts of other universities to form organizations to start companies to develop university discoveries. The cold-fusion controversy at the University of Utah, clearly caused by the university's desire to realize a large financial return, resulted in a great deal of embarrassment for the university and damage to its academic reputation and may have led to the resignation of the university's president when it was discovered that he had improperly transferred funds to support cold-fusion development. Michigan Technological University's Venture Group, Incorporated, a profit-seeking investment company, has been controversial since it lost $1.6 million in 1989 because of mismanagement and embezzlement by its officers. The University of South Carolina's research and development foundation has been under intense public scrutiny since 1987, and this scrutiny led to indictments and convictions against the university's former president, James B. Holderman. These cases and many others offer warnings to universities preparing to step into the marketplace.

Despite these painful examples, the lure of large financial returns and a desire to facilitate the commercialization of university-developed technology for the good of the public are pulling almost every research university into some new arrangement for technology development and investment. Based on a study conducted in 1984 by SRI International for the National Science Foundation, Gregory and Sheahen (1991) conclude that start-up investments are more successful than simple licensing in the commercialization of university-owned intellectual property. The financial returns are greater, and the range of inventions that achieve financial viability is wider. They point out that a technology licensing program based upon a patent licensing approach must be highly selective, which leads to the neglect of many middle-of-the-road inventions (that is, those promising a market under $100 million in sales per year). They also conclude that an arms-length licensing agreement can often inhibit commercialization. Lacking the involvement of the university, licensees frequently lose interest in pursuing commercialization of the technology.

PROTECTIVE MECHANISMS

Universities are beginning to learn from their mistakes and to recognize the importance of developing policies and practices to protect themselves from the dangers inherent in taking an active part in technology transfer. Several common patterns are beginning to emerge. To begin with, most universities are seeking to buffer themselves by establishing separate for- or not-for-profit organizations to administer some or all aspects of the commercialization of intellectual property. A major exception to this trend is MIT, which, perhaps because of the arrangements it has been able to make with the well-established venture capital community in the Boston area and the resistance it would have from that community if it were to set up a buffer organization, has proclaimed publicly that it would not separate itself from its intellectual property management functions.

Universities have also become better at articulating technology transfer initiatives to their public and legislative constituencies. Such articulation often means emphasizing the public benefits of these initiatives and playing down the benefits to the university, including the increased resources made available to the university through these efforts. At the same time, gaining acceptance for technology transfer within the university often requires emphasizing the potential of such activities for resource generation. Striking a balance between the arguments required for internal and external acceptance can be very difficult.

Universities are experimenting with different approaches to the conflict-of-interest issues raised by aggressive technology commercialization programs. For instance, most universities do not allow university researchers to receive research funding from companies in which they own stock. The problem is that, once a university becomes involved in ownership of research-based companies, there are so many possible kinds of conflict of interest that policy formation is difficult. The trend therefore is toward process policies, that is, policies that require full disclosure of the circumstances and then a review of those circumstances by a designated body. Johns Hopkins is a leader in this approach.

Unless these elements—buffer organizations, public policy rationales, and policies to deal with conflict of interest—are in place, universities are vulnerable to scandals associated with aggressive commercialization efforts. When a scandal does erupt, it colors the university's efforts to engage in technology transfer of any kind and often retards progress toward a stable balance between economic service and traditional university values.

With these general trends in mind, let us now turn to the case of UC. Its unsuccessful efforts to form a separate organization to manage and market its intellectual property illustrate many of the dangers of and obstacles to an expanded university technology transfer program.

THE CASE OF THE UNIVERSITY OF CALIFORNIA

This story begins in about 1990. In the fiscal year 1990–1991, UC, through its nine campuses and the three major research laboratories it manages for the federal government (Los Alamos, Lawrence Livermore, and Lawrence Berkeley), conducted $1.36 billion in research, with about 10 percent of the basic research funded by the federal government. UC's intellectual property is managed through a centralized Office of Technology Transfer (OTT) and several campus-based offices, including offices at Berkeley and Los Angeles (UCLA). In fiscal year 1992 the OTT (not including the Berkeley and UCLA offices) received 352 invention disclosures, filed 197 patents, received 68 patents, issued 102 licenses, had 621 licenses in effect, and received $28.8 million in royalty revenue.

History

The history of UC's management of its intellectual property through 1988 has been described elsewhere. To summarize, until about 1989, UC's intellectual property administration was oriented primarily toward protecting intellectual property through patents and copyrights, rather than toward the active marketing of the property. To some extent, this stance was dictated by the staffing level authorized for the office, then called the Patent, Trademark, and Copyright Office (PTCO). In 1980 PTCO had ten employees; in 1987 it had twenty employees.

With this orientation and at these staffing levels, PTCO simply was not getting the job done. UC researchers complained vigorously about the lack of attention given to invention disclosures, and the press made the public aware of the problem in a front-page article in the *San Francisco Examiner* (Best, 1987).

In response to these criticisms, the UC hired a new director for PTCO, Carl Wootten. Wootten changed the emphasis of PTCO to marketing. He acted quickly to increase the staff and licensing activity of the office, which was renamed the Office of Technology Transfer (OTT) to reflect its new charge. The number of staff increased from 20 in 1987 to 43 in 1989 and an authorized 57 in 1994. These efforts apparently paid off, as royalty and fee income increased from $5 million in 1987 to $44.7 million in 1993.

Despite this seeming success, a number of issues surfaced that caused concern among UC administrators. First, a review of UC's inventory of undeveloped inventions revealed a large number that, with a relatively small investment, might be brought to commercial attractiveness, yet the UC had no funding to dedicate to their development. This is known as the "funding the gap" problem. Second, in a number of cases, licensees for what appeared to be very promising technology could not be found. In both these situations it seemed that UC, through an appropriate arrangement, could attract the necessary funding from outside sources. In still other cases, in the opinion of Wootten and others, UC was not getting the best result in terms of financial return or technology transfer effectiveness from deals restricted to the issuance of licenses.

Furthermore, it became clear that there were a number of difficulties in operating the OTT under the full force of the UC's regulations, policies, and cumbersome bureaucracy. The OTT needed to be responsive and to be able to make decisions quickly, and its licensing officers needed to have the freedom to structure deals. High turnover in licensing professionals also indicated that UC's compensation structure was inappropriate. Salespeople should be compensated in part on an incentive basis, but UC was uncomfortable with such an arrangement.

For the administrators involved, including Wootten and UC's vice president, Ron Brady (to whom Wootten reported through an associate vice president), these concerns argued strongly for the separation of the OTT into some combination of for-profit and not-for-profit organizations. The remainder of this case study is a description of the unsuccessful efforts by these administrators to establish these entities. These attempts fall into four distinct phases, which might be called "white paper," "DU-1," "Pilot Project," and "state sponsored."

The White Paper Phase. Shortly after his arrival at UC in May 1989, Wootten wrote a "white paper" describing the need for an external structure to manage UC intellectual property and recommending a particular configuration. This proposal has remained essentially the same during all the subsequent phases of the effort.

The white paper called for a not-for-profit foundation to absorb all the functions performed by the (then) PTCO. In addition the paper recommended formation of a for-profit corporation to be called the California Technologies Ventures Corporation (CTVC), which would provide gap funding for undeveloped technologies and venture capital for start-up companies. CTVC would also help start-ups in other ways: for example, CTVC could assemble management teams and provide subsequent rounds of venture capital. UC would own a majority of the shares in CTVC. The remainder of the shares would be held by corporate investors whose purchase of those shares would provide the initial capital to fund technology developments and prepare start-up efforts for first-round financing. The foundation would release technology to CTVC for development, and CTVC would then develop or sell that technology to the greatest advantage, returning licensing fees to the foundation and profit from equity appreciation in start-ups to UC through distributions to its stockholders.

The Patents and Technology Transfer Executive Committee, composed of senior officials from the Office of the President and the nine campuses and three laboratories, met to consider Wootten's proposal in early 1990. The committee decided that the proposal was too far-reaching and complicated for the committee to pass on without a more complete review. Committee members felt they were unfamiliar with many of the issues, and they were ignorant of any alternatives to the plan. They also saw that achieving consensus across so many campuses and laboratories was going to be difficult. In the usual academic fashion, a subcommittee was formed to consider the proposal further and report to the full committee.

The DU-1 Phase. Impatient with the pace of the discussions and feeling that the value of the proposal could be proven if given a chance, Wootten and his colleagues decided to just "do one," that is, to choose a very hot, promising technology and, on an exception basis and with the approval of the administration, secure venture funding and create a start-up company. They expected that in the process the policy and operational issues that would have to be addressed during a larger effort would become more clearly defined. Beginning approximately in early March 1990 and continuing through September 1990, a group of UC officials, with help from experts outside UC, met to review the inventory of technologies in order to select one for intense development. The group finally chose a ceramic-metal composite with wide potential applications, from golf clubs to tanks.

The OTT prepared a proposal for the DU-1 effort and a business plan for the commercial development of the composite material. These were presented to the subcommittee on October 10, 1990. The subcommittee members questioned almost every aspect of the proposals. They wondered whether the selected technology really did have a good chance for success. They questioned the wisdom of risking the entire program on only one technology, and they echoed the criticisms of the previous phase—that the philosophical, policy, and informational framework for such a project had not been developed. In his report of the meeting, the chair of the subcommittee voiced the subcommittee's opposition to the DU-1 project and suggested that the next effort, whatever it might be, be preceded by an examination of the efforts of other universities in this area and an all-university conference of campus representatives to build the knowledge, background, and consensus needed for proper implementation.

The Pilot Project Phase. The next chapter in the story began with a major reorganization in the advisory structure supporting the technology transfer efforts. Two major committees, the Intellectual Property Advisory Committee and the PTCO Executive Committee, were merged into a single Technology Transfer Council (TTC), in August 1991. This committee, like its predecessors, was composed of high-ranking campus and laboratory officials, often the number two official in each organization. The committee immediately formed a subcommittee, called the CTVC Task Force, to consider the next step in the CTVC project.

Wootten revised his white paper and presented it to the new committee in November 1991. Another plan was then developed, focusing on a pilot project to be based at a single campus. The University of California, San Francisco (UCSF) had the most to gain from such a plan because of its large portfolio of undeveloped technologies. At a May 1992 meeting, therefore, the TTC approved a study of the feasibility of developing a CTVC pilot program at UCSF.

During the summer of 1992, the feasibility study was made. Faculty members were interviewed, the experience of other universities was examined, and alternatives were proposed and evaluated. The study supported the feasibility of a CTVC pilot program at UCSF, and the proposal for such a program was endorsed by the UCSF faculty and administration.

A meeting of the CTVC Task Force was held on October 12, 1992, to consider the study. The task force expected to recommend that the TTC approve the pilot project at its scheduled meeting on November 6. The day before the task force meeting, however, the chair of the task force, a vice chancellor at UCSF, met with Vice President Brady to review the study and the project proposal. The report of this meeting astounded the members of the task force. Brady raised serious questions about the study, despite his ongoing knowledge of its development, and basically vetoed the project. The TTC meeting scheduled for November 6 was canceled.

The State-Sponsored Phase. This sudden reversal had come about because events had overtaken the proposal, calling for more aggressive and visible efforts by UC. The new president of the university, Jack W. Peltason, who had just assumed office on October 1 under intense budget pressure and strong demands that UC demonstrate its economic value to the state, had quickly developed what were called his economic initiatives, a prominent feature of which was a full-blown foundation and CTVC proposal, as opposed to the relatively small-scale and seemingly tentative pilot project. UC made a deal with the state whereby the state's share of royalty revenue (about 25% after administrative costs), which was based upon the premise that the state had provided some of the means by which the inventions had been made, was capped at 1992 levels. Any additional amounts would go to fund foundation and CTVC efforts.

This plan gained immediate and enthusiastic support from the state government, which was desperate to improve California's economy. The response has been less enthusiastic among members of the business community, particularly among biotechnology and venture capital firms, who view it as a potential competitor. They were concerned about what is called "pipelining," the practice whereby the most promising technologies are chosen for in-house development rather than offered openly to the business community. This is a particularly touchy issue for a public university, which is generally held to have a duty to make sure that the public is served before its own treasury.

The UC faculty also has expressed reservations. In a letter to President Peltason dated March 8, 1993, and endorsed by 43 colleagues from five campuses of UC, UCLA Professor Emeritus Paul Boyer objected to the foundation (now called UCTDF) and the CTVC (now UCTDC) in the following terms:

Pursuit of basic knowledge in biological, biomedical and agricultural research has achieved remarkable success in enriching our culture, promoting our health, and launching the biotechnology industry. The accomplishments document the rewards to society from University support and illustrate the success of interactions with private enterprise under present policies and procedures.

Based on this experience and other considerations, we believe that the proposed UCTDF/UCTDC would be a mistake. Such action is unnecessary and could seriously detract from the teaching, research, and public service functions of the University. Any changes aimed at improving technology transfer should not undermine the primary mission of the University. (P. D. Boyer, personal communication, March 8, 1993)

This letter received wide circulation and was featured in stories in the state and national press.

Complicating Factors

Much has been left out of this story. One complicating feature is the tension between the OTT and the individual campuses regarding the administration of intellectual property. In May 1989, the chancellors of the campuses voted to permit the campuses to open their own technology licensing offices and control their own intellectual property. Berkeley and UCLA have done so, and several other campuses began considering this alternative. As the president's proposal appeared to threaten this recently won campus autonomy, there was cause for campus opposition to the plan. Underlying this opposition was the understandable tension between two practical concerns. On the one hand, technology licensing officers need to be close to faculty researchers and develop personal relationships with them in order to elicit invention disclosures and help in marketing technology. On the other hand, there is also a need in a multiple-campus organization for intellectual property matters, including policy formation and administration and marketing, to be administered and coordinated on a system-wide basis.

Then there was the series of controversies and scandals that shook public confidence in UC's ability to manage its affairs in the public interest. In March 1992, a controversy erupted over the retirement package granted to President Gardner that was reported to be over $1 million. This package came to light at a time when UC was raising student fees significantly (by over 40%), laying off employees, and freezing salaries in order to meet a budget shortage caused by a reduction in support from the state. Other aspects of UC fiscal policy and practice came under intense, and often hostile, public scrutiny at the same time, including (unfortunately for the proposal being described) elements of UC's technology transfer efforts.

In 1989, the then-PTCO moved into new administrative space in Harbor Bay Isle, a large real estate development in the city of Alameda. Ron Cowan, the developer-owner of Harbor Bay Isle, offered PTCO ten years' free rent in the hope of attracting not only it but other UC units and spin-off companies based on UC technology. Cowan and Vice President Brady apparently formed a close friendship. Cowan also retained the services of Willie Brown, a lawyer but also the powerful speaker of the State Assembly and a UC regent by virtue of that post. Furthermore, when UCSF, frustrated by local opposition to its efforts to locate a "second campus" within the city and county of San Francisco, began looking for space in nearby cities, Cowan presented UC with a proposal for using Harbor Bay Isle for that campus as well.

Fearful of the loss of jobs and economic benefits that the removal of part of UCSF would cause, the city of San Francisco, as well as the San Francisco press, began looking for improprieties in the relationship between UC and Cowan. It came to light that a number of meetings held in 1990 about technology development projects were held in the offices of Cowan's development company, a practice that continued until one of the committee members questioned the propriety of holding meetings about university business in such a setting. Brown was rumored to have attended some of the meetings (although this was never verified). To make matters worse, several high-ranking UC officials, including Brady and the chancellor of UCSF, appeared in a promotional videotape for Harbor Bay Isle, extolling its virtues and mentioning the fact that the OTT was located in the development. A subsequent independent investigation by the university cleared UC officials of substantive violations in these matters, although there were some "technical violations" and "the strong appearance of impropriety."

The Present Situation

All this publicity cast the proposal for the state-sponsored foundation and for-profit company in a very questionable light. In mid-May 1993, Theodore Hullar, chancellor at UC-Davis on special assignment to direct President Peltason's economic initiatives, announced that the plans for the for-profit CTVC were "off the table." In late June 1993, under the headline "UC's Secret Stock Deals," the *San Francisco Chronicle/Examiner* reported that UC had "taken ownership in at least 10 start-up high-tech firms" in return for the licensing of university-owned technology, in spite of a UC policy prohibiting such ownership. The newspaper protested the secrecy and UC's refusal to provide information about the deals. The same issue reported incorrectly the failure of one of the companies and suggested that Wootten had a conflict of interest in dealings with the man who had been named chief executive officer (CEO) of the failed company, a suggestion that Wootten has disputed exhaustively.

In the light of all this, the foundation initiative was put aside. Yet another faculty committee was formed by Vice President V. Wayne Kennedy, who replaced Brady when Brady retired. It has recommended that many functions of the OTT be decentralized to the campuses. The proposed plan has been carried out over the last three years. Director Wootten left the university, and some elements of the controversy have abated. The Cowan-UCSF controversy seems to have blown over; UCSF has decided, at least for now, not to consider the Harbor Bay Isle site. The underlying factors in favor of increased technology transfer activity—especially against the backdrop of salary cuts for UC employees and the elimination of schools and departments—are more important than ever. However, this is very much a story to be continued. Its outcome is anything but clear.

Lessons from the UC Case

Much may seem idiosyncratic in the evolving case of UC's attempts to create a full-service technology transfer program. Few universities compare to UC, for example, in sheer size and in complexity as a multicampus, multilaboratory organization. However, UC's story clearly offers parallels with the experience of other universities. Some lessons from the UC case thus may be valuable for other universities and for policymakers involved in technology transfer initiatives.

Avoid Real or Apparent Conflict of Interest. As universities step aggressively into the marketplace, they become enmeshed in the threads that form the fabric of commercial relationships. The problems UC officials faced because of their associations with real estate developers and outside commercial interests are not unique, as the experiences of Boston University, the University of Utah, the University of South Carolina, and several others attest.

University trustees often are selected precisely because they are well-connected with the commercial world, and university presidents must deal with people in that world every day. As the university starts trying to make money through aggressive commercialization of its intellectual property, conflict of interest problems are likely to arise. It is natural and valuable for trustees and presidents to be involved directly in establishing the basis and mechanisms for university commercial involvement, but it is also important that, from the beginning, appropriate mechanisms be put in place to avoid conflict of interest or the perception of conflict of interest. Review committees, scientific panels, strict guidelines, and appropriate buffering mechanisms, all supported by a careful public relations effort, are important early components of any effort to commercialize university research.

Articulate a Clear and Timely Public Policy Agenda. Only in late 1992, about three years after the first efforts to establish separate organizations for the purpose, did the president publicly endorse an expanded technology transfer effort. His statement came in response to a crisis and, at least in regard to the elements described in this case study, was done without the full advice and consent of the faculty or even of the committees established to oversee the efforts. His statement also included a specific and controversial proposal (for the establishment of the foundation and CTVC). A university administration's support for technology transfer efforts is crucial, but in UC's case that support was not fully effective. It came late, it appeared to be reactive to a crisis, it was put together hurriedly without a broadly based consultative effort, and it mixed policy elements with policy implementation steps, some of which were controversial. Such errors can be avoided.

General policies, expressing the university's support of technology transfer and explaining how this support fits with the institutional mission, should be formulated and adopted formally by the board of trustees after a process involving extensive consultation with faculty. Such consultation is also necessary for the next step, the setting of appropriate implementation plans, which should involve expanding the consultative process to members of the university's external constituencies, including, where appropriate, governmental bodies.

Provide a Forum and Process for Internal Debate. Most universities, certainly including the UC system, lack a structure or forum and a process by which the members of the university community can reach consensus on broad policy issues such as the nature of the university's role in economic development or technology transfer. A new forum and process thus must be invented each time the university faces such issues. Such invention takes time and effort and may mean that the discussion never happens. This was the case with UC. After the failure of the DU-1 initiative, the chair of the CTVC Task Force proposed a university-wide conference to consider alternatives, but nothing was ever done to organize such a conference until early 1996, when planning began for a conference to be held in early 1997.

The process of consideration was also flawed. Although the experiences of several other universities were examined, no serious consideration was given to models for organizing technology transfer efforts other than the one laid out in Wootten's original white paper. Each effort, then, took on the appearance of a selling job for the original proposal, rather than an objective examination of what was best for UC. University faculty are unlikely to respond positively to such an approach. As many large universities have had to face technology transfer issues, there are many models and much data for university administrators to consider and evaluate. No process of examination can be considered legitimate unless it includes an objective study of available alternatives.

Avoid the Appearance of Unfair Advantage. Traditionally, universities, particularly public and land-grant universities, are not supposed to make money from the knowledge they produce. Although this principle steadily is being modified, many members of the general public (including university alumni), government officials, and faculty members still believe in it. The public policy justification for university technology transfer activity, therefore, must emphasize the good to society that such efforts are likely to bring and place the benefits to the university treasury in a secondary position of importance. The guiding principle for a full-service technology transfer program is the increased commercialization of university-developed technology, which means, among other things, that the best mechanism for economic development for each technology should be sought and found, even when that mechanism does not maximize financial return to the university.

In the UC case, it was not always clear exactly what privileges the foundation and CTVC would have with regard to university-owned intellectual property. Would CTVC, for instance, have the right of first refusal over UC technology, or would it have some kind of facilitated access to information about the technology? Either way, UC would be vulnerable to the charge of pipelining. Another problem with the UC proposal was the combination of functions proposed for CTVC. The public policy argument in favor of funding the gap is much easier to make than is the argument in favor of the university's investing in start-up companies. Thus the controversy over UC's involvement in start-ups may have prevented progress on the funding-the-gap issue. Universities can avoid these problems to some extent by establishing procedures designed to find interest in university technology from a wide pool of potential commercial developers. University-sponsored commercialization should be undertaken only after the technology has been marketed, and then only according to established criteria.

Choose Appropriate Partners. So many universities have run into difficulties because of a poor choice of partners in technology development that this problem begins to seem unavoidable. UC's association with real estate developer Cowan, while not related directly to a technology commercialization proposal, illustrates this point. Universities can protect themselves to some extent, however, by establishing standard procedures and criteria to evaluate the background, reputation, and capabilities of potential partners (both individuals and organizations).

Seek External Support. Wilson and Szygenda (1991) claim that the keys to successful technology transfer are a wide range of tools, clear university policies, and a supportive capital community. They also stress the importance of supportive governmental policies. Until now, however, UC initiatives have been primarily internal, with little involvement from outside UC. Only in a late stage did it receive the endorsement of the state government. Members of the capital community remain skeptical of UC initiatives, and some view them as potentially competitive to their own interests. Without strong external support, the UC initiative had trouble passing internal reviews. In developing technology transfer initiatives, universities should seek the early involvement of external groups to assure that university programs mesh with and support related efforts, rather than compete with them.

Establish Appropriate Oversight. Universities face a dilemma when they decide to become more aggressive in developing commercial technology. On the one hand, they must engage professionals who are experienced in selling intellectual property, which means making deals with sophisticated commercial interests. On the other hand, they must constrain those professionals with policies designed to protect the university from the problems described in this chapter. Licensing professionals are bound to be frustrated by restrictive policies, and they will desire independence and autonomy. An appropriate balance between autonomy and restriction is difficult to strike, both for in-house efforts and for buffer organizations where the issue is defined primarily in terms of ownership and control relationships between the university and the organization. However, the balance must be established and defined in order to avoid continued frustration, both in the professionals who carry out the technology transfer activities and in those with whom they must deal.

Integrate Technology Transfer Activities on a Broad Scale. Technology transfer is part of such a sweeping trend in higher education that no single initiative, even one as significant as that proposed by UC, can be taken without serious implications for other parts of the institution. Related university policies, particularly those concerned with conflict of interest, consulting, use of university property, graduate student employment, and leaves of absence, must be examined and revised if such initiatives are adopted.

New forms of organization, such as the foundation and CTVC, must be devised, evaluated, and created. The activities of previously unrelated existing organizational units must be coordinated, as one major university discovered: It found that its patent office was suing a corporation for patent infringement at the same time its development office was making a major pitch for research support to the same corporation! In addition, efforts to alter the culture of the university in favor of the desired changes must be undertaken—campaigns to educate faculty about the value of technology transfer, public relations efforts describing successful initiatives, and so on. Even with such efforts, there is no assurance that humanities faculty, for instance, will support technology transfer efforts.

In any event, in the UC case there is clear evidence that no such broad-scale effort was ever contemplated seriously, let alone carried out. On the contrary, the DU-1 and the pilot project phases can be seen as attempts to take a shortcut around this difficult and time-consuming task. Their failure illustrates what is perhaps the most important lesson of all: There are no shortcuts.

CONCLUSION

As the university is called upon to assume new roles in society, in this case as an important contributor to national and regional economies, some of its traditions inevitably are challenged and even overturned. The process by which traditional and new demands are balanced is and always has been vital to the university, allowing it to adapt to changing social conditions and at the same time maintain its legitimacy and integrity. However, this process is carried on in a fragile shell. There is always the danger of a rupture, either as a catastrophic loss of public confidence or as a fracture of the internal cohesiveness of collegiality. If change occurs without the self-awareness and free debate necessary to define the issues and come to some consensus, the whole structure and basis of the university is threatened. Such a danger is present now.

The trend toward increased university and faculty involvement in commercial activity is irreversible: The commitment to economic development and commercialization of intellectual property is too strong and too advanced to be undone or even slowed down very much. Having stepped into the marketplace, the university will find itself governed by new rules. It will have to take legal action against others, as in the defense of patent rights, and it will be sued in its turn. Errors of judgment or association that bring negative attention to the university inevitably will occur. Danger to the university arises not so much from these individual occurrences (although some of the cases cited have been very serious indeed) as from the fact that universities are unlikely to be ready for them.

Most American universities have a poor understanding of the scope of the changes related to their increasing commercial activity. They see problems that arise as isolated instances of bad judgment or bad luck, calling for ad hoc solutions, rather than as symptoms of an underlying trend. Most universities also lack provision for the kind of debate and interchange of ideas that is necessary for informed decisionmaking on such issues. University faculty and administrators, thus, are poorly equipped to handle the crises, large and small, that are sure to come as commercial involvement increases.

Since universities have not yet marshaled sufficient administrative and faculty support for their new role, scandal or financial failure related to commercialization or economic development might well crystallize traditionalist opposition and allow it to carry the day. The result could be a temporary retreat from the new course. The consequences of such a retreat are likely to be as little foreseen or understood as the consequences of the advance that preceded it. The university's resultant unsteady course will condemn the institution to further loss of public confidence.

University leaders must strike a careful balance between the traditions of their institution and the new demands placed on it by constituencies both inside and outside the university. This balancing act starts with increased awareness of underlying issues and activation of debate between groups or individuals within the university. The balancing will never end, but if it is successful long enough, it should become more like riding a bicycle than like walking a high wire.

CHAPTER 7

Translating Academic Research to Technological Innovation

YONG S. LEE AND RICHARD GAERTNER

Technology transfer policy in the United States encourages academics to explore various avenues by which to transfer the new knowledge, technology, and know-how to industry.[1] One approach examined in this chapter is a process by which university scientists and engineers peer into their own scientific advances from which to identify industrially useful ideas and concepts and "transform" them to advanced technologies. The process may also include instances in which academics work with extant generic inventions and explore other applications. In technology transfer literature, as well as in policy debate,[2] much of this transformation process is assumed as though it is linear. In other words, it is understood simply as a matter of "translating" the ideas on the shelf to applications and "transferring" them out the door to firms. As this chapter will show, the transformation process involves extensive market interaction and requires an expenditure of large R&D resources.[3] Policy based on a neat, yet simple, notion of linearity is bound to disappoint many. To improve policy discourse a need exists for a better understanding of what is actually required to transform academic science to industrial innovation.

The purpose of this chapter is to discuss the recent experience of Iowa State University, which has experimented for a number of years with the concept of transforming academic research to technological innovation.[4] This concept is often referred to as "university-based technology development" (see Chapter 6). The experiment began in 1987 with funding from the U.S. Department of Commerce, joined later in 1992 by the Iowa General Assembly, and by industry thereafter.[5] Discussion and analysis of this chapter is based on our own "participant" observation and extensive case studies of the firms that participated in the ISU experiment.[6] In the first part of this chapter we discuss the "ideal" process of university technology transfer that initially guided the ISU experiment, and in the second part we focus on the dynamics of university-firm interaction. In conclusion we discuss what we have learned from the experiment.

We note at the outset that the idea of university-based technology development is not without controversy because it represents a departure from the traditional norm of university research as we know it (Feller, 1990). The "postwar social contract" that emerged from Bush's *Science—The Endless Frontier* (1945) is that the federal government should support university research, according the university community "a high degree of self-governance and intellectual autonomy, in return for which its benefits would be widely diffused through society and the economy" (Brooks, 1986, p. 126). The concept of university-based technology development arguably goes against the traditional norm because academics must get their hands "dirty" with "downstream" applied research, the result of which is intended to benefit private firms and, only in the aggregate sense, the public. Note, however, as discussed in Chapter 1, the legislative intent of the Bayh-Dole Act of 1980 and the Stevenson-Wydler Act of 1980 was to do just that. Strong support for the legislative intent has been expressed by the National Academy of Sciences (1992), the Carnegie Commission on Science, Technology, and Government (1992), and the President's Council of Advisors on Science and Technology (1992). Still, controversy continues—and it is important to make note of it because the national technology transfer policy is periodically under review. Our objective here is not to become an advocate of this approach but to describe the process and what it actually entails.

THE THEORY OF UNIVERSITY-BASED TECHNOLOGICAL INNOVATION

To understand the underlying rationale for university-based technology development it is important to discuss what is referred to in the literature as "technological gap theory."[7] The theory suggests that a large gap exists between scientific advances made in academic research and technologies exploited in the market. Scientific discoveries advanced in academic research are recognized as scientific investigation of fundamental natural phenomena whose interest is driven largely by intellectual curiosity or by particular scientific problems. Even where academic research is conducted with applications in mind, they still represent the very early stage of technological innovation, requiring many years of focused applied research and large sums of R&D funds. Because of this requirement, coupled with market uncertainty, firms consider academic research too high a risk in which to invest their fortune. If academic research is to be deployable by industry, it is necessary that this technological gap be narrowed.

In Figure 7.1 we present an organizational process model that attempts to bridge academic research to technological innovation. The model, developed at ISU,[8] has guided the experiment in its early stage. The model, as shown in Figure 7.1, describes the process of university-based technological innovation,

Figure 7.1
The University-Based Technological Innovation Process

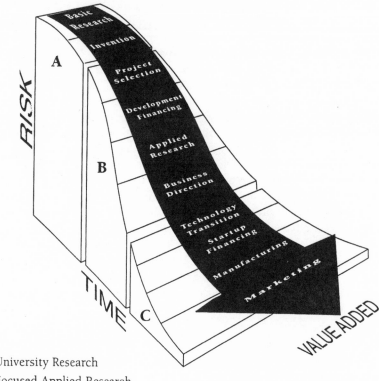

A = University Research
B = Focused Applied Research
C = Commercialization

which is structured on a downward slope. In this model, the risks normally associated with academic discovery are reduced to a level at which firms feel safer to invest in commercialization. It is important to stress that the model focuses on academic technological innovation, not ''product development.''

Area ''A'' in Figure 7.1 is the relative risk associated with academic research considered to have strong commercial potential. This is a phase in which companies would not normally get involved. To bring the risk down to a commercially palatable level, the model incorporates the second phase, Area ''B,'' ''focused applied research.'' Focused applied research is the process of technological innovation in which theoretical concepts and ideas are *reformulated* into useful applications. Patentable inventions, processes, designs, prototypes, and software exemplify the results of focused applied research.

Typically, focused applied research is protracted research; and it often leads to many more technological spin-offs and inventions, which also require additional focused applied research. The evolution of "thin-film" resonator technology at Iowa State University may illustrate the nature of spin-offs. In 1988, the Center for Advanced Technology Development at Iowa State University (the organizational unit that carried out the experiment) awarded a grant to ISU's Microelectronics Research Center (MRC) in response to a proposal to further expand the "thin-film resonator" concept (developed earlier under a contract from the Departments of Energy and Defense). The MRC group believed that the thin-film resonator concept could be extended to industrial applications. One of these involved the use of special chemical coatings on etched semiconductor composites. The special coatings, which were yet to be identified, would generate "electrical pulses" when activated by environmental stimuli such as adsorbed gases or liquids. Such electrical devices could be used for a variety of industrial and public applications. The center was persuaded, and it funded the proposal. After two years of focused applied research, the MRC was successful in developing new chemical substrates that were sensitive to families of gases and liquids. This opened a window for a large number of sensing applications. Other forms of resonator technology also led to the development of micro-antennas and other unique devices that show high promise for use in several specialized areas of microelectronics. By 1995, with additional funding and involvement of other additional research teams, the thin-film research has produced fifteen patents and five licenses to different companies.

The third phase in the transfer slope, Area "C," involves commercialization. The process involves a range of commercial activities from technology licensing to beta-testing (experimental testing of the market), raising venture capital, scale-up production, capital investment, manufacturing, and marketing. This "commercialization" phase is an area in which the university, being ill-equipped to deal with it, typically phases out in the transfer process. What typically remains for the university is the management of intellectual property, including royalties, license fees, disputes, and potential or actual litigation. To further assist firms in the commercialization phase some entrepreneurial universities establish "research parks" in which to incubate new start-up firms, share equity, and provide technical assistance.

Thus far, we have described an organizational process model on a linear slope. We now must point out that this is only a very rough road map. In reality, as we learn from the ISU study, the transformation process zigs and zags, often haltingly, and repeats itself in response to a multitude of forces: an unexpected increase in cost of research, a technical snag, pressures from market competition, university politics, legislative vicissitudes, and luck. But the two most central aspects, not explicated in the model above, are about (1) the dynamics of university-industry interaction and (2) the requirement for new R&D resources. We turn to these topics below.

THE PROBLEM OF THE "FUNDING GAP"

As pointed out earlier in the chapter, focused applied research (Area "B" in Figure 7.1) requires an expenditure of large R&D resources. This is the money that universities do not have and that firms are unwilling to underwrite. This is called the "funding gap," an incidence of the "market failure."[9] In recent years, U.S. research universities, particularly state universities, have been under pressure to translate their research for industrial applications and state economic development.[10] However, the universities have not been provided with needed R&D resources to assume this new responsibility. This is a dilemma, and it often invites conflict of interest on campus, as Gary Matkin so vividly demonstrates in Chapter 6 of this volume in the case of the University of California.

The ISU study reported here is a special case because the federal government has filled the funding gap. Of course, we do not argue here that this is the way the funding gap ought to be addressed. Historically, though, as Johnson and Teske discuss extensively in Chapter 3, this is a public policy tool by which under special circumstances the federal government has often intervened to fill the void created by the market.

In 1987, ISU became a recipient of federal funding to study the feasibility, as well as the efficiency, of converting new scientific advances that were originating from the university and its affiliated Ames Lab into advanced (or cutting-edge) technologies.[11] The coordination of the experiment (a term used not in a scientific sense) was placed under the Center for Advanced Technology Development (CATD), a newly established center charged with university technology transfer. From 1987 to 1995 the center received a total of $29.6 million: $22.4 million from the Department of Commerce, $3.7 million from the State of Iowa, and $3.5 million from private firms. State and industrial support continue to date, but federal funding ended in 1995.

MARKET INTERACTION

Technology transfer literature introduces two models of innovation: "technology-push" and "market-pull" (Kline and Rosenberg, 1986). Whereas technology-push theory argues that innovation is driven (or "pushed") by scientific research, market-pull theory counters that innovation is rather driven (or "pulled") by market forces. Previously, we presented in Figure 7.1 the university-based technological innovation process as though it were "pushed" by the university, since the process begins with academic research as a point of departure.

Our experience with the ISU experiment is that the two models (technology-push and market-pull) really run in parallel in almost every stage with extensive market interaction. Thus, in practice, the process works more like a flow chart (Figure 7.2) where the entire process runs in iteration, with continuous feedback

Figure 7.2
The Dynamic Model of the University-Based Technological Innovation Process

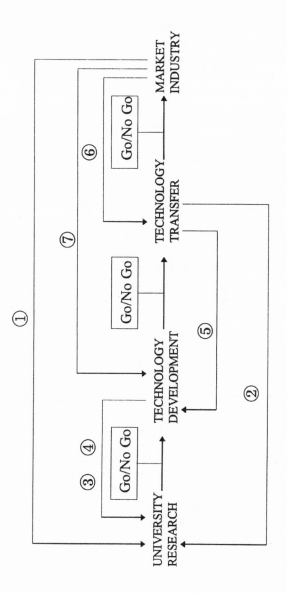

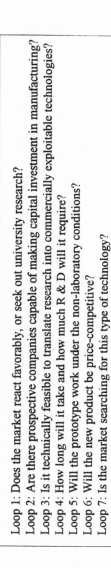

Loop 1: Does the market react favorably, or seek out university research?
Loop 2: Are there prospective companies capable of making capital investment in manufacturing?
Loop 3: Is it technically feasible to translate research into commercially exploitable technologies?
Loop 4: How long will it take and how much R & D will it require?
Loop 5: Will the prototype work under the non-laboratory conditions?
Loop 6: Will the new product be price-competitive?
Loop 7: Is the market searching for this type of technology?

from the market. Since this interaction is central to academic technological innovation, we look at the process in detail.

Phase I: Search for Industrially Promising R&D Projects

As we indicated earlier, the first step in the university-based innovation model is the process by which academic scientists and engineers peer into their own research and identify industrially promising concepts and ideas. As discussed in Chapters 8 and 9, academics vary in their response to this search. This is the point at which interested faculty disclose their new patentable ideas for further research and declare their intention to file a patent through the university.

Each year during the period of its experiment, the center called for preproposals from the ISU community, particularly from those who conduct research in the physical sciences, engineering, and sciences related to a new material, device, process, or software. The announcement called attention to two principal requirements. One was that the proposal be based on the completion of basic research in which the proof of concept already has been demonstrated; and the other was that the proposed invention show strong potential for commercial applications. In addition, the applicants were asked to (1) outline the scope of the focused applied research that would be completed within a one- or two-year funding period, (2) identify unique attributes of the invention that will give a competitive advantage over other existing technologies, and (3) demonstrate its patentability. The maximum two-year requirement was set largely in response to the prevailing industry concern that academic research presents too high a risk for commercial exploitation and that the time required to develop usable technology from basic research is too long to be of much value to industry. But, more important, there was a practical limit on the extent of available funding.

During the initial stage of the experiment, market inputs on the proposals were sought in a two-step process, first by the center's advisors, representing academia and the business community, and second by an external consulting group.[12] For each step the proposals were rated on two criteria: technological and commercial potential. For the technological potential, emphasis was placed on whether basic research has already been accomplished and proof of concept demonstrated, whether the idea is patentable, and whether the proposed project can be completed in two years or less (see Loops 3 & 4 in Figure 7.2). Concerning commercial potential, the emphasis was on whether there is (or will be) a market for the new technology and whether the technology will have sufficiently distinguishing features to create a competitive advantage (see Loops 1 & 2).

The proposals that survived this gauntlet were awarded funding for one to two years. Funding was considered a *contractual* agreement between the principal investigator (PI) and the center. The center, however, was careful not to keep PIs from publishing their research results, provided that they could take the necessary steps to protect the intellectual property through the prompt filing of patent applications. Occasionally, financial support was extended to a third year, when the request was considered exceptionally meritorious. It was understood by the PI, however, that the project could be terminated if changing circumstances threatened its commercial potential, technical feasibility, or future patent position. Throughout the project the applied research was conducted according to an agreed-upon technical plan prepared by the PI. Progress according to this plan was reviewed on the specific dates when key technical milestone objectives were to be achieved, as well as any new developments pertaining to the market, patent, and licensing.

The search process described up to this point has emphasized the academic initiative. As it turned out, surprisingly, the market response was rapid, changing the center's original search strategy. Soon after its inception, the center began receiving inquiries from companies about certain technical information and possible R&D collaboration. Company scientists and engineers read scientific papers and announcements printed in professional journals, go to academic conferences, and scan university bulletins in search of new ideas and commercially promising research. When they detect items of interest, they contact faculty authors, expressing interest in applications or collaborative work. In other cases, company representatives contact university departments, labs, and research centers, inquiring about faculty research in particular areas of their interest. At Iowa State University, these inquiries were directed to the center (CATD) for evaluation and coordination. The center realized that market initiative greatly simplified the time-consuming and costly (market & technology) assessment process, compared to the university-initiated marketing approach.

Phase II: Focused Applied Research

We indicated in the previous section that focused applied research is the R&D phase (Area "B" in Figure 7.1) in which scientific advances made in the university are reformulated into a form of advanced technology for industrial and public applications. Figure 7.1 may have imparted an impression that focused applied research is carried out by a faculty scientist or a team in an academic setting. We now must point out that this is true only to a very limited extent.

The impression is correct to the extent that when they encounter conceptual anomalies during focused applied research, academics immediately return to their own basic research for further conceptualization and state-of-the art review. Parenthetically, this is a great advantage of technological innovation projects orchestrated in the academic community. With the fundamental research capacity incorporated, the projects are internally evaluated and reevaluated in light of new scientific advances, other breakthrough discoveries, and possible demand shifts (see Loops 5, 6, and 7 in Figure 7.2).

This internal process, however, is only part of the story. From the ISU study we find that market interaction is an integral part of focused applied research. This is particularly true when a project includes an industrial partner, the partner who is interested in the proposed technology. In the ISU study, companies became a research collaborator with ISU when the center (CATD) located prospective companies and reached a basic agreement with them with respect to licensing options and R&D support, partially or fully. Companies also became an industrial partner with ISU when they had proposed a research agenda, invariably with some original ideas of their own. When industrial partners had been found, the center assembled research teams—not an easy task at all—combining academic scientists and industry engineers. Our observation is that without exception these teams develop a close working relationship and interact intensively. The university-industry team would meet frequently, weekly or monthly, alternating between university and company labs to discuss progress, identify technical snags and problems, study solutions, and reprioritize the work required. The case study of the center's clientele firms (Lee et al., 1996) led us to believe that this interaction was the key to successful technology transfer from ISU to industry. It also seemed that the earlier the partnering firm enters the process, the greater the possibility for successful technology transfer.

A caveat, however, is in order. The "university-*firm* collaboration thesis," as opposed to the "university-*industry* (a consortium of firms) collaboration thesis" is not without controversy because it has a policy implication of "privatizing" university resources (see Feller, 1990). While philosophical debate is beyond the scope of this chapter, we wish to point out that this is really a matter of public policy and law. In a sense, a decade of federal legislation on technology transfer is largely an economic justification for public-to-private transfer (see Chapter 1, particularly the example of CRADAs). In the case of the ISU experiment, the terms of the federal grant, state funding, and industrial support defined the center's task unequivocally: to translate academic research into industrial application and state economic development.

Phase III: Technology Commercialization and Intellectual Property Management

Technology commercialization is the process (Area "C" in Figure 7.1) by which the university licenses technology to a company and the company in return invests in fine-tuning the product to meet specific market and manufacturing needs in preparation for the start-up of production. If a technology development project was undertaken without a company collaborator, the task of transfer was much more difficult. The center, in our study, had to identify potential licensees, engage in market studies, develop networks with industry, and screen companies from various databases, including industry directories, and trade associations. This takes time and resources. The center also assisted faculty or student inventors who were interested in commercializing their research and establishing new start-up firms.[13] In cases where a more diffuse marketing approach was desirable, the center sought other communication channels such as published papers, press announcements in trade literature, and domestic or international trade shows.

While searching for prospective firms, the center's preference was to work with small or medium-size firms. The center found it not easy to work with large corporations with strong in-house R&D capabilities. In the center's view and as has been observed by others (see National Academy of Engineering, 1995, p. 39), large firms had a complicated decisionmaking structure and invariably exhibited a strong risk-averse behavior. After a licensee had been identified and the terms and conditions negotiated, the center turned over the final agreement to the university's Research Foundation for implementation.

When a firm has been a partner to the technology development project, the intellectual management negotiation can become potentially complicated. When a company has contributed original ideas to the project and even partially defrayed the R&D expenses, it may demand the ownership or at least co-ownership of the patent resulting from the project. This demand can create a dilemma for the university, because such transfer of ownership is tantamount to "privatization of research." Moreover, the university would be deprived of an opportunity to collect rent (royalties and license fees) needed to reinvest in basic research and also to fill the funding gap created by a market failure. The faculty inventor also is deprived of his or her reward for invention.

During the period of this experiment, the center encountered a few of these disputes. However, in most cases the center entered into up-front agreements with the partner companies before they committed to investing in the research. The agreements confirmed that the university owned all patent rights and fixed the maximum royalty rates to be paid by the partner companies depending on the extent of their intellectual and financial contributions to the collaborative development. It was not unusual for those companies who made major contributions to the development of the technologies to secure licenses that were totally royalty free, as well as to receive exclusive rights to the technologies in all markets and applications within their scope of business interest. Notwithstanding, the commercialization of university technology, even in the most ideal partnership, still can have the potential for misunderstanding, controversy, and even litigation.

THREE ARCHETYPES

With a total investment of $29.6 million in university-based technology development projects over a span of nine years (1987–1995), the center produced a total of 220 invention disclosures, 129 patent applications, 67 patents, 59 license agreements, and 9 start-up companies. A recent evaluation study conducted by Lee, Roessner, Bozeman, and Shapira (1996) showed that the rate of return (the firm's benefit from R&D investment) is roughly at 3.45, significantly better than for federal lab projects (2.69)[14] After an extensive analysis of the records supplemented by the company survey, the Roessner group concluded,

"Relative to the Fedlab projects, CATD projects can be characterized as 'safe bets, yielding a good return.' "

And yet, because our interest in this chapter is in the "real world" process of innovation, it is important to discuss some exemplars of university transfer. For this purpose, we have selected three transfer archetypes (X, Y, Z) reconstructed from field interviews.[15] The first incidence (X) is a case of the university initially "pushing" its idea to the market, the second incidence (Y) is a case of the market initially "pulling" innovation from the university, and the third incidence (Z) is a case of serendipity.

The Incidence of "Technology-Push"

Company "X" is a firm that was founded by two ISU professors and two of their students. Located at the University Research Park, the company (in 1996) has 145 employees, 90 of whom are full-time permanent employees. The company manufactures software involving computer-based three-dimensional (3D) visualization and offers consulting services by providing 3D analysis. Three-dimensional computer-animated technology has a wide range of practical applications, including the reconstruction of accidents and crime scenes and the charting out of medical surgical procedures.

In 1988, the two professors, interested in developing 3D computer animation software that would allow users to create realistic, detailed animation at high speed, received three competitive research grants (a total of $476,000) from CATD in order to convert their 3D animation concept to commercial applications. (The total development fund over a span of seven years amounted to several million dollars.) After two years of focused applied research, the two professors, in 1990, were able to perfect their 3D animated software, and the center obtained its patent for the university. In the same year, the two professors and their two students co-founded a start-up firm. Since then, the firm has expanded its 3D technology and won several national awards for invention. In 1996, the firm went public and captured $120 million of assets.

The Incidence of "Market-Pull"

Company "Y" is a start-up firm that developed surgical fiber optics in collaboration with ISU scientists. The firm, founded by an ISU alumnus and medical doctor, is currently being incubated at the ISU Research Park. The new technology applies to the surgical procedure, and it helped him win a national medal of invention in 1993.

Doctor "S" has long been interested in laser research in clinical trials. His interest grew out of his own experience with laser application in surgery. When optical fiber contacted tissue at levels of high energy, 2,000–3,000 degrees Fahrenheit, the tip routinely fractured, losing efficiency. He conjectured that some sort of coating should overcome fractures; and to understand the underlying pattern, he collected a large amount of tissue data. In 1990, the medical doctor called ISU, his alma mater, to inquire whether the university would be interested in the fabrication of optical fiber suitable for laser surgery. Subsequently, the center identified a professor of materials and engineering (Professor "M") whose specialty is in ceramics. After initial investigation, Professor "M" presented his conceptual analysis of the "degradation problem," which, in the view of Doctor "S," solved half of the problem. Professor "M" speculated that there may be a way to develop what later was labeled as "ultra low expansion (ULE) glass," which would be less susceptible to thermal degradation. If the assumptions underlying the ULE glass were correct, the professor believed, it would take about two years to develop new technology of fabricating surgically usable optical fiber.

Doctor "S" proposed to finance the project from his own sources, at least in its initial phase. Over the next three years he contributed to the project in the amount of $300,000; the center also partially funded the professor's proposal, in the amount of $50,000. After three years of focused applied research, the project resulted in a successful development of ULE fibers that could deliver high-energy (2,000°F–3,000°F) without creating tip fractures while in use. The technology subsequently received approval by the Food and Drug Administration for medical use, and it is now undergoing commercialization.

The Incidence of Serendipity

Company "Z" is a medium-sized firm that manufactures magnets for automotive industries, industrial products, security systems, computer/fax machines, aerospace industries, and telecommunications industries. While Company "Z" saw growth in the world demand for magnets, it also was keenly aware that the magnets it produced could not withstand a high-temperature environment of 180–200 degrees Celsius. To be competitive in the rapidly changing global market the company engineers felt it imperative to develop new magnets that could withstand high-temperature environments.

At Ames Lab, operated by ISU, Scientist "R" and her research assistant "J" found a way to blend powdered metals and binders for precision shaping called "Powder Injection Molding (PIM)." The PIM technique involves using materials in powdered form that are mixed with binders to create a viscous, gel-like compound. This compound is then pulverized into pellets and fed into an injection molding machine. The molding machine heats and flows the material into cavities of the desired shape where it hardens as it cools. In this process, production rates are high, scrap generation is low, the molded shapes can become complex, and dimensions can be maintained to a close tolerance. The ISU scientist has used PIM to identify resins that can be blended with magnet materials, which results in increased temperature resistance up to 200 degrees Celsius.

In early spring of 1994, the chief engineer of Company "Z" attended a regional conference on materials science held in Chicago at which ISU Scientist "R" gave a presentation on her recent findings. Intrigued by the presentation, the company engineer decided to pursue the matter further. Because the PIM discovery had been patented by ISU, the ISU scientist introduced the engineer to CATD to work on the necessary technology transfer arrangement. Subsequently, a collaboration between ISU Scientist "R" and Company "Z" commenced, to apply the PIM technology to the manufacturing process. For two full years (1993–1994) the ISU scientists and Company "Z" engineers had meetings almost every two weeks to discuss the progress of the project and prioritize the next phase of the work. The interaction between the ISU scientists and the company engineers was intensive, and the transfer of technology and know-how was rapid.

After two years of intensive collaborative work with ISU scientists, Company "Z" constructed a new laboratory and was able to design a new manufacturing process from which to produce three new products of high-temperature-resistant magnets and improve the quality of other products.

LESSONS FROM THE ISU EXPERIMENT

In this chapter, while focusing on university technology transfer in general, we also have narrowly focused on a process whereby the university transforms its academic research to industrially exploitable technologies. The purpose of the chapter was to present not so much the merits of this particular approach as the transformation process itself—how it works and what it requires.

First, we wish to stress that the *technological innovation gap* between academic research and commercially exploitable technology is real and large. This is shown by the intensity of R&D required in the transformation process, especially in focused applied research. In this connection, the second important point to be stressed is that focused R&D for technological innovation requires large expenditures of resources and time. The cost of innovation research is much higher than that of basic academic research. The Government-University-Industry Research Roundtable has estimated the cost ratio of basic research to development research to be one to ten (1991). That is, every one dollar for basic research requires ten additional dollars for product development research. The ISU study did not focus on product development but on development of advanced technology. Still, focused applied research is expensive and requires a large R&D expenditure. Therefore, should universities play a substantive role in technological innovation and economic development, government and industry must be prepared to address the problem of the funding gap.

Third, with regard to the theory of university innovation, we find that the theories of technology-push and market-pull are without much force in explaining technological innovation. The two concepts actually run in parallel. Just as with industrial innovation, university-based technological innovation requires extensive interaction with the market in all stages. In fact, creative "body contact'' between academic and industry scientists is the key to the transfer of knowledge, know-how, and technology between university and industry.

Our fourth lesson is that, insofar as our interest is in the acceleration of technology transfer, the earlier companies get involved in the R&D process, the better, even at the early stage of formulating research agenda. This saves the time and expenses required for technology and market assessment. Moreover, this can give the prospective firm a head start on technological innovation.

Fifth, the management and negotiation of intellectual property issues are far more complicated than generally understood. The issues annoy industry as well as the university. At the core of this tension is the collusion of different perspectives held by university and industry. For the university the concern is about the privatization of university research and the opportunity to collect rent. The participating firms, on the other hand, feel that they are entitled to have a share of the public good or to rent it at the lowest possible cost.

Finally, as the study by Roessner and his colleagues has demonstrated, industry satisfaction with the ISU projects runs high. Although a full economic impact is yet to be assessed with the passage of time, available first evidence shows that the research university in the United States, as shown by Iowa State University (a typical state university), is fully capable of "transforming" basic research into practically useful technologies—with speed and efficiency.

NOTES

1. Technology transfer occurs when industry hires graduates with advanced training; calls on academic scientists and engineers for consultation; sponsors industry-specific research; enters collaborative research with academics; participates in seminars, workshops, and conferences; and licenses patents from the university.

2. See the legislative history of the Stevenson-Wydler Technology Innovation Act of 1980 (PL 96–480) as amended by the Federal Technology Transfer Act of 1986 (PL 99–502).

3. National Academy of Sciences, *Government-University-Industry Research Roundtable* (Washington, DC: National Academic Press, 1991).

4. The term "experimentation" is used here in the context of the "social experimentation" that Campbell (1971) wrote about in his unpublished paper "Experimenting Society." The ISU experimentation was not designed as a controlled experiment.

5. The Department of Commerce ended its funding in 1995; as a result, the experimentation continues on a reduced scale.

6. David Roessner, Yong Lee, Philip Shapira, and Barry Bozeman, *Evaluation of Iowa State University's Center for Advanced Technology Development (CATD)* (1996). The case studies were part of this evaluation study. Richard Gaertner had been director of the CATD from 1987 to 1994.

7. Tom Noble, "CATD: A Unique Technology Development and Transfer Engine at ISU." Paper delivered at the 15th Annual Meeting of the Technology Transfer Society, Dayton, Ohio, 1990. See also National Academy of Sciences, *The Government Role in Civilian Technology: Building a New Alliance* (Washington, DC: National Academy Press, 1992).

8. Richard Gaertner, director of the Center for Advanced Technology Development from its inception in 1987 to 1994, was responsible for the creation of this pictorial representation as well as for the overall methodology used by the center. This model was based on Gaertner's industrial experience of over 25 years in the management of applied research and new product innovation.

9. David C. Mowery and Nathan Rosenberg, *Technology and the Pursuit of Economic Growth* (Cambridge: Cambridge University Press, 1989). See Chapter 1, Introduction, pp. 3–21.

10. Karen M. Paget, "State Government–University Cooperation," in Jurgen Schmandt and Robert Wilson (eds.), *Growth Policy in the Age of High Technology* (Boston: Unwin Hyman, 1990), pp. 344–380.

11. The project was an award by the Commerce Department to a proposal submitted by an Iowa State University scientist in 1986.

12. Later in the experiment, the two processes were combined into one with an expanded internal review capability.

13. This is a controversial topic. In the 1980s, when there was a perception of crisis in American competitiveness, faculty were allowed on many campuses to form start-up firms as a way to commercialize their inventions. As the crisis perception has subsided in the 1990s, while issues about faculty conflict of interest loom large, support for faculty entrepreneurism appears to have waned considerably.

14. Roessner et al. (1996).

15. Case studies were part of the CATD evaluation carried out by Roessner et al., ibid.

CHAPTER 8

Patterns of University-Industry Interaction

DIANNE RAHM

INTRODUCTION

Global technological competition has made technology transfer from universities to firms an important public policy issue. The policy objective is for the universities to assist firms with their innovation efforts and, in so doing, to increase national economic prosperity. While the goal is clear, the implementation process is not yet well understood. How exactly is university knowledge best transferred to private-sector firms?

Technology transfer interactions between academic researchers and companies are complex. Universities and firms have different missions, objectives, structures, organization cultures, and research orientations. For instance, the university researcher is evaluated based largely upon published research, but industry, concerned with keeping information from competitors, may demand that no publications come from collaborative efforts. University researchers often are more focused on basic research questions, while industry is interested in application and development. University researchers openly involve visiting foreign students in research projects, while industry may tend to see these students as future international competitors. Ownership of patents and rights to profits coming from inventions can be thorny issues to resolve when both university and firm personnel are involved. While these and other barriers exist, overcoming obstacles can lead to winning linkages. There are encouraging success stories.

A public policy emphasis placed upon moving knowledge, know-how, and technology from universities to firms should be informed by a better understanding of the details of the technology transfer process. Why do some academics engage in technology transfer activities while others do not? What facilitates technology transfer? What inhibits it? This chapter attempts to answer these questions from the vantage point of academic researchers. After briefly review-ing some pertinent literature, findings from a survey of academic researchers in the nation's top 100 research universities are presented. An assessment is made of academic researchers' technology transfer activities and attributes that differ-entiate researchers who engage in technology transfer from their nonparticipat-ing colleagues. Conclusions are drawn regarding the barriers to and facilitators of university technology transfer to industry.

A REVIEW OF THE LITERATURE

What factors are at work when academic researchers collaborate with firms? Geisler and Rubenstein (1989) suggest reasons why firms cooperate with uni-versities, including access to students and professors, access to university-based, state-of-the-art knowledge and technology, the prestige associated with university collaboration, and more efficient use of their limited resources through access to university facilities and personnel. Universities cooperate with industry for other reasons, they suggest, including access to scientific or technical areas in which industry has expertise, exposing students to practical problems, use of earmarked government funds, and potential employment for graduates. Geisler and Rubenstein argue that formal institutional firm-friendly offices and programs facilitate technology transfer to firms. These formal institutional programs and offices include industrial extension services, offices of patents and technology licensing, offices to negotiate cooperative research agreements, spin-off enter-prises, incubators, and research parks.

Geisler and Rubenstein (1989) also discuss barriers to technology transfer, including the ineffectiveness of university-industry mechanisms for collabora-tion as well as the inability to measure adequately the success of interactions and a consequent failure to set reasonable goals. Crow and Emmert (1984) add to the barrier concept. They argue that one reason for lack of success in industry-university interactions is the inability of professors to reach beyond their aca-demic discipline lines for communication with firm personnel.

Stewart and Gibson (1990) concentrate on departmental curricular firm-friendly offerings. Their study of high-tech firms in the Austin, Texas, region highlights the importance of classroom interactions. Firms need to have their personnel stay current, given the rapid rate of technological change, and may encourage periodic refresher courses. Classroom, face-to-face interactions result in interpersonal networking, not only between student and teacher but also among students (industry professionals) as well. Stewart and Gibson suggest that universities offering evening and weekend classes so that full-time day workers might attend will have advantages in establishing classroom technology transfer linkages. Also of consequence might be such firm-friendly curricular offerings as satellite broadcasts to firm sites and classes held at firm locations so that firm personnel might have increased access to university courses.

Stewart and Gibson (1990) also direct attention to the barriers to technology transfer that result from the different organizational cultures and internal reward structures of universities and firms. These differences take on particular importance when it comes to decisions regarding the freedom to publish research results coming from collaborative research. The demand of firms to delay or prohibit publications in an effort to assure secrecy creates a barrier to technology transfer. Researchers must be willing to accept this restriction, should it be imposed by the firm, yet such acceptance may mean that the traditional avenue of internal university rewards will not be realized. This line of thought also draws attention to other organizational culture issues that arise. Researchers engaging in technology transfer activities somehow must reconcile themselves to the conflicts that exist between the basic research mission of the university and undertaking applied industrial research.

Taking the firm's perspective, Frye (1985) concentrates on effective ways of moving technology from the university lab to the market. Seeing the process thwarted in the earliest stage of creating the initial link between university and industry personnel, Frye sees the solution in opening channels of communication, in large part through industry-sponsored multi-university technology transfer conferences at which universities are given the opportunity to showcase their research projects and describe their patent policies. For firms, Frye argues, these conferences provide the opportunity to contact a large number of universities in a very short period of time. For the universities, the conferences provide the opportunity to become aware of what technologies various industries seek. Frye also discusses the usefulness of university-sponsored technology expositions and university efforts to reward academic researchers for activities leading to patents.

Owen and Entorf (1989) report the results of a survey sent by Entorf and Katuri, of the University of Wisconsin-Stout, to selected faculty in technology-based educational institutions. They found a correlation between faculty engaging in technology transfer activities and faculty consulting for firms, ongoing co-op or internship programs, graduate students doing field work for industry projects, the presence of a clear university patent policy, and universities receiving gifts or grants from industry. Ties with government are also suggested by Owen and Entorf as a facilitator of university-industry interactions. State and local governments increasingly are attempting to use technology for state and regional economic development, just as the federal programs attempt to foster economic growth and national competitiveness.

Owen and Entorf look at the National Science Foundation (NSF) Engineering Research Centers as models for university-industry interactions. They suggest several features designed into the centers that seem likely to promote successful interactions: cross-disciplinary research, team research, meetings on both campus center and member company facilities so that the cultures of each environment may be learned, and research priorities defined by participating firms within the broad areas of NSF program guidelines.

This literature is helpful in suggesting many of the factors at work when academic researchers collaborate with firms. It also points out potential barriers to and facilitators of university technology transfer to firms. Scholars argue that technology transfer is promoted by the presence of firm-friendly formal institutional offices and programs, as well as firm-friendly curricular offerings. Informal contacts between university professors and firms, such as those established by paid industrial consulting, are also suggested by the literature as being important promoters of technology transfer activities. The literature suggests that research organization based upon interdisciplinary research teams (as opposed to the traditional university organization of single investigators within a single discipline) promotes technology transfer. This scholarship also calls our attention to the conflicts that emerge for researchers as they move toward an applied industrial research focus. Many of these conflicts can be traced to the differing organizational cultures of the firm and the university. Failure to resolve these conflicts may act as a barrier to technology transfer.

RESEARCH METHODS

The study was designed to improve our understanding of the current circumstance of university-firm technology transfer efforts, as well as the barriers to and facilitators of university-firm interaction. In an effort to make findings widely generalizable, the population to be studied was defined as researchers and technology administrators within the top 100 U.S. research universities. The initial population list of the top 100 universities was drawn from NSF data ranking universities by annual research and development (R&D) expenditure. These universities, including a high percentage of land-grant colleges, are geographically well distributed across the nation. The top 100 universities account for the vast majority of R&D expenditure at all U.S. universities.

This chapter reports data gathered as one part of the overall study. In phase one of the study, two specially tailored surveys were developed. One, emphasizing researcher concerns, was sent to academic researchers. The other, stressing administrative issues, was sent to those university administrators most likely to be the focus of campus technology transfer efforts. Three researcher surveys were sent to chairpersons of the departments of biology, chemistry, computer science, electrical engineering, and physics. All of these disciplines are ranked highly as recipients of R&D funds, and research results coming from these areas are likely to be related directly to industry. Each department chairperson was asked to fill out one survey and to select two other researchers from the department to complete the others. A sample of centers affiliated with targeted departments was taken. Directors of these centers also received a researcher survey. In this way, each university received a minimum of seventeen survey forms (two administrative surveys and at least fifteen researcher questionnaires). The number of centers varied by department and university. The total identified sample frame, including administrators and academic researchers, was 2,049. The total researcher sample frame consisted of 1,849 (1,500 department researchers and 349 center researchers). The administrative sample frame was 200.

In August of 1993, the questionnaire was pretested; and an alert letter requesting assistance with the study was sent to the selected administrators, department chairpersons, and center directors. The survey was mailed in September, and a second-wave mailing to nonrespondents occurred in October. Each questionnaire included a return, postage-paid envelope with a preprinted address. Personally addressed cover letters were sent to technology managers, center directors, and department chairpersons. The cover letter included an office phone number and electronic mail address so that respondents could make contact should they have any questions. Eighty-eight identified respondents declined to be included in the study, thus reducing the effective sample frame to 1,961 (1,774 researchers and 187 administrative officials). Of those, 1,134 completed surveys were returned, yielding an overall response rate of 58 percent. Returns included 1,013 researcher and 121 administrative questionnaires.

The results of the administrative survey are not reported here. Instead, this chapter concentrates on university academic researchers only. From the university perspective, there are two types of academic researchers: the researcher with no technology transfer experience (hereafter referred to as the *university-bound researcher*) and the researcher who has interacted with firms in an effort to transfer knowledge, know-how, or technology (hereafter referred to as the *spanning researcher*). The sample contains responses of 254 university-bound researchers and 759 spanning researchers. More than 80 percent of both bound and spanning researchers are tenured associate or full professors.

RESEARCH RESULTS AND DISCUSSION

The main focus of this section is to address the question of differences between university-bound and spanning researchers. Do spanning researchers differ from university-bound researchers? If so, how? Is there evidence to suggest that these differences are important in understanding better the process of university-firm technology transfer?

As might be expected, one of the ways in which spanning and university-bound researchers differ is in their description of contacts with companies. Spanning researchers tend to initiate communication with firms personally, and they are far more inclined than their university-bound colleagues to have informal links to firms. Eighty-seven percent of spanning researchers report they have independently approached firms, 95 percent of spanning researchers testify they have been contacted directly by firms, and 45 percent of spanning researchers suggest they have been introduced to firm personnel by university technology transfer staff. Several other informal links to firms are of considerable importance. Seventy-five percent of spanning researchers say they engage in paid industrial consulting. Perhaps more important, 80 percent of spanning researchers say that former university students now working in industry sometimes or often contact them regarding firm needs.

University-bound researchers are less likely to have any of these types of contacts. Table 8.1 summarizes these differences. Nonparametric correlation analysis also reveals a strong and statistically significant pattern. Correlations were run, assigning a value of one to spanning researchers and zero to bound researchers. There are strong positive correlations between spanning researchers and the researcher taking the initiative personally to contact a firm as well as being personally contacted by a firm (Kendall's tau-b values of .51 and .50, respectively). Introduction to firms by university technology managers weakly correlates with spanning behaviors (tau-b of .20). Undertaking consulting activities and contacts from former students both correlate moderately with the designation of spanning researcher (tau-b values of .43 and .30, respectively).

The literature suggests that university-based, firm-friendly class offerings, organizations, or programs act to foster university-industry interaction. Do spanning researchers tend to come from departments with firm-friendly curricular offerings? Do they differ from their university-bound colleagues in the extent to which they report the presence of firm-friendly university-wide organizations and programs on campus? To explore this possible relationship, the survey asked a series of questions regarding department and university offerings that might be considered supportive of industrial linkage and firm interactions.

Academic researchers were asked, first, about department firm-friendly offerings, such as whether their departments offered graduate courses regularly scheduled in the evening (to facilitate access to firm personnel), student internships with firms, professional workshops or short refresher courses, satellite courses broadcast to firm sites, classes held at firm locations with the professor traveling to the firm to give the class, or weekend classes (again to facilitate access to firm personnel). Are there differences between the firm-friendly offerings reported by spanning and by university-bound researchers?

Twenty-eight percent of spanning researchers indicate their department offers night classes, 40% sponsor student internships with firms, 33% offer professional workshops or short refresher courses, 23% broadcast classes to firms, 22% say their department offers classes at firm sites, and 6% of spanning researchers indicate their department offers weekend classes. Statistically significant differences exist between spanning researchers and bound researchers on most of these variables. Table 8.2 reports these differences.

The correlation between each of the variables (night classes, student internships, professional workshops, satellite courses, classes held at firm locations, and weekend classes) and spanning researchers are all statistically significant but weak.

The respondents were also asked to comment on whether or not their university has or sponsors any firm-friendly organizations or programs, including research consortia, technology transfer conferences, industrial extension services, cooperative R&D agreements with firms, technology expositions, research parks, industry-supported university facilities, start-up firm incubators, or personnel sharing between the university and firms. Sixty-two percent of spanning researchers say their university sponsors research consortia, 44% know about

Table 8.1
Differences between Spanning and University-Bound Researchers by Firm Contacts

	Spanning Yes	Spanning No	Bound Yes	Bound No	X^2
Researcher Contacts Firm	663 87%	95 13%	91 36%	163 64%	267.0****
Firm Contacts Researcher	717 95%	40 5%	135 53%	119 47%	247.9****
Technology Manager Introduces Researcher to Firm	343 45%	413 55%	57 22%	197 78%	41.93****
Researcher Consults for Firms	564 75%	191 25%	67 26%	187 74%	189.4****
Alumni Contacts	608 80%	146 20%	126 15%	120 49%	100.2****

Source: Author's data.
Numbers in cells are observed frequencies and percentages.
**** = prob. < .0001

Table 8.2
Differences between Spanning and University-Bound Researchers by Firm-Friendly Class Offerings

	Spanning Yes	Spanning No	Bound Yes	Bound No	X^2
Student Internships	288 40%	471 60%	72 28%	182 72%	7.65***
Professional Workshops	249 33%	510 67%	41 16%	213 84%	25.86****
Satellite Courses	171 23%	588 77%	23 9%	231 91%	22.31****
Courses Taught at Firm Site	164 22%	595 78%	24 9%	230 91%	18.61****
Weekend Classes	46 6%	713 94%	8 3%	246 97%	3.19
Night Classes	209 28%	550 72%	42 17%	212 83%	12.35****

Source: Author's data.
Numbers in cells are observed frequencies and percentages.
  *** = prob. < .001
  **** = prob. < .0001

technology transfer conferences, 33% of industrial extension services, 70% of cooperative agreements with firms, 42% of spin-off enterprises, 14% of technology expos, 41% of research parks, 45% of industry-supported university facilities, 31% of start-up firm incubators, and 29% of personnel sharing with firms.

The cross-tabulation results reported in Table 8.3 show that there are statistically significant differences between spanning researchers and university-bound researchers on all but two of the variables, and correlation analysis reveals a significant but weak relationship.

Spanning researchers are more likely than university-bound researchers to come from universities that have in place firm-friendly curricular offerings, as well as institutional firm-friendly programs and organizations (or perhaps they are more likely to know that such organizations and programs are in place).

The literature emphasizes the importance of several organizational components of the research effort and suggests that these will be associated positively with undertaking technology transfer efforts. Of prime consideration are interdisciplinary research, team research, and center affiliation. The organization of the research effort can be described along the dimension of traditional departmental, single-disciplinary, primary-investigator focus and the extent to which the researcher departs from this locus.

The organization of the research effort by spanning researchers reflects a stated emphasis on interdisciplinary teams. Only 20% of spanning researchers respond that they are primarily single investigators, while 60% of spanning researchers state they are affiliated with one or more research centers and 77% describe their research as interdisciplinary or multidisciplinary. Statistically significant differences in the organization of research exist between spanning researchers and bound researchers. These results are reported in Table 8.4.

The literature suggests that the distinct organizational cultures of universities and firms create barriers to successful collaborations. The present data support this assertion. For instance, despite the university norm of openness, almost half of spanning researchers report that firms, in an attempt to protect the secrecy of a potential commercial product, have placed restrictions on their sharing information regarding R&D breakthroughs with colleagues. Spanning researchers say this restriction has created a feeling of conflict for them between loyalty to the firm and the university value of open knowledge. Fifty-three percent of spanning researchers also respond that firms they have dealt with have sought to prohibit or delay publication of research results coming from university-firm R&D interactions.

Spanning researchers differ from bound researchers in that they are more likely to hold patents than their colleagues. There is a moderate to strong correlation (tau-b of .33) between being a spanning researcher and having filed for or been granted a patent. Nearly 60 percent of spanning researchers indicate they hold or have applied for a patent, as compared to 17 percent of bound

Table 8.3
Differences between Spanning and University-Bound Researchers by Firm-Friendly University Programs and Organizations

	Spanning Yes	Spanning No	Bound Yes	Bound No	X^2
Research Consortia	474 62%	285 38%	139 55%	115 45%	4.75**
Tech Transfer Conferences	336 44%	423 66%	97 38%	157 62%	2.87
Industrial Extension Services	248 33%	511 67%	58 23%	196 77%	8.74***
Cooperative R&D Agreements with Firm	534 70%	225 30%	123 48%	131 52%	40.15****
Spin-Off Enterprises	315 42%	444 58%	68 27%	186 73%	17.56****
R&D Expos	106 14%	653 86%	39 15%	215 85%	0.299
Research Parks	309 41%	450 49%	85 33%	169 67%	4.20*
Industry Funded University Facilities	342 45%	417 55%	83 33%	171 67%	11.98***
Incubators	237 31%	522 69%	57 22%	197 78%	7.12**
Personnel Sharing with Firms	217 29%	542 71%	40 16%	214 84%	16.57****

Source: Author's data.
Numbers in cells are observed frequencies and percentages.
* = prob. < .05; ** = prob. < .01; *** = prob. < .001; **** = prob. < .0001

Table 8.4

Differences between Spanning and University-Bound Researchers by Organization of Research Effort

	<u>Spanning</u> <u>Yes</u>	<u>Spanning</u> <u>No</u>	<u>Bound</u> <u>Yes</u>	<u>Bound</u> <u>No</u>	X^2
Work Primarily as Sole-PI	154 20%	605 80%	70 28%	184 72%	5.83**
Inter- or Multi-disciplinary	584 77%	166 23%	157 62%	96 38%	27.6****
Affiliated with a Research Center	456 60%	303 40%	113 44%	140 56%	23.17**

Source: Author's data.

Numbers in cells are observed frequencies and percentages.

** = prob. < .01

**** = prob. < .0001

researchers (the results are highly significant statistically, with a chi-square test statistic value of 137.5).

Faculty reward systems also come into play when patents are discussed. Nearly half of the spanning researchers insist that patents are given minimal or no consideration in faculty annual reviews or in promotion or tenure decisions. Only 23 percent of spanning researchers say patents are evaluated as the equivalent of peer-reviewed articles appearing in highly (or less-highly) ranked professional journals.

The respondents were asked a series of questions to determine their perspectives on the impacts of applied industrial research efforts on the university. When asked if they thought the emphasis on industrial outreach was having a negative effect on the basic research mission of the university, 41 percent of spanning researchers and 54 percent of bound researchers say yes. Table 8.5 shows the responses of bound and spanning researchers regarding how highly they think universities value work that leads to patents, the extent to which they feel pressured to undertake applied research because they believe government granting agencies or university administrations will look favorably upon such activity, and their beliefs regarding the harm done to the basic research mission of the university by the recent emphasis on applied industrial outreach.

Spanning researchers are slightly less apt than bound researchers to believe the university rewards researchers for undertaking patenting activity. The tau-b correlation (of -0.11) is statistically significant, but weak. Spanning researchers are a bit more likely than others to feel pressured to become involved with applied industrial research efforts because they sense that granting agencies, as well as university, department, or center administration, will look favorably upon such activity. Finally, spanning researchers are less prone to consider the recent emphasis on industrial outreach to improve national competitiveness as negatively impacting the university's basic research mission (tau-b of -0.13).

CONCLUSION

To implement public policy that emphasizes university technology transfer to firms, decisionmakers must consider several simple, yet crucial, questions. What researchers participate in technology transfer activities? How do they differ from those who do not participate? What facilitates or inhibits university technology transfer to firms? This chapter has presented an analysis of data that attempts to answer some of these questions.

From the data reported in this chapter, it is clear that many researchers participate willingly in technology transfer activities with firms. Spanning researchers, that is, those who make technology transfer linkages, are confronted with several dilemmas that arise primarily out of the conflicting organizational cultures of the university and the firm. Dealing with patents, publications, and secrecy is troublesome for many respondents.

Researchers who participate in technology transfer activities differ from their

Table 8.5
Differences between Spanning and University-Bound Researchers by Attitude Variables

	Spanning Yes	Spanning No	Bound Yes	Bound No	X^2
Efforts to get Patents are Rewarded by University	331 44%	346 56%	71 33%	144 67%	18.27****
Feel Pressured to Adopt Applied Research Focus	417 55%	336 45%	122 48%	132 52%	9.09**
Think Applied Research Focus Hurts Basic Research	308 41%	440 59%	134 54%	115 46%	16.56****

Source: Author's data.
Numbers in cells are observed frequencies and percentages.

**= prob. < .01
****= prob. < .0001

nonparticipating, university-bound colleagues in several important ways. They tend to come from departments and universities that provide firm-friendly curricular offerings, organizations, and programs (or, perhaps, they are just more aware of these than their university-bound colleagues). The spanning researchers organize their research efforts differently than do university-bound researchers. Spanning researchers are more likely to be cross-disciplinary than are bound researchers, they affiliate with research centers more than do university-bound researchers, and they are less likely than bound researchers to work as independent investigators. Researchers who participate in technology transfer activities contrast with their nonparticipating colleagues in that they are far more prone to have applied for or been granted a patent, they are more apt to have taken the initiative personally to approach a firm regarding their research expertise, and there is a greater probability that they have been sought out by a firm for their expertise. These researchers are far more liable to indicate that they engage in paid industrial consulting and that former students now in firms contact them regarding firm problems. They differ in that they are less likely to view applied industrial outreach efforts as threatening the basic research mission of the university. Researchers who participate in technology transfer activities vary also in that they are more inclined to say that the university system does not highly value patents in annual evaluations or in tenure or promotion decisions.

While technology transfer interactions between universities and firms are complex, there do seem to be systematic relationships at work. University-bound researchers vary predictably and clearly from researchers who span the university and link with firms. Barriers to technology transfer exist. Understanding what inhibits university researchers from engaging in technology transfer activities, however, is a step in the direction of lowering barriers.

CHAPTER 9

Technology Transfer and Faculty Attitudes

YONG S. LEE

INTRODUCTION

Since the passage of the Stevenson-Wydler Technology Innovation Act (PL 96–480) and the Bayh-Dole Act (PL 96–517) in 1980—legislation that created a policy framework for technology transfer—the last decade in the United States has seen a significant growth in university-industry collaboration on technology transfer. This growth is evidenced by a large number of university-industry research centers (more than 1000) established within universities (Cohen et al., 1994), the breadth of interaction taking place between university faculty and industry scientists (Blumenthal et al., 1986; Rahm, 1995), and an increasing number of university patents licensed to industry followed by a dramatic increase in royalty income (Association of University Technology Managers [AUTM], 1995). The commercial impact of university licenses was estimated conservatively at $17 billion in 1994 (AUTM, 1995) and at over $20 billion in a recent MIT study (Pressman et al., 1995).

Notwithstanding this growth, controversy continues—and it is not likely to be settled anytime soon—over what the proper relationship should be between university and industry in technology transfer collaboration. Proponents of university-industry collaboration argue that in a democracy such as the United States universities are no different from other public organizations and must be accountable to the public will. Since economic development and global competition have now become issues of central importance to the nation, it is well that universities incorporate these concerns as part of their mission (Armstrong, 1991). Similarly, political observers caution that times have changed from when universities received generous research funding from Congress. The Cold War is over, and grassroots support for university science is waning. To receive research support, the argument goes, universities must present a new case to taxpayers (Bruce Smith, 1990; Neal Smith, 1993).

Not all arguments, however, are based on political grounds. Some point out that basic research is not the only legitimate activity in academia; strong technological development is in fact an engine for science, not the other way around ("Mary Good," 1995). This argument gains force from those who take into account the historical roots of American higher education, particularly the early land-grant movement. Rosenberg and Nelson (1994) argued that it is only after World War II that practical research has not been awarded much credit in U.S. universities. For much of U.S. history, in their view, the dominant rationale for university research funding has been the expectation that the research would yield practical benefits. Examining congressional testimonies by university presidents in the early 1980s, Slaughter (1993) observed that while the presidents still viewed basic science as the key component of academic research, they were now redefining *basic* in such a way that "*basic* and *applied science* were no longer treated as dichotomous, but as complementary parts of a whole entity [in] the . . . innovation process" (italics added).

Nevertheless, skeptics question whether university-industry collaboration is really key to economic development and competitiveness. Feller (1990), after reviewing the literature on the privatization of research, argued that efforts to foster "privatization of research" may actually slow down the rate of technological innovation. "Academic research flows to the market are likely to become blocked," Feller reasoned, "as universities limit existing flows of information in order to divert faculty findings to specific firms. This shift runs counter to other trends within academic research designed to correct the debilitating effects that a close identification with commercial needs has had on the quality of research." Bok (1991) joined the debate by pointing out that there are dangers of shifting emphasis in the university from the great utilitarian purpose (e.g., the welfare and betterment of all humankind) to economic development and competitiveness. "I fear," declared Bok, "that if we continue to justify our research in those terms [economic development and competitiveness], to try to exploit competitiveness as a reason for building science and links with industry, we are likely to end by disappointing our constituencies to our ultimate disadvantages." While attempting to clarify industry perspective, the Government-University-Industry Research Roundtable (1991) offered that what industry really needs from universities is not the development of technology but a close linkage to fundamental research.

At this point one may wonder how American university faculty, in general, regard the issue of university-industry collaboration on technology transfer. To be sure, academics, especially science and engineering faculty, are the ones who must carry on much of the transfer task; yet their views have not been fully documented in the literature. This chapter attempts to fill part of that void. The questions examined in this chapter are, What role do U.S. academics believe that they, or their university, should play in university-industry collaborations, and why?

PAST RESEARCH

Empirical research in this area is beginning to accumulate. In her question-naire survey, as reported in Chapter 8, Dianne Rahm found that the behaviors of industry-linked researchers are manifestly different from the behaviors of those who pursue traditional university-bound research; they respond to transfer demand more favorably. Many of the industry-linked faculty are from engi-neering disciplines and, compared to their colleagues in the basic sciences, tend to be more interdisciplinary in orientation, more actively involved in university-industry research collaboration, and more supportive of extension-oriented ed-ucation programs. In their recent survey Campbell and Slaughter (1995) also observed that university-industry collaborative experience per se is in fact a significant factor that differentiates the attitudes of those involved from those not involved. Compared to those who have *not* been involved in university-industry collaboration, those who do collaborate—whether academics or indus-try representatives—are far less concerned or worried about conflict of interest issues or possible organizational disloyalty.

Based on a national survey that I conducted and reported earlier (Lee, 1995), I found that faculty attitudes vary widely among different transfer methods. While U.S. faculty generally appeared to support their university's participation in regional economic development and commercialization of academic research, they were not particularly sanguine about the idea of providing start-up assis-tance to new technology-based firms or making equity investments in firms based on university research. I also found that the reasons for faculty support or opposition were quite complicated, requiring further analysis. On the one hand, for example, academics seemed to support university-industry collabora-tion in part out of their sense of social responsibility (i.e., economic develop-ment) and in part out of their own need for research funding. And yet, they were fearful that a close collaboration with industry might derail the university from its fundamental mission—teaching and basic research. The impression was that academics were pulled apart by opposing forces.

To gain a better sense of how various and possibly idiosyncratic views and attitudes are all interrelated, in this chapter I reanalyze the survey data by ap-plying Bollen and Long's (1993) structural equation model (SEM). Since faculty attitudes appear to vary in relation to the nature and type of university-industry collaboration, I hypothesize (on the basis of my previous work) that the aca-demic climate (that is, the immediate work environment) supporting or opposing university-industry collaboration would have a significant impact on faculty at-titudes (Lee, 1996). The academic climate, on the other hand, would be miti-gated by the collision of two powerful but opposing motives: the need for external funding versus the need to preserve academic freedom and independence. With the SEM technique I evaluate this hypothesis.

DATA AND MEASUREMENTS

The data for this analysis come from a mailed questionnaire survey I administered during the spring of 1994.[1] The data include approximately 1000 faculty responses representing nine academic departments and 115 research universities. In the survey I used a multistage sampling process. First, I borrowed the sampling framework from Feller and Geiger's (1993) study, in which all research universities (N = 194) on the NSF list of academic science and engineering institutions were ranked on the basis of faculty research and doctoral programs. To ensure that my study sample would have a broad representation from public (non-land-grant) universities, (public) land-grant universities, and private universities, I classified the universities according to their characteristics (public, private, or land grant). I then applied the stratified random sampling technique, which yielded a total of 123 universities, including 44 land-grant universities, 40 public non-land-grant universities, and 39 private universities. The sample represented about 64 percent of the research university population in the United States.

Next, I targeted three broad disciplinary groupings: basic, applied and engineering, and social sciences. It was reasoned that the disciplinary orientation would be an important cultural factor that might help delineate various academic responses. Included in the disciplinary groupings were three basic science departments (biology, chemistry, and physics), four engineering applied-science departments (chemical engineering, electrical engineering, computer science, and materials science), and two social science departments (economics and political science).

Finally, I selected three potential respondents from within each department: (1) the chair, (2) the person most recently promoted to associate professor, and (3) the person most recently promoted to full professor. Since not all institutions have representation in all nine disciplines, the selection process resulted in a total of 764 academic departments and a faculty pool of 2,292. The mailed questionnaire, along with two reminder letters, produced a 43 percent faculty response (n = 986).

This chapter examines four sets of attitudinal variables and their structural relationships. The variable sets (or factors) include (1) faculty attitudes toward university-industry collaboration on technology transfer, (2) the immediate work climate supporting or opposing university-industry collaboration, (3) pressures for research grants, and (4) the concern for academic independence. In addition to these four variable sets, in the model I examine the effects of other contextual variables frequently discussed in the literature. These variables are academic disciplines (Morgan et al., 1993; Rosenberg and Nelson, 1994; Rahm, 1995), public-private distinction of universities (Paget, 1990), and institutional prestige ranking (Feller & Geiger, 1993; Mansfield, 1995). The faculty attitude toward university-industry collaboration is the dependent variable in this study.

Faculty Attitudes toward University-Industry Collaboration

University-industry (UI) collaboration on technology transfer involves many different interactions. A simple but valuable transfer activity is the interaction, formal or informal, that occurs between academic scientists and industry scientists/engineers in seminars and workshops and through personnel exchange programs. The value of this type of interaction is the sharing of and access to new knowledge and research findings. This kind of interaction might also be formalized by means of consortia or alliances. Given their educational mission, academics appear least troubled by this type of interaction, but not when they are faced with commercial transactions involving, for instance, intellectual property, confidentiality agreements, and business development. Academics in the United States are divided over the issues of commercial transactions (Matkin, 1994). No single measure, therefore, will sufficiently capture the full spectrum of faculty attitudes toward technology transfer.

The concept *faculty attitudes toward UI collaboration on technology transfer*, as employed here, is inferred from faculty response to a five-item question about their agreement or disagreement on their university's participation in various types of industry-bound technology transfer activities. The five-item question, employing a Gutman-type structure, asked the faculty respondents to express the extent of their agreement or disagreement on whether a research university like theirs should (1) get involved in the economic development efforts of their region and state, (2) get involved in commercialization of academic research by setting up and operating technology transfer centers, (3) set up their own development foundation to help start new technology-based businesses, (4) encourage faculty to provide consulting services to private firms, and (5) own equity (stock) in companies derived from university research. Each item was recorded on a five-point Likert-type scale: Strongly Agree (coded as 5), Agree (coded as 4), Indifferent (coded as 3), Disagree (coded as 2), and Strongly Disagree (coded as 1).

For the purpose of analysis, I combined these five items into a single scale. Cronbach's reliability test yields Alpha = 0.724. This suggests that the five items can be added and averaged for the purpose of statistical analysis. In other words, each respondent can be assigned a single average attitudinal score, albeit roughly estimated, with respect to university-industry collaboration.

Academic Climate Supporting or Opposing UI Collaboration

In this study academic climate is defined as the immediate work environment of the faculty, the department or its equivalent, as it relates to and affects potential UI collaboration. To ascertain the work environment of faculty respondents the questionnaire asked the respondents whether they would approve or disapprove of a colleague in their work unit working closely with industry in precommercialization research (e.g., contract research, development of new technologies or processes). The assumption underlying this item was that the faculty who approve or disapprove of their colleague's *application-oriented research* (or *user-oriented research*) would set the tone of their departmental or unit environment with respect to university-industry collaboration. Thus, approval or disapproval serves as a surrogate measure for the academic climate. Responses were obtained on a five-point Likert scale: Strongly Approve (coded as 5), Approve (coded as 4), Indifferent (coded as 3), Disapprove (coded as 2), and Strongly Disapprove (coded as 1). Parenthetically, this "academic climate" item drew significantly more voluntary comments from the respondents than any other item in the questionnaire, perhaps a testimony to its importance.

Pressure to Seek External Funding

Funding pressure is defined as the extent to which the individual faculty member feels pressured to seek research funding from external sources. Underlying this question is a recent trend in which federal funding for university research is increasingly tight, whereas industry support is showing relative growth. To capture the "flash point" of faculty perception I asked the respondents to express their "pressure or no pressure" experience in connection with their academic career progression: (1) tenure/promotion, (2) promotion to full professor, (3) annual performance evaluation and salary increase, and (4) recognition and prestige. Again, responses were sought on a five-point Likert scale to indicate how important it is for the faculty to seek external research funding as a means of academic advancement: Absolutely Important (coded as 5), Very Important (coded as 4), Important (coded as 3), Somewhat Important (coded as 2), and Not Important (coded as 1). "Absolutely Important" is translated as higher pressure, and "Not Important" as lower pressure. Cronbach's reliability test of the four items resulted in Alpha = 0.896, suggesting that the four items are additive for statistical analysis. The hypothesis underlying this measure is that the greater the funding pressure, the more flexible the faculty would be toward research collaboration with industry.

Need to Preserve Academic Freedom

Following World War II, the federal government and the universities entered a new era of unprecedented "patron-client" relations (England, 1982; Brooks, 1986). In Harvey Brooks's view, the federal government, for the first time, committed to continuing support for academic research; and it conferred on the university a high degree of self-governance and intellectual autonomy, provided that the benefits of research would be diffused widely throughout society and the economy. Brooks believed that universities took this new relationship to heart, particularly "intellectual autonomy," as though it were a "social contract." Whatever the interpretation, the fact remains that "academic freedom"— the freedom to pursue disinterested research—is part of the central ethos of American universities. In recent years, as national concern shifted from the Cold War to economic development, a sense of erosion is felt to be occurring in the "cherished" social contract (Guston & Keniston, 1994). Federal support in real dollars for university research has been declining, yet universities are under pressure to increase the flow of new knowledge, know-how, and trained people to industry (National Academy of Sciences, 1992; National Science Board, 1992). Meanwhile, industry support for university research has been on the rise, from 3.3 percent in 1980 to 7.5 percent in 1993, as a percentage of total academic research. This creates a perception in the minds of many faculty that another patron-client relationship may be in the offering between the university and industry. Academics are uneasy about this development because, in their view, industry is neither generous with its support for research nor interested in intellectual autonomy (Matkin, 1994). Some academics also fear that efforts to foster commercialization of academic research might actually slow down the social rate of innovation (Feller, 1990).

Against this backdrop, my survey questionnaire attempted to ascertain the extent to which American faculty are concerned about their traditional university values, including academic independence, if their universities are to work closely with industry. The more fearful they are of a possible loss of independence, I reason, the greater the reluctance on their part to support closer university-industry collaboration. To understand the extent of faculty concerns about university values, including independence (as indirectly as possible), respondents were asked to estimate the likelihood that a close university-industry cooperation will (1) disrupt the university mission, (2) interfere with intellectual freedom and autonomy, (3) increase pressure for short-term research, (4) depress long-term basic research, and (5) increase conflict of interest. Responses are recorded on a five-point Likert scale: Almost Certain to Happen (coded as 5), Likely to Happen (coded as 4), Possible to Happen (coded as 3), Unlikely to Happen (coded as 2), and Most Unlikely to Happen (coded as 1). Cronbach's reliability test of these five items yields Alpha = 0.824, again ensuring that these five items may be added and averaged to a single score for statistical analysis.

RESULTS OF THE SURVEY

The results of faculty responses to four variable sets are summarized in Tables 9.1 through 9.4. Since the tables are self-explanatory, only brief comments will be made on each.

Table 9.1 summarizes the frequencies of faculty response to five items defined as *faculty attitudes toward UI collaboration on technology transfer*. On a five-point scale, from 1 as "Strongly Disagree" to 5 as "Strongly Agree," the scale mean is about 3.5, which is about between "Agree" and "Indifferent." A pe-

Table 9.1
Frequency of Faculty Response to a Set of Five Items Defined as the Faculty Attitude toward University Transfer

The research university like yours should:	Strongly Agree (5)	Agree (4)	Indifferent (3)	Disagree (2)	Strongly Disagree (1)	N of Observations
Get involved in regional economic development efforts	30.1%	52.5%	11.5%	4.6%	1.2%	963
Set up and operate technology transfer centers in order to facilitate commercialization of academic research	18.5	45.2	23.8	10.9	1.6	962
Encourage faculty to provide consulting services to private firms	14.9	41.3	29.6	11.3	2.9	964
Set up a development foundation to help start up new technology-based businesses	12.0	32.0	27.5	23.7	4.7	955
Invest equity (stock) in companies based on university research	7.2	19.3	34.3	26.0	13.3	943

Scale Mean = 3.46
Cronbach's Alpha = .724

Table 9.2

Frequency of Faculty Approval/Disapproval of a Peer Engaged in User-Oriented Applied Research (e.g., precommercialization research)

	Strongly Approve (5)	Approve (4)	Indifferent (3)	Disapprove (2)	Strongly Disapprove (1)	N of observation
Approve or disapprove of a colleague working with industry in user-oriented research	17.3%	37.5%	32.6%	11.1%	1.5%	954

Mean = 3.92

Table 9.3
Frequency of Faculty Response Indicating Importance of Seeking External Research Grant in Relation to Tenure, Promotion, Annual Evaluation, and Recognition

Academic Rewards	Absolutely important (5)	Very Important (4)	Important (3)	Somewhat Important (2)	Not Important (1)	N of Observations
Tenure & Promotion	58.6%	22.2%	9.6%	6.5%	3.2%	973
Promotion to Full Professor	57.0	24.0	10.3	5.6	3.1	968
Annual Evaluation	26.5	37.5	22.3	8.8	4.0	970
Recognition & Prestige	38.4	36.7	17.1	6.2	1.6	973

Scale Mean = 4.08
Cronbach's Alpha = .896

Table 9.4

Frequency of Faculty Assessment with Regard to the Likely Impact of a Close University-Industry Cooperation for Technology Transfer and Commercialization

Nature of Impact	Almost certain (5)	Likely (4)	Possible (3)	Unlikely (2)	Most unlikely (1)	N of observations
Displacement of the University Mission	9.5%	19.9%	43.1%	23.9%	3.5%	953
Loss of Academic Freedom and Autonomy	6.0	18.8	40.4	30.3	4.4	950
Pressure for Short-term Research	25.5	43.5	24.6	5.3	1.0	954
Reduction in Basic Research	20.5	38.1	30.3	9.5	1.6	954
Increased Conflict of Interest by Mixing Research and Business	10.7	25.2	46.8	14.8	2.5	949

Scale Mean = 3.36
Cronbach's Alpha = .824

rusal of the individual item responses shows that faculty views vary substantially and systematically from item to item, displaying a pattern similar to a Guttman scale. The Guttman reproducibility test yields a Lambda of 0.73, which is close to Cronbach's Alpha of 0.72. With regard to university participation in regional economic development (e.g., participation in the policy or planning process) faculty support is strong: More than 88 percent either agree or strongly agree with this objective, producing a scale mean of 4.05. Also, a fairly strong majority (64 percent) either agree or strongly agree with the concept of the university establishing and operating technology transfer centers as a way to facilitate commercialization of academic research. The scale mean for this measure moves slightly downward to 3.7, which is roughly between "Agree" and "Indifferent." On the proposition that the university provide consulting services to private firms, only a 56 percent majority either agrees or strongly agrees, with the scale mean being 3.5. This is as far as majority support holds.

Concerning the idea that the university set up its own development foundation to help start up new technology-based businesses, 44 percent either agree or strongly agree, with a scale mean being 3.2, which is about "Indifferent." On the idea that the university invest equity in companies based on university research, only 27 percent agree or strongly agree. The scale mean drops to 2.8, which is about between "Indifferent" and "Disagree." Data seem to indicate that those who agree with the idea of equity investment (i.e., a proprietary role) tend to agree with all five items, but those agreeing with the university participation in economic development efforts (i.e., public function) do not necessarily agree with items of more proprietary implication, especially start up assistance or equity investment propositions. Guttman's reproducibility test (Lambda = 0.73) supports this interpretation, suggesting that there may be an internal structure in faculty responses. My suspicion is that faculty respondents might have "sorted out" the five items on the basis of "publicness-privateness."

Table 9.2 is a summary of faculty responses on the academic climate as it relates to application-oriented industry research (or precommercialization research). On a five-point scale, with 1 being "Strongly Disapprove" and 5 "Strongly Approve," the overall mean is 3.92, which is close to "Approve." Specifically, about 55 percent of the respondents either approve or strongly approve of the colleague who works closely with industry on technology transfer. A significant number of the faculty (about 33 percent), however, remain indifferent, with a proviso that the colleague needs to fulfill academic obligations.[2] A small minority (about 13 percent) disapprove of application-oriented industry research as not appropriate in the academic setting. Note that the individual agreement/disagreement represents the respondent's own state of mind, not an interpretation of how others might think. The questionnaire item asked the respondents the extent to which they *personally* would approve or disapprove of a colleague in their department working closely with industry in precommercialization research.

Table 9.3 describes the extent to which academics feel pressured to seek external funding for research. As discussed, the weight of pressures was ascertained on a scale of five for four related items: tenure and promotion, promotion to full professor, annual evaluation and salary increase, and recognition and prestige. The scale mean of these four items is 4.1, which is slightly above "Very Important." While responses to all four items appear to have clustered to form a single dimension, the response mode is "Absolutely Important." About 58 percent of respondents rated it as "Absolutely Important" for tenure and promotion.

Why this is the case in the United States may not always be obvious to nonacademics or some international audiences. In the U.S. university, research and publication are critical elements for tenure and promotion decisions. But this requires funding. Research funds allow faculty to purchase new lab equipment, hire bright students, and possibly reduce their teaching load so as to devote more time to research. Institutional administrators are also known to put pressure on faculty, subtly and sometimes not so subtly, to seek external funding. The external funding generates overhead that allows the university to upgrade its research infrastructure, hire graduate students, and generate "seed grants" for other start-up research.

Finally, Table 9.4 summarizes faculty responses to their own concerns (fears) about a possible erosion of traditional university values as a result of a close UI collaboration: university mission, academic freedom, no pressure for short-term research, long-term basic research, and no conflict of interest. Frequencies show that all five items are clustered around the mean of 3.36, indicating that faculty in general believe that close university-industry cooperation is likely to interfere with academic values. It is of interest to note that, of all values, faculty respondents appear to be most concerned about the issue of intellectual autonomy. A large majority, 69 percent, are concerned that a close university-industry collaboration may generate undue pressure for short-term research, thereby disrupting their long-term basic research mission.

STRUCTURAL EXPLANATION

By now it is clear that faculty attitudes toward UI collaboration do vary considerably from one faculty member to another and from one type of collaboration to another. A perusal of the data also shows that attitudes vary in an orderly manner, not chaotically, suggesting an underlying structure. The next level of our interest is, Why do some academics exhibit a favorable attitude toward UI collaboration (even if it involves several different activities), and others do not? How are these varying attitudes related to and affected by their own sense of what academics should be doing? How does their instrumental need for external grants affect and shape their attitudes toward UI collaboration? In the same vein, how does their intrinsic need to preserve academic freedom and autonomy affect and shape their attitudes toward UI collaboration? Or, are faculty attitudes toward UI collaboration predetermined by structural artifacts such as academic disciplines and institutional characteristics (public versus private)?

Note that at the outset of this chapter a causal structure was hypothesized that the academic climate (that is, what academics should or should not be doing) would have a significant impact on faculty attitudes. The academic climate, on the other hand, would be affected by the collision of two powerful but opposing motives: the need for external funding versus the need to preserve academic freedom and independence. Figure 9.1 is the result of Bollen and Long's structural equation models (SEMs) for all variables included in the design. The standardized (path) coefficients are reported in the final hypothesized causal structure (a path diagram) in Figure 9.1.

As various goodness-of-fit indicators[3] suggest, a causal structure appears to exist between faculty attitudes and other variable sets considered in the model. In the main, as indicated by the arrows in bold, the *academic climate* variable appears to exert a determining influence on faculty attitudes toward UI collaboration on technology transfer. On a closer look, it should not come as a surprise that faculty who *approve* of their departmental colleagues working closely with industry would also exhibit a supportive attitude toward UI collaboration on technology transfer. Although it is unnecessary to belabor the obvious logic, the importance of the academic climate cannot be overemphasized. The academic climate, in a sense, is a peer-evaluation culture. While approval by colleagues, especially by senior colleagues, is a blessing for one's career advancement, their disapproval often is a "kiss of death."

If the academic climate plays such a powerful role, what causes it or mitigates it? Within the limits of the data, SEM analysis shows that the two motives—*the need for external funding* and *the need to preserve autonomy*—are operating in opposite directions. On the one hand, the need for intellectual autonomy, including publishable research, makes some faculty think twice about working with industry. The intrinsic need for freedom and autonomy causes faculty to expostulate about the dangers of application-oriented, firm-specific research. Hence, the path coefficient is negative. This point was explained eloquently by one faculty member who commented in his response: "I believe that the research university should concentrate on the basic research. Applications and transfer are best left to businesses. Our comparative advantage is in the basic research and the history is clear that is where our greatest productivity and contribution to society are. It is a mistake to shift our emphasis to more applied problems."

On the other hand, in the environment where funding for academic research is becoming increasingly scarce and competitive, academics may not be able to afford to be "too picky." One respondent's comment, "All money is the same color," appears to capture today's temper of the academic climate. Another commented to the same effect, "Money is required; its source is not so important; it's hard to get from any source." The instrumental need for external funding, therefore, seems to make a convincing case for faculty to become more realistic about funding sources. In the final analysis, realism mitigates the oth-

Figure 9.1
The Structural Relationship of Faculty Attitudes as Indicated by Path Coefficients

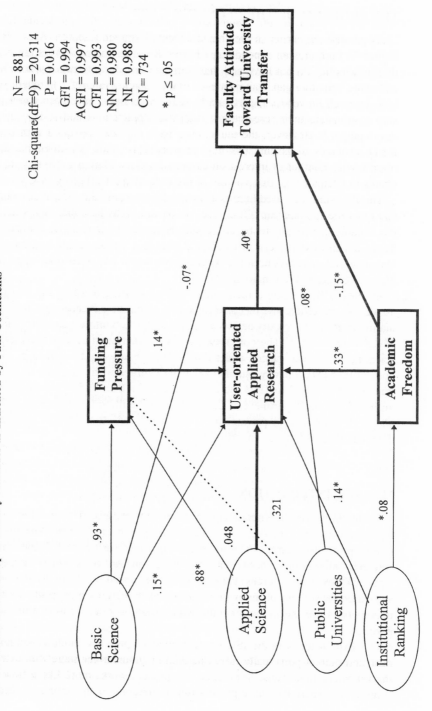

N = 881
Chi-square(df=9) = 20.314
P = 0.016
GFI = 0.994
AGFI = 0.997
CFI = 0.993
NNI = 0.980
NI = 0.988
CN = 734

* p ≤ .05

erwise "purist" position and helps faculty accept the need for application-oriented, firm-specific research. Thus, the path coefficient between funding pressure and user-oriented research is positive. Notwithstanding, one may not push this type of interpretation too far. Faculty from certain academic disciplines, such as industrial engineering, may argue that their mission is to work with industry and conduct industry-related research. And yet, they also would emphasize the fact that their industry orientation does not mitigate their academic obligation to generate knowledge and diffuse it.

Structural analysis (Figure 9.1) also provides interesting but not surprising directional information about the behavior of academic disciplines. Faculty in basic sciences and engineering (coded as "1") show a significantly more supportive attitude toward UI collaboration than their counterparts in the social sciences (coded as "0"). Engineering faculty's support for UI collaboration is slightly stronger than that of basic science faculty. The influence of institutional characteristics (public or private) does not appear to be significant. This does not mean, however, that public universities are not under pressure by their state legislatures to contribute more to economic development. The pressures may not have worked their way through to the individual faculty level enough to make a difference in attitude as compared to faculty in private institutions. The effects of institutional ranking also are not strong in connection with the academic climate (user-oriented research) or with the need to preserve *academic freedom*. A breakdown of the ranking data, however, shows a tendency that, compared to the institutions ranked either high or low in prestige, those ranked in the middle are more supportive of application-oriented, industry-specific research.

SUMMARY AND IMPLICATIONS

Whether real or anticipated, the perception of a competitiveness crisis in the 1980s raised the issue of university-industry collaboration to a national policy agenda. Since then, depending on the ups and downs in competitiveness, American research universities have been cajoled and pressured to generate greater benefits to the economy and society out of their research. This, in practice, has meant that universities work with industry to increase and diffuse technological innovation, help industry become more competitive in the global marketplace, and thereby improve the national standard of living. While, in principle, this policy objective (as articulated in the 1980 Stevenson-Wydler Act) seems to be generally shared, it has never been made clear just how universities and academics should go about collaborating with industry—for example, what kind of R&D collaboration (basic, precompetitive, or technical), what level of collaboration (firm or industry), what kind of intellectual property and other asset transactions, and how to finance it. Debate still continues in the search for workable solutions.

This chapter looked at *what academics, in turn, believe their role, or their*

university's role, should or should not be. The chapter also explored *why* academics think as they do—so we may gain some insights for future policy debate.
My interest in the chapter, in particular, was to gain an ecological perspective
on faculty views and attitudes—that is, how their views and attitudes are *related
to* and *affected by* their social and environmental milieu: normative orientation
(academic climate), ethos (academic freedom and intellectual autonomy), needs
(funding versus intellectual autonomy), disciplinary orientation, institutional
characteristics (public versus private), and institutional prestige.

If faculty views are to be "summed up" from the survey data, it can be said
that they are not opposed to university-industry collaboration. However, a more
interesting finding, in my view, is in the details and the underlying pattern.
Analysis shows that American academics are actually very favorably disposed
to a close university-industry collaboration—insofar as such collaboration is
structured to contribute to public welfare or economic development. When university-industry collaboration is perceived as a move toward privatization of
university research, narrowly benefiting individual companies, faculty views are
negative, or split at best. It is not altogether clear, though, what this really means
in practice. Are there ways, one might ask, in which academics and their institutions can address the collective needs of firms without actually working with
individual firms? If so, what could they be? This is an issue that is beyond the
scope of this chapter and requires further investigation.

Perhaps a more interesting finding, in my view, is why the survey respondents
appraised the issue of UI collaboration as they did. Analysis shows that at the
heart of the issue is what academics believe they ought to be doing or ought
not to be doing as part of their research mission. For convenience I labeled this
"sense-making" as the *academic climate* (normative orientation) and measured
it in terms of their approval or disapproval of application-oriented or user-
oriented research. Data show that faculty support for (or opposition to) university-industry collaboration is initially determined by this normative orientation.

If the academic climate (or the normative orientation) is central to the shaping
of faculty attitudes toward university-industry collaboration, what causes it?
Data evince that academics are troubled by two powerful but not necessarily
complementary motives: *the instrumental need for external funding for research*
and *the intrinsic need to preserve academic freedom and intellectual autonomy.*
To the extent that academics are dependent upon external funding for research,
the emergent R&D funding environment has a seductive quality to it. The need
for funding forces academics to become more realistic and worldly in their
search for external resources, even if the sources that they seek are not entirely
compatible with their fundamental research mission. But the intrinsic need for
academic freedom and intellectual autonomy of the faculty points up the potential dangers of being side-tracked from fundamental research. Academics con-
tend that they are already making valuable contributions to the economy by
leading the nation to the frontiers of knowledge that engender important technological breakthroughs. They believe that this is their strength and that the

United States is most competitive on this knowledge frontier. Academics fear, justifiably or not, that too close a university-industry collaboration will undermine their fundamental research mission. Clearly, a strain exists between these two forces.

If this interpretation is correct, it seems important that public policy continue to emphasize the need for cooperation between university and industry on technological innovation. The economy requires it, and the complexity of technological innovation requires it. It would be disingenuous, however, for policymakers to make academics and their institutions increase their financial dependence on industry or practically private firms. To academics this is disquieting, and they are fearful of its long-term consequence.

Finally, in spite of continuing debate over whether academics can afford to get involved in application-oriented research, analysis shows that application-oriented research per se is not really an important point of debate—insofar as science and engineering faculty are concerned. As opposed to the social science faculty, most science and engineering faculty do not see much problem with their colleagues who work closely with industry on "pre-competitive" research, *provided* that they do their "academic chores"—teaching and publication. There now is a sense of datedness in this debate. We need to move forward in search of new creative ways for universities and industry to collaborate with one another, with an emphasis on the longer time horizon.

NOTES

1. This study is partially funded by the National Science Foundation, SBR-9314. The questionnaire was pilot-tested on sixteen chairs of science departments from four research universities. The result of the pilot test indicated that the instrument might generate a dataset of reasonable variability for analysis.

2. This proviso has been stated by many respondents in their comments.

3. In Figure 9.1 the null hypothesis is $\Sigma = \Sigma(\Theta)$, where Σ is the population covariance matrix of the observed variables, $\Sigma(\Theta)$ is the covariance matrix implied by a specific model, and Θ is a vector containing the free parameters of the model. Thus, to reject the null hypothesis means the model would have little empirical reality. Conversely, a failure to reject the null hypothesis indicates that the hypothesized model has a good fit. Figure 9.1 includes several goodness-of-fit indicators. The reason for this multiple indicator approach is that structural equation modelists generally agree that no single test statistic is sufficiently reliable for testing the null hypothesis. According to Bollen and Long, there is no consensus among structural equation modelists on the best ways to assess the model fit, and no single measure of overall fit should be relied on exclusively. In Figure 9.1 all goodness-of-fit indicators except the Chi-square test show a strong fit. A possible reason for the significant Chi-square test statistic is that, as Bollen and Long note, "in large samples even trivial deviation of a model from the actual structure could be detected and could lead to a rejection of the null hypothesis" (Bollen and Long, 1993, p. 3).

PART IV

Federal Lab–Industry Interaction

CHAPTER 10

Cooperative Research and Development Agreements

EVAN MICHAEL BERMAN

Throughout the 1980s, the federal government pioneered new strategies for the commercialization of defense and other federal technologies. Cooperative Research and Development Agreements (CRADAs) were first authorized in 1986 and are defined as comprehensive legal agreements for the sharing of personnel, equipment, funding, and intellectual property rights in joint government-industry research. Initially introduced to increase U.S. technological competitiveness in the global economy, CRADAs remain at the heart of commercialization efforts in the current era of downward pressures on public and private R&D budgets (U.S. Department of Commerce, Office of Technology Policy, 1996), because CRADAs help industry to gain access to new research in cooperation with federal laboratories. Since 1986, over 2,200 CRADAs have been signed, making CRADAs the chief way by which federal labs and industry work together. Examples of CRADAs include research on adapting antisubmarine warfare sonar technology for deep sea exploration, the development of oral vaccines, innovative software for parallel computing, lightweight automotive materials, neural network imaging, and other applications. CRADAs are also used by R&D consortia such as SEMATECH in their research collaborations (U.S. Department of Commerce, 1993, 1994; White House, 1993; Marshall & Schramm, 1993; Andrews, 1993).

Notwithstanding the growing use of CRADAs, a continuing concern is of their legal procedural difficulties (see Ham & Mowery, 1995). In congressional testimony, some leading firms have stated that the CRADA process is unsatisfactory and fraught with legal and other difficulties. Of most serious concern to industry is that CRADAs are very slow to negotiate and cumbersome to implement. This chapter offers a "midterm" assessment of CRADAs, focusing on the barriers that frustrate federal lab–industry collaborations (RD&D Report,

1993; U.S. Congress, 1992; National Academy of Sciences, 1992; General Accounting Office, 1989).[1,2]

FRAMEWORK

Technology transfer is a complex process involving the utilization of existing knowledge, facilities, or capabilities in another field, organization, or sector (Stewart, 1987; National Academy of Sciences, 1992). From a policy-analytic perspective, the evaluation of technology transfer programs is complicated because the impacts of technology transfer occur over long periods of time, for example, five to fifteen years. CRADAs are best regarded as the seeds from which subsequent commercialized products "sprout," and it is often difficult to trace commercialization back to the original seeds of collaborative research. Furthermore, the practical utility to policymakers of long-term evaluations is often limited (Betz, 1993).

In response to these problems, technology transfer programs sometimes use "built-in" or "real-time" evaluation in order to assist policymakers with meaningful and timely information. The National Competitiveness Transfer Act of 1989 mandates that the Department of Commerce provide to Congress a biennial report on the use of CRADAs, which is an opportunity for real-time evaluation. To date, these reports have been limited in scope (for example, relying on administrative data, such as the number of CRADAs signed); some observers believe that the Commerce Department is overly optimistic in its assessment of barriers and that complementary and independent assessment is needed (U.S. Department of Commerce, 1993).

This midterm evaluation focuses on two sets of concerns. The first involves the efficacy and outcomes of CRADAs: What is the current utilization of CRADAs? What kinds of firms benefit most? How satisfied are firms with the results of their collaborative efforts? The second set of concerns focuses on barriers and processes related to CRADAs. In this regard, the literature discusses (1) legal issues, (2) agency priority and support, and (3) lack of familiarity.

Legal Issues

CRADA negotiations involve the following legal issues: the financial and staffing obligations of each party, timely reporting of inventions, sharing of intellectual property rights, filing of patent applications, sharing of royalties, the granting of commercialization licenses to third parties, rights to applications beyond intended fields of use, pricing of inventions, access and ownership of research results and data, protection of proprietary data, publication rights, standard clauses concerning indemnification, dispute settlement, contract termination, written waivers, and severability (National Institute of Standards and Technology, 1992). While most agencies have drawn up standard or model

CRADAs, each agreement presents different circumstances and must be negotiated separately.

Priority and Support

Technology transfer is a secondary mission for agencies. As a result, an agency may provide limited funds for CRADAs[3] and may be slow in resolving negotiation obstacles. First, agency technology transfer offices, which provide administrative and legal services, are reported to be understaffed and inconsistently directed (Council on Competitiveness, 1992; General Accounting Office, 1989). Second, Executive Order 12591, signed in 1987, aims to increase CRADAs by delegating negotiating authority from the agencies to the laboratory directors, but in many cases this order still has not been implemented fully (U.S. Congress, 1992). Third, while the Clinton administration calls for heightened technology transfer efforts, to date no official has been appointed responsibility for overseeing this objective. This lack of administrative follow-through is an important barrier to technology transfer.

Lack of Familiarity

Many industry researchers are unfamiliar with the research activities of the federal laboratories (Atlantic Council, 1992; Baron, 1990). Unfamiliarity occurs because (1) a considerable amount of Department of Defense and Department of Energy research is classified, (2) few industry researchers have past employment or training experience in federal laboratories, and (3) most federal laboratories lack expertise in manufacturing technology (Bozeman, 1992). Recent initiatives attempt to reduce this problem. For example, the Federal Technology Transfer Act (FTTA) provides an incentive to federal inventors to seek collaboration by awarding them a minimum of 15 percent of the royalties paid to the government by firms. Networking services exist to assist industry in locating relevant federal research, such as the Federal Laboratory Consortium (FLC) created in 1974 and the National Technology Transfer Center (NTTC) created in 1992. However, their effectiveness has not been formally evaluated (Federal Laboratory Consortium, 1992).

METHODS

A sample of CRADAs was drawn and analyzed in relation to different firms and industries. CRADAs were analyzed that were signed between November 1, 1992, and January 31, 1993. In addition, over 40 exploratory, in-depth telephone interviews were conducted with technology transfer program managers at the Department of Energy, Department of Defense, Department of Commerce, and National Institutes of Health (NIH), as well as technology transfer directors and managers at eleven large laboratories of these agencies.[4] Large laboratories were selected because these labs are more likely to have many CRADAs with industry and thus more experience. Within each laboratory, technology transfer directors and managers were interviewed because they have more experience than individual lab scientists in negotiating CRADAs.

Federal technology transfer managers provided a list of companies with which agencies have CRADAs. From these lists, five large, five medium, and five small companies were selected for additional case study in-depth interviews. Those who were interviewed were the participants in CRADA research and negotiations. They were asked about barriers that they experienced in CRADA negotiations, as well as perceived benefits from collaborative research.

STUDY RESULTS

Level of Use

Table 10.1 shows the use of CRADAs by agencies. The growth of CRADAs appears to be extraordinary, although the trend data since 1987 are not strictly comparable. The Departments of Army, Agriculture, Commerce, and Health and Human Services are approximately equal leaders in the use of CRADAs. Aggregate data for all federal agencies show that the total number of active CRADAs has increased from 732 in 1991 to 1250 in 1992, 1847 in 1993, and 2607 in 1994 (U.S. Department of Commerce, Office of Technology Policy, 1996). The pattern of utilization suggests that CRADAs address a research need by industry.

Table 10.2 analyzes a sample of CRADAs in connection with firm size and industry. In congressional testimony it was suggested that large firms may be primary beneficiaries of CRADAs, because of the complexity of the negotiation process (U.S. Congress, 1992). However, the sample shows no such bias: 43 percent of CRADA participants are from small firms (fewer than 500 employees), 21 percent from medium-sized firms, and 36 percent from large firms (more than 10,000 employees). The participation by small and medium-sized firms is further confirmed by interviews with technology transfer officers. Based on agency records, interviewees estimate that 25 percent to 30 percent of firms are small, 40 percent to 45 percent are large, and the rest, 25 percent to 35 percent, are medium in size.

Table 10.2 also shows that many CRADAs involve firms in high-technology industries. Many participating firms have extensive research and development (R&D) programs. While few of the companies are known leaders in their areas, none of the firms in the sample can be classified as "catching up." This result reflects selection criteria requiring that firms are familiar with best industry practices. Industry participants are also relatively R&D intensive. Although R&D expenditures generally are not available for private firms and subsidiaries of public firms, such data are available for 27 of the 30 large firms in the sample.

Table 10.1
Cooperative Research and Development Agreements (CRADAs)

Agency	1987	1988	1989	1990	1991[a]	New[b] CRADAs 1992	New CRADAs 1993	Total[b] CRADAs 1987–93	S&Es[c]
Defense									
Army	3	8	27	80	115	103	82	303	25,000
Navy	0	0	2	20	52	24	45	119	10,000
Air Force	0	2	7	13	26	26	72	149	23,000
Agriculture	9	51	98	128	177	43	61	315	2,300
Commerce	0	9	44	82	115	85	152	411	3,900
Energy	0	0	0	1	43	153	258	486	35,000
EPA	0	0	2	11	31	23	4	66	850
HHS	22	28	89	110	144	116	21	316	6,200
Interior	0	0	1	12	11	2	25	37	6,300
DoT	0	0	0	1	9	7	14	33	500
Veterans	0	0	1	2	8	0	0	4	2,500
CIA	0	0	0	0	0	0	1	1	n/a
Total	34	98	271	460	731	(582)	(735)	(2240)	115,550

Notes: [a]Department of Commerce, 1993. Numbers reported for 1987–1991 are active CRADAs in fiscal years, that is, collaborative research in progress. Update for 1992 and 1993 not available (as of March, 1994).

[b]*Cooperative Technology RD&D Report*, Technology Publishing Group, Washington, DC, December 1992, 1993. Numbers reported are new CRADAs signed in calendar year, including *active and inactive* CRADAs.

[c]Federal scientists and engineers employed by agencies (estimate). However, not all are engaged in RD&T activities.

Source: Cooperative Technology RD&D Report.

Table 10.2
Federal CRADAs: Firm Size and Industry

Industry[a,b]	Total Firms	Large Firms	Medium Firms	Small Firms	Size Unknown
Software	15	4	3	6	2
Aerospace	4	3	0	1	0
Microelectronic components	6	2	1	0	3
Materials	14	1	2	7	4
Electronic components/ equipment	6	3	0	0	3
Ceramics	3	2	0	0	1
Electronic networks	7	1	0	0	6
Glass	2	1	1	0	0
Lithography	2	1	0	1	0
Textiles	1	0	1	0	0
Jet Engines	3	3	0	0	0
Refuse management	2	0	1	1	0
Telecommunications	2	2	0	0	0
Machinery	5	0	2	3	0
Biomedical equipment	1	0	0	1	0
Optical equipment	5	1	1	3	0
Instruments/test equip. n.e.c.	4	0	0	4	0
Biomedical research	7	0	1	4	2
Biological/pharm.products	3	1	1	0	1
Research, n.e.c.	7	2	1	2	2
Agr. vaccines and pesticides	10	0	0	0	10
Chemicals, plastics	5	3	2	0	0
Unknown	5	0	0	2	3
Total	119	30	17	35	37

n.e.c. = not elsewhere classified.

Notes: [a]Small is defined as fewer than 500 employees (U.S. Small Business Administration). Large is defined as greater than 10,000 employees. Subsidiaries of firms are analyzed based on their number of employees. Some names of industry participants are withheld by agencies for reasons of confidentiality. Information on firms was obtained from agencies and sources stated below.

[b]Industry classification is based on company SIC code. When companies have multiple codes, determinantion is made based on the CRADA project description. When the description is unclear with regard to industry, multiple SIC codes are identified and weighted. In the absence of a company name, the CRADA project description is used as the basis of classification.

Source: CRADAs obtained through Technology Publishing Group, Washington, DC. Sample 11/92–1/93. Company information obtained through telephone interviews, *Dun's Market Identifiers* (Dialogue File 516) and *Business Infotrack*.

Within their respective industry categories, these firms rate on average within the top 26th percentile of R&D expenditures per employee.[5]

Industry interviewees also expressed a high level of satisfaction with the assistance and cooperation received from federal scientists, indicating the usefulness of federal technology. This finding is consistent with Roessner and Bean (1991), who examined informal interactions between industry and federal labs. Outcomes of CRADA research are varied and generally involve (1) applications of federal technology to problems of industrial manufacturing, (2) assistance in the development of commercial products, (3) access to test equipment in federal laboratories, and (4) research results. Although in only one instance did an interviewee report the commercialization of a new product, overall industry values the technology that is received. Participation is often viewed as a strategic asset, and many firms opt to keep their participation confidential in order to keep their competitive edge over rivals. Many firms also stated that they would not have participated in CRADA research if it had included a competitor.

Overcoming Legal Barriers

Legal issues were mentioned by all federal interviewees as the most important barrier in CRADA negotiations. According to federal interviewees, CRADA negotiations take about two to four months when no complicated issues are raised.[6] However, when legal complications arise, negotiations often last from four to six months and in some instances from twelve to eighteen months. Delays are longest at the Department of Energy, because the organization has authorized its contractor-operated labs to negotiate only a limited set of preapproved departures from model CRADAs. Five legal issues were mentioned in interviews: (1) United States manufacturing preference laws (important to the Department of Energy and the National Institute of Standards and Technology), (2) product liability and indemnification (Department of Energy), (3) fair access (National Institute of Standards and Technology, Department of Energy), (4) intellectual property rights (Department of Defense), and (5) future pricing clauses (National Institutes of Health).

U.S. Manufacturing

The FTTA mandates that preference be given to companies that substantially manufacture CRADA inventions in the United States. The term "substantially" is not clarified in the law, and the Department of Energy instructs its labs to interpret this as a per se requirement, that is, regardless of circumstances. As a consequence of this strict interpretation, one CRADA opportunity fell through when the manufacturer of an aviation braking system would not guarantee that the entire brake, which is manufactured by a subcontractor, would be manufactured in the United States. One large firm with overseas operations also argued that compliance with the FTTA could result in a competitive disadvantage in global manufacturing, because it shifts production away from low-cost sites. It also argued that compliance with the FTTA may conflict with the local content laws of other nations. To avoid these problems, the Department of Defense interprets "substantially" by rule of reason, that is, with regard to circumstances. Specifically, the Department of Defense instructs its CRADA participants to demonstrate that they will manufacture resulting products as much as possible in the United States, and they must back up their positions with data from manufacturing operations. Department of Defense interviewees report that firms understand the intent of the law, and that no CRADA negotiations have stalled as a result. Consequently, only a few CRADAs were signed that do not increase United States manufacturing. In these instances, the reason for signing the CRADAs was that technological gains to the Department of Defense resulting from the research activity were considerable.

Product Liability

Product liability issues arise because, although the United States government accepts royalties for use of patents and licenses, it nevertheless insists on being indemnified in future lawsuits from damages that may result from the sale and use of developed products. The United States government argues that this position is fair because it has no control over industrial engineering and design decisions subsequent to CRADA research. However, firms argue that indemnification implies that the government wants benefits without taking its share of risks (U.S. Congress, 1992). This problem has arisen in Department of Energy negotiations. The National Institute of Standards and Technology and the Department of Defense attempt to overcome this barrier, granting industrial partners indemnification from lawsuits involving other firms that are granted a license by the United States government. By accepting this provision, firms acknowledge that the U.S. government has little control over subsequent development work, while the government acknowledges that firms have little control over government decisions to grant licenses to third parties. Finally, to avoid future liabilities arising from these third-party licenses, the government negotiates that these parties will indemnify both the government and its license-partners in the event of assessed damages.

Fair Access

Selecting a few partners from among many is a potentially difficult legal problem for agencies. The FTTA does not provide criteria for selecting partners, nor does it rely on the usual federal fairness-of-opportunity rules. While firms do not have legal rights to participate in CRADAs, agencies fear that firms that are intentionally or for lack of communication left out of CRADA bidding processes may have rights to research results. While no such claim has yet been heard in court, damages would be assessed against the government if it was found that firms had been discriminated against in the selection process. This fear has caused the Department of Energy to cancel a preliminary CRADA worth $70 million with Cray on supercomputer programs, after rivals complained that it was tantamount to a subsidy to Cray for underwriting the development costs of the next-generation model computer. The rivals wanted similar deals, and the Department of Energy backed off from the deal (Andrews, 1993). To avoid this problem, the National Institute of Standards and Technology (NIST), whose industry partners are mainly small and medium-sized businesses, advertises its CRADA opportunities in a wide range of trade journals as well as in the *Federal Register*. The institute also has decided that when multiple qualified firms respond to a CRADA opportunity, it will organize itself with these firms into an R&D consortium, rather than selecting a single partner. However, the negotiation of R&D consortia is more complex and takes longer, because it involves a larger number of partners.

Intellectual Property

Intellectual property (IP) issues were mentioned only by the Department of Defense as being a concern to CRADA administration. IP issues occur because the government insists on preserving royalty-free, nonexclusive use of any invention that is made jointly with the industry partner under the CRADA or solely by the partner in the course of the CRADA project. The government is required to obtain these IP rights by the FTTA. However, firms are concerned that the government may grant a license to third parties, including rival firms. This fear usually is allayed by government granting a three-year (NIH) or five-year (NIST) nondisclosure period for inventions developed under CRADAs. During this period, no third-party license is possible. Firms eventually agree to this formula, but sometimes only after prolonged negotiation. In interviews, firms were asked whether they trusted the government to ensure nondisclosure of proprietary information in view of staff turnover and the possibility of policy changes. Industry interviewees stated that they trusted the laboratories to protect this information, just as the laboratory does with company proprietary information that is provided during the course of CRADA research. Two interviewees stated that the basis of this trust in government is that the information is being held at the laboratory, not at the parent agency where ''administrative and political types do not fully understand its commercial significance.''

Pricing

Finally, NIH CRADAs contain a clause that gives NIH the right to request that firms establish a reasonable relationship among the pricing of licensed products, the public investment in products (for example, through in-kind CRADA contributions), and the health and safety needs of the public. Firms may be required to provide reasonable evidence in support of this relationship. The

FTTA does not provide a definition for "reasonableness," nor does it state when the agency should request evidence of a reasonable relationship. However, this issue has not yet arisen, and companies did not expect it to. Still, when the Clinton Administration announced in January 1993 that it was concerned about the high level of profits in the pharmaceutical industry, NIH CRADA negotiations stalled as firms became concerned that NIH might invoke the clause in the future. At present, NIH is considering whether modifications should be made to this clause.

Interviews suggest that these barriers are more commonplace in CRADA negotiations that involve large firms. Compared with larger firms, smaller firms are characterized by (1) the absence of international manufacturing operations, (2) the direct involvement of the chief executive officer in CRADA negotiations, and (3) the absence of large legal staffs, all of which decrease the likelihood of legal issues becoming barriers. Among the larger firms, electronic and automobile firms were concerned particularly with United States manufacturing preference laws, and most medium-sized and large firms were concerned with the length of Department of Energy negotiations. One industry interviewee lamented that Department of Energy lawyers were attempting to make their CRADAs "Dingell-proof," that is, the department was trying to secure too many government rights in view of possible allegations by that congressman's staff about "giving the (public) store away."

OTHER BARRIERS

Agency Priority and Support

Many technology transfer managers at Department of Energy and Department of Defense laboratories stated that their agency had been slow to implement technology transfer legislation and directives. They had not received additional personnel and funds for marketing their laboratories' resources to industry. Despite new responsibilities, technology transfer budgets in each laboratory remained stable, with staffing ranging between two and five full-time professionals. Agencies had been slow to develop policy and legal opinions concerning the above legal issues. Technology transfer managers attributed this slowness to a lack of priority given by federal agencies to their new technology transfer mission. Department of Energy and Department of Defense interviewees did, however, mention that in recent months they had been authorized to hire some additional staff.

Federal in-kind support for CRADAS is an important determinant of research collaboration. Federal in-kind support is said to contribute 40 percent to 60 percent of total project costs. Most interviewees stated that in the absence of this support, firms would not collaborate with the federal government. However, both the NIH and Naval Research Laboratory (NRL) interviewees stated that their facilities and the quality of researchers were very high and that industry appeared willing to collaborate with NIH and NRL regardless of cost-sharing considerations. This view was supported by industry representatives. One NRL representative stated that the majority of its CRADAs include an industry contribution of almost 90 percent of total project costs, including federal research salaries. Overall, however, it appears that in-kind support, with these unusual exceptions, is an important determinant of industry's participation in CRADAs.

At the Department of Energy, unlike other agencies, each laboratory receives a separate budget allocation for in-kind and project costs related to CRADAs. These annual CRADA budgets may not be exceeded, nor may funds from other accounts be transferred into CRADA budgets. This arrangement causes delays of up to twelve months in the CRADA approval process when CRADA requests exceed previously budgeted levels, and laboratory directors must negotiate with Department of Energy headquarters for additional CRADA funding. Consequently, more complaints were heard from national lab interviewees than from any other agency about the level of agency funding as a barrier to technology transfer.

Familiarity

Both laboratory and industry interviewees stated that industry is generally unaware of the capabilities of federal labs. Many mentioned that the lack of a central information source was a very important barrier in learning more about the research activities of federal labs. Initial contact often occurred in an indirect way, informally, in an effort to solve a technical problem; the possibility of research collaboration was usually discussed two to six months after this initial contact was made. One large company has employees at the corporate level whose job is to visit the federal laboratories and identify areas of joint interest, but only a few companies have resources of this type available. None of the industry interviewees mentioned the FLC or NTTC as a source of networking. Several Department of Energy technology transfer directors mentioned that they recently had started to increase their networking activities through trade shows, seminars, and advertising, thereby contacting non–Department of Energy contractors.

CRADAs are sometimes viewed as a means to supplement falling laboratory budgets, because the FTTA provides federal inventors with a share of royalties. In most instances, royalties from CRADA research have yet to occur. However, Argonne National Laboratory received $700,000 in royalties and licensing fees from industry between 1987 and 1992, based on inventions involving 52 researchers. At this lab, each inventor received 25 percent of gross proceeds from his or her own invention or, on average, less than $3,500.

For almost a decade now, government-industry research collaboration is clearly increasing. Industry continues to show growing interest in federal technology. While improvements have been made in the CRADA process, as noted in this chapter, negotiations of CRADAs are still often slow, and certain legal and organizational barriers still impede the use of CRADAs. Small firms some-times find CRADAs difficult to negotiate. An important barrier is also the lack of central information sources about research in the federal activities and ca-pabilities of the labs. Complaints are most frequent at Department of Energy laboratories, some of which are still going down the "learning curve." CRADAs appear to be an increasingly important cornerstone of U.S. technology policy to ensure that public technologies are transferred and/or co-developed with industry in a timely and cost-effective way. Many companies benefit from CRADAs, although the overall effect on job creation and economic growth is still uncer-tain. The history of past technology efforts suggest that as long as industry remains committed to this concept and as long as ideologies do not change to oppose cooperative R&D (including co-production), there is every reason to believe that CRADAs will continue to be an important vehicle of technology transfer and co-development (Berman, 1992).

NOTES

1. This study examines the federal laboratories. Although laboratories of the Depart-ment of Energy (DOE) sometimes are called "national" laboratories, in this study the term "federal" includes both DOE and federal laboratories. The study excludes, how-ever, NASA technology transfer efforts, because NASA elected to remain under the provisions of the Space Act. The NASA "equivalent" of CRADAs is not considered here. It is estimated that over 800 federal laboratories exist. However, federal laboratories are highly diverse in R&D types and range in size from 10,000 people to small field offices staffed by only a few researchers. Only 300 laboratories are estimated to have more than 30 researchers. Combined, the federal laboratories perform over $20 billion of research annually (Council on Competitiveness, 1992).

2. The relationship of CRADAs to other federal technology transfer efforts is as fol-lows. While technology transfer sometimes occurs through written reports, articles, casual person-to-person interaction, purchases of devices, and patent disclosure, there is wide-spread agreement that sustained, person-to-person interactions, such as those provided by CRADAs, are more effective. This is because commercialization frequently involves further research and ongoing communication. In this regard, CRADAs differ from R&D consortia, which are also formal approaches, in that the former provide for a high degree of confidentiality and proprietary research in applied research. By contrast, R&D con-sortia include many rival firms and a high degree of disclosure. It is believed that R&D consortia are best suited for long-term, high-risk strategic research (Berman, 1990).

3. CRADAs are based on a model of partnership with industry in which each partner is expected to pay its own expenses. The government typically contributes by paying the salaries of researchers and the research costs related to the activities of its researchers. The government is prohibited from making payments to firms.

4. These four agencies were selected based on their use of CRADAs. According to Table 10.1, these four agencies account for almost 80 percent of the total number of CRADAs. The eleven laboratories are the Naval Research Laboratory; Army Research Laboratory; Rome Air Force Laboratory; Oak Ridge National Laboratory; Lawrence Berkeley National Laboratory; Sandia National Laboratory; Argonne National Labora-

tory; National Institute of Standards and Technology (Department of Commerce); National Cancer Institute; and National Heart, Lung and Blood Institute. The four national laboratories belong to the Department of Energy. Because of the selection of large laboratories, the findings in this study do not pertain to smaller labs.

5. For these 27 large firms, the ratio of company-funded R&D expenditures to sales is 4.4 percent, which is higher than the average of 3.6 percent for all reporting firms with sales over $45 million and company R&D expenditures over $1 million. Within their respective industry categories, these firms rate on average in the top 26th percentile regarding their average R&D expenditures per employee between 1987 and 1991, which is $6,277 (in 1991 dollars). The sources for these results are R&D data and industry classification based on companies' SEC 10-K forms as published in *Business Week*, June 29, 1992 (the "R&D Scoreboard Issue").

6. CRADAs are preceded by Joint Work statements, which discuss the proposed collaborative research. The time frame stated here is the elapsed time between the signing of the Joint Work statement and the signing of the CRADA.

CHAPTER 11

The Cooperative Technology Paradigm: An Assessment

BARRY BOZEMAN

EMERGENCE OF THE COOPERATIVE TECHNOLOGY PARADIGM

Economic decline has a way of encouraging the reexamination of fundamental values. In the wake of the perceived crisis in United States competitiveness (Massachusetts Institute of Technology Commission on Industrial Productivity, 1989; National Academy of Sciences, 1978; National Governors' Association, 1987; President's Commission on Industrial Competitiveness, 1985), many core assumptions have been reconsidered, including even the bedrock faith in the private sector as the source of virtually all significant innovation. As other nations, especially Japan, forged ahead with government support of technology development, the federal government's characteristic hands-off approach—its "market failure paradigm"—seemed less compelling (Bozeman & Crow, 1990; Bozeman & Crow, 1987).

During the 1980s, a number of policy initiatives challenged the preeminence of the market-failure paradigm for technology policy with a new one, "cooperative technology." As used here, cooperative technology is an umbrella term for a set of values emphasizing cooperation among sectors—industry, government, and university—and cooperation among rival firms in development of precompetitive technologies and "infratechnologies" (Link & Tasey, 1987). To be sure, cooperative technology has not supplanted classic free-market economics as a basis for technology policies. For example, such comparatively recent initiatives as the R&D tax credit provisions from the Economic Recovery Tax Act of 1981 assume that industry is the progenitor of innovation and the role of government is chiefly limited to staying out of the way (Bozeman & Link, 1984, 1985; Bucy, 1985; Landau & Hannay, 1981). Similarly, the strongest medicines prescribed by the cooperative technology paradigm, those entailing a fully developed industrial policy (e.g., Magaziner & Reich, 1983) have not been adopted (though the Clinton administration's policy statements seem sympathetic). Moreover, cooperative technology has made sufficient inroads so that there is no longer a single dominant technology policy paradigm. Now, there are two alternative paradigms, largely incompatible, vying for the public's and policymakers' support.

The cooperative technology development policies that have attracted the most attention are those pertaining to domestic technology transfer, especially the use of government laboratories as a partner in the commercialization of technology (Herman, 1983; Rahm, Bozeman, & Crow, 1988; General Accounting Office, 1989). Although the federal labs had been previously aloof from commercial concerns, indeed prohibited by law from developing technology specifically for private vendors, the legislation of the 1980s gradually changed the mission, tenor, and climate of the federal labs. The intellectual property dictum "If it belongs to everyone, it belongs to no one" began to take hold as the government labs increasingly moved from a sole focus on public domain research to a mandated role as a technology development partner to industry.

The cooperative technology development paradigm seems to have gathered momentum—but does it work? Is the optimism of Argonne National Laboratory director Alan Schriesheim (1990) and others (Conference Board, 1987; Kearns, 1990; Krieger, 1987) warranted, or is the more pessimistic view of former National Science Foundation director Erich Bloch (1991) and other skeptics (Morone & Ivins, 1982; General Accounting Office, 1989; Werner & Bremer, 1991) more accurate? Have the technology transfer and competitiveness policies of the 1980s had a significant impact (U.S. Congress, House of Representatives, 1985)?

Evaluating the technology policy changes of the 1980s and early 1990s is well beyond the scope of this or any single research project. However, this chapter seeks to shed some light on the degree of success of one of the jewels in the cooperative technology development crown—technology transfer from government laboratories to industry. The research presented here draws from a national study that includes data from 189 government laboratories, about half of the larger government laboratories. Based on questionnaires mailed to laboratory directors, the study seeks to determine the extent of technology transfer activity and degrees of success. Several effectiveness measures are employed, some based on subjective self-ratings, others based on objectives measures.

The present study builds on earlier efforts to document technology transfer impacts. According to data derived from comparable surveys, the level of technology transfer in government laboratories is significant and growing. In a study based on 1987 data (Rahm, Bozeman, & Crow, 1988), about half (52.3%) of government laboratories were significantly involved in technology transfer. However, 1990 data (Bozeman & Coker, 1992) taken from many of those same laboratories indicate that 74.2 percent now report significant technology transfer activity. Activity does not, of course, equate to effectiveness, and the present study is a preliminary analysis of impact.

STUDY METHODS AND PROCEDURES

Data for this study are taken from the master database of the National Comparative Research and Development Project (NCRDP). This section describes the NCRDP, sampling procedures, and measures employed for the present study.

Begun in 1984, the NCRDP is an ongoing study of the technical enterprise in the United States and other industrial nations. Sponsored at different points by a number of government agencies,[1] the NCRDP has developed in three phases.[2] This study is based on Phase III data. Designed as a panel study, Phase III sought data from all government labs, all respondents from Phase II, and focused intensively on technology transfer and cooperative research and development (R&D). Questionnaires were mailed to directors of R&D laboratories in June and July of 1990. The Phase III sample was 1,137 laboratories; 533 questionnaires were returned, for an overall response rate of 47 percent.[3] By sector, questionnaires were sent to 594 industry labs (260 received, 44% response rate); 164 university laboratories (71 received, 43% response rate); 23 nonprofit or hybrid laboratories (12 received, 61% response rate), and 356 government laboratories (189 received, 53% response rate). Given a concern to measure change, most of the sample (939 of the 1,137) and most of the respondents (420 of the 533) were drawn from the pool of respondents to a 1988 Phase II questionnaire.[4] However, given a particular concern with government laboratories, all government laboratories in the United States (meeting sample criteria) were mailed questionnaires. The data used here are entirely from the government laboratory subsample (n = 189) of the Phase III data.[5]

MEASURING TECHNOLOGY TRANSFER EFFECTIVENESS

Regardless of the approach taken to measurement,[6] a major obstacle to the study of technology transfer effectiveness is that there is little agreement on the conceptualization of effectiveness (O'Keefe, 1982). Bozeman and Fellows (1988) have presented distinct models of technology transfer effectiveness; the focus here is on two of their approaches, the "out-the-door" model and the "market impact" model.[7]

The most pervasive approach to effectiveness determination is the out-the-door model, which asks: "Did the technology (or information) get transferred to another organization?" Under this concept of effectiveness, it is the transfer itself that is important, not the impact after the transfer. The out-the-door model has the advantage of focusing on matters that are, to a large extent, under the control of the transferring organization. The market impact model, as the name implies, assesses effectiveness according to the commercial success of the transferred technology or information. The advantage is that it is a richer notion of success—there is little appeal to technology transfer that proves commercially and instrumentally barren—but it entails conceptual difficulties. If the transfer is not commercially successful, is it because the product or process transferred is of limited value, because the transferring agent has not taken the actions necessary to ensure its success, or because the recipient organization has had problems in development, manufacture, marketing, or strategy? These problems are particularly troublesome if one plans to use an effectiveness evaluation to recommend action and change.

The measures of technology transfer effectiveness are operationalized from responses to the Phase III NCRDP questionnaire. Laboratory directors were asked to fill out a (branched) section on technology transfer only if their laboratory was involved in technology transfer.[8] A first measure of effectiveness, objective but crude, is the number of licenses [variable name: LICENSE].[9] The out-the-door model of success is further measured by an item that requires the directors to rate the lab's ability to get organizations to use their technology [variable name: T-DOOR].[10] Similarly, the market impact model of technology transfer effectiveness [variable name: T-MARKET] required lab directors to rate the lab's technology transfer in terms of its commercial impact on the organizations receiving the technology.[11]

A variant of the market model considers the impact of the commercial activity on the laboratory itself. Does the laboratory generate profit from this activity? Do the individuals in the laboratory benefit personally? Two items were geared to determine these possible pecuniary benefits to the laboratory. Respondents were asked to assess[12] the level of pecuniary benefit to the laboratory [variable name: PROFITLAB] and to the individual scientists and engineers working in the laboratory [variable name: PROFITSCI].

WHO IS INVOLVED IN TECHNOLOGY TRANSFER?

While technology transfer is now a mandated activity for many federal laboratories, it is so only for those of a certain size. Further, not all the government laboratories in our database are *federal* government laboratories. Thus, examining the results presented in Table 11.1, we see that about one-quarter of the 182 reporting government laboratories are, effectively, not involved in technology transfer (collapsing the "not a mission" and "mission of little importance" categories). As expected, there are very few laboratories, only four in this sample, that view technology transfer as the major mission of the laboratory. Thus, we can conclude that technology transfer activity is ubiquitous in government laboratories and that about half the labs view it as an important mission.

Another way of determining the importance of laboratories' technology transfer activity is in terms of the budget devoted to technology transfer. On average, the 187 laboratories spent about $191,000 each on technology transfer activities, some 6.28 percent of their total R&D budgets. This percentage figure serves, however, to distort the wide range of variance in budget allocations to technol-

Table 11.1
Level of Technology Transfer Activity

TECHTRANS[a]	Frequency	Percent	Cumulative Frequency	Cumulative Percent
0	17	9.3	17	9.3
1	30	16.5	47	25.8
2	53	29.1	100	54.9
3	78	42.9	178	97.8
4	4	2.2	182	100.0

Notes:

0 = Not a mission

1 = Mission of Little Importance

2 = Somewhat Important Mission

3 = Important Mission

4 = Single Most Important Mission

[a]TECHTRANS = Response to request to indicate importance of "Technology transfer, including physical devices, processes, or 'know-how' from this laboratory to private firms or industrial organizations."

ogy transfer (standard deviation = 11.48), with one lab reporting its entire budget devoted to technology transfer and with many reporting none of their budgets devoted to that activity.

HOW EFFECTIVE IS GOVERNMENT LABORATORY TECHNOLOGY TRANSFER?

One might expect that using a range of quite different effectiveness criteria would result in an equally wide range of answers to the effectiveness question. Such does appear to be the case. Table 11.2 gives the means for the various effectiveness measures.

The average of 1.5 licenses per laboratory is quite deceptive. The distribution of licenses by laboratory is heavily skewed; just a few laboratories have most of the licenses. One of the study laboratories had twenty licenses in effect, another had fourteen; but among those having licenses, all but those two were in the range of one to eight. Most important, nearly 60 percent of the laboratories had no licenses at all. While the production of patents is not a focus of this study, it is useful to examine briefly (and for comparison to licensing) the patenting activity of the government labs. Similar to licensing, the average number of patents reported by the laboratories (in 1989) is not vast, at 4.5. Also, again, there is a highly skewed distribution, reflected in the fact that the median number of patents for all laboratories is just one. While fifty (35.2%) of the laboratories reported no patents, eight (5.6%) reported more than twenty.

The level of perceived benefit from the two indicators of profit—for the lab and for the individual—indicate that the benefits typically are modest. With the average score indicating that the benefits are insignificant, we see that only a

Table 11.2
Means for the Effectiveness Indicators

Variable	Label	N	Mean
T-MARKET	success in commercial impact	150	5.22
T-DOOR	success in getting tech. out	150	6.04
LICENSE	# licensed technologies in 1989	138	1.51
PROFITSCI	profit for individual scientists	147	0.73
PROFITLAB	profit for the lab	145	0.49

Notes:

T-MARKET, T-DOOR: 0–10, where 0 = "No impact," 10 = "Excellent."

PROFITSCI, PROFITLAB: 0 = "No Benefit," 1 = "Minor Benefit," 2 = "Major Benefit," 3 = "Single Most Important Benefit."

few labs have experienced much in the way of remuneration, either for the lab or for the scientists and engineers involved in technology transfer. An examination of the original data indicated that only two (1.3%) of the laboratories considered profit for the lab as the most important benefit and only eleven (7.5%) considered it a major benefit. Similarly, only five (3.4%) considered profit for the lab scientists and engineers as the most important benefit, and only fourteen (9.5%) considered it a major benefit.

DETERMINANTS OF TECHNOLOGY TRANSFER EFFECTIVENESS: AN ORGANIZATIONAL MODEL

Simply knowing the types and levels of technology transfer effectiveness is much less interesting than knowing what causes effectiveness. The simple model tested here is loosely derived from the literature on organizational technology. Since the late 1960s, organization theorists have examined the dynamic relationships among organizations' structures, technologies, and strategies (Thompson, 1967; Woodward, 1965). Most early studies examined technology-intensive organizations (such as Scottish electronics firms [Burns & Stalker, 1961]) and were motivated by the fact that certain organizational structures seemed to be better adaptations to changes in organizational environments. The term "contingency theory" was adopted to describe this work, because a fundamental premise is that the organization's structure is contingent on its technology and its mission and that effective strategy flows from the relationship between technology and structure. Later studies included analysis of additional contingencies including size (Blau & Schoenherr, 1971; Hage & Aiken, 1969), routineness of task (Hall, 1968), and control mechanisms (Child, 1972).

While there are many variants even of this basic premise—some, for example, assume that technology mitigates the interactions among mission, structure, and strategy—all contingency theory is rooted in conceptualization of structure-strategy-technology relations. Some analyses are more theoretical in orientation (e.g., Thompson, 1967), providing propositions or research findings about the relations among these factors; others are more prescriptive and concerned with the active design and reformulation of organizations (e.g., Galbraith, 1977; Starbuck & Nystrom, 1981). While in most cases contingency theory–oriented studies have not focused on government organizations (an exception is Hood & Dunsire, 1981), many include government organizations in their samples.

The conceptual model employed here assumes that technology transfer effectiveness is a function of much the same set of factors examined by the contingency theorists. The reasoning is that technology transfer effectiveness flows directly from the technology transfer strategy employed by the organization, which, in turn, is a function of the organization's structure and its motives for engaging in the technology transfer task. Both structure and task motivation are viewed as determined by the nature of the organization's mission. In the case of research and development (R&D) laboratories, it is assumed further that the mission is conceived in terms of the technical activity of the laboratory (e.g., basic research, applied research, technology development). In regard to structure, not only are traditional structural variables important (e.g., hierarchy, size, complexity), but the way in which technical activity is structured is especially important.

The approach involves simply posing a number of questions about possible determinants of technology transfer (based on the components of the model) and examining nonparametric (Kendall's tau) correlation coefficients. The analysis is grouped according to a series of questions posed as to possible determinants of effectiveness. Naturally, there is considerable possibility for statistical confluence among the variables hypothesized, but in the interest of space more sophisticated regression model results are not included here.

HOW DOES MOTIVE RELATE TO TECHNOLOGY TRANSFER EFFECTIVENESS?

For many government laboratories technology transfer is mandated, and transfer activity may simply be a matter of (possibly unenthusiastic) compliance. For others, technology transfer may represent other possible ends, including economic development opportunities, profit for the laboratory or its scientists, and exchange of information. It seems reasonable that the degree and type of success in technology transfer might relate to the motive for pursing the mission.

Laboratory directors were asked to evaluate[13] the importance of the following motives for their laboratory's technology transfer activity (variable names appear adjacent):

—Legislative requirements or statutory mandate [MOTIVE-MANDATE]

—Economic development emphasis of the lab [MOTIVE-ECONDEV]

—Outgrowth of cooperative R&D or research consortium [MOTIVE-COOPR&D]

Table 11.3
Kendall's Tau Correlation between Technology Transfer Effectiveness Indicators and Technology Transfer Motives

	T-DOOR	T-MARKET	LICENSE	PROFITSCI	PROFITLAB
MOTIVE-MANDATE	.069	.043	.039	.043	.102
MOTIVE-ECONDEV	.198^^	.299^^	.248^	.194*	.246^
MOTIVE-COOPR&	.162**	.113	.055	.050	.079
MOTIVE-R&DCENTER	.129*	.144*	.234^	.123	.124
MOTIVE-EXCHANGE	.103	.122	.027	-.077	.021
MOTIVE-BUDGET	-.033	-.010	.003	.055	.176*
MOTIVE-SATISFY	.074	.050	.021	.070	-.037
MOTIVE-WEALTH	.080	.120	.282^	.446^^	.352^^

Notes: $*p < .05$; $**p < .01$; $^p < .001$; $^^p < .0001$.

—Participation in industry-university or government-university research center [MOTIVE-R&DCENTER]

—Exchange of technical information or personnel [MOTIVE-EXCHANGE]

—Hope to increase lab's or parent agency's budget [MOTIVE-BUDGET]

—Scientists' and engineers' personal satisfaction at seeing their ideas or technology developed [MOTIVE-SATISFY]

—Scientists' and engineers' interests in entrepreneurship and personal wealth [MOTIVE-WEALTH]

One might assume that emphasis on the legislative mandate as a motive for technology transfer would be negatively related to success, simply because such a desultory motive (''we're in the technology transfer business because we have no choice'') would rarely lead to success. However, as shown in Table 11.3, the correlations display no significant relationship between MOTIVE-MANDATE and the transfer effectiveness measures.

Three motives seem especially important, according to the correlations. The economic development motivation is significantly and positively associated with all the success measures. The entrepreneurial motivation is significantly and positively associated with benefit both to the lab and to the individual scientists, but also with the number of licenses. Perhaps the most interesting finding, at least from a public policy standpoint, is the positive relationship between technology transfer success of various types (T-DOOR, T-MARKET, LICENSE) and the motive of participating in a research center; that is, labs that view technology transfer as an outgrowth of center participation are more likely to have success.

DO LABORATORIES' OTHER MISSIONS COMPLEMENT TECHNOLOGY TRANSFER EFFECTIVENESS?

Few laboratories exist for the sole purpose of technology transfer. Does the laboratory reporting basic research as a major mission enjoy greater or lesser

Table 11.4
Kendall's Tau Correlation Between Technology Transfer Effectiveness Indicators and Lab Missions

	T-DOOR	T-MARKET	LICENSE	PROFITSCI	PROFITLAB
BASIC	-.131*	-.080	.129	.138	-.003
PREAPPLIED	.086	.157*	.085	.065	.053
APPLIED	.030	.174**	.140	.075	.291^^
DEVELOP	.052	.035	-.009	-.006	.129
GOVTECH	-.050	-.023	-.122	-.065	-.055
INDTECH	-.005	-.028*	-.152	-.163*	-.130
PARTECH	.160*	.170**	.117	-.012	.036

Notes: *p < .05; **p < .01; ^p < .001; ^^p < .0001.

technology transfer success? Are technology development laboratories more successful? Are laboratories with a greater number of missions more successful?

The mission variables are based on items asking the laboratory directors to identify the significance of each of the following missions:[14]

—Basic research (knowledge for its own sake without any particular application in mind) [BASIC]

—Precommercial applied research (focused on bringing new products and processes into being, but not directed at a specific design) [PREAPPLIED]

—Commercial applied research (focused on product or process with specific design in mind) [APPLIED]

—Development (developing existing prototypes, modifying existing products/processes, or applications engineering) [DEVELOP]

—Providing technical assistance to government agencies [GOVTECH]

—Providing technical assistance to private firms and industrial organizations [INDTECH]

—Providing technical assistance to this laboratory's parent organization [PARTECH]

One might expect that some lab missions would be compatible with technology transfer and that others would not. For example, one might assume that basic research—science for its own sake—might be at odds with science and technology for commerce's sake. Table 11.4 gives some modest support for this expectation in the relationship between BASIC and T-DOOR. Similarly, one might assume that laboratories involved in applied research and technology development would likely be more compatible with the technology transfer mission. However, this assumption needs to be refined. Apparently, there is no significant relationship between a technology development mission and technology transfer success, but several significant relationships exist with the two applied research missions: commercial applied and precommercial applied. Technical assistance missions of laboratories appear related to technology transfer effectiveness, but with opposite effect according to the object of the assistance. Technical assistance to a parent agency is negatively related to technology transfer effectiveness in terms of licenses and profit for lab scientists and engineers. Technical assistance to industry is positively related, at least for out-the-door success and market impact.

DO THE ORGANIZATIONAL STRUCTURES AND DESIGNS OF LABORATORIES AFFECT TECHNOLOGY TRANSFER EFFECTIVENESS?

Are more centralized laboratories more successful, and are more hierarchical ones less successful, at technology transfer? Are laboratories with greater administrative intensity (high administrator-to-scientists ratios) more or less successful? Questions related to design and structure are particularly important because there is often some possibility of making relatively quick changes in these areas.

A first structure variable worth considering is the size of the laboratory, measured in terms of total personnel [SIZE]. Arguably, larger organizations would have more slack resources to use in technology transfer. Arguably, smaller organizations would be better at the informal, person-to-person activities so often cited as crucial to technology transfer. Possibly, the ratio of the administrative component is even more important than sheer size; thus, we consider administrative intensity [ADMINT], measured as the total number of scientific and technical personnel divided by the total number of personnel.

Organizational complexity is measured in terms of the type and number of organizational schemes used for the laboratory. Respondents were asked to indicate whether their laboratory was organized according to principal investigator–led research groups [ORG-PI], departments, divisions, or branches [ORG-DEPT], on a more-or-less ad hoc basis based on the needs of the particular project [ORG-ADHOC], or on any other basis [ORG-OTHER]. Respondents could indicate more than one organizational type; thus, organizational complexity [COMPLEX] is measured in terms of the total number of organizational schemes used by the laboratory. Hierarchy is measured in the traditional manner: the number of layers of authority [variable name: HIERARCHY].[15]

Table 11.5 provides Kendall's tau correlations between the various organization structure and design variables and the technology transfer effectiveness indicators. While there are some significant relationships, the overall lesson is that the structures, at least as measured by these variables, don't necessarily have much bearing on technology transfer effectiveness. The relationship of SIZE to number of licensed technologies is important because it implies that there may be certain threshold requirements of resources for success in licensing technology. The number of hierarchical levels (HIERARCHY) is modestly but significantly related; however, this relationship may be, in part, an artifact of the importance of SIZE. Total number of personnel is also importantly related

Table 11.5
Kendall's Tau Correlation between Technology Transfer Effectiveness Indicators and Organization Structure Measures

	T-DOOR	T-MARKET	LICENSE	PROFITSCI	PROFITLAB
LOGPER	-.022	-.027	.287^^	.137*	.062
ADMINT	.011	-.023	-.015	.016	-.026
HIERARCHY	-.059	-.070	.136*	.050	-.014
ORG-PI	.096	.199**	.095	.072	.051
RESORGAH	.063	.028	.057	.039	.054
COMPLEX	.080	.172*	.168*	.134	.135

Note: *p < .05; **p < .01; ^p < .001; ^^p < .0001.

to pecuniary benefits of technology transfer for the lab's scientists and engineers. This may be because the larger labs are more likely to have administrative support and more detailed procedures for entrepreneurial employees.

The group-level organizational scheme (PI, departmental, ad hoc) doesn't seem to have much bearing on transfer effectiveness. The conspicuous exception is the strong relationship between ORG-PI and T-MARKET. One might expect just the opposite: that principal investigator–led labs would be more traditional, science-oriented labs and less adept at market-oriented technology transfer. If the particular structure is not very relevant, the number of structural types (as reflected in COMPLEX) does seem to have an impact on both market-based success and the number of licenses.

WHICH TECHNOLOGY TRANSFER STRATEGIES ARE THE MOST EFFECTIVE?

Presumably, some technology transfer strategies work better than others (Weijo, 1987). While we cannot assume that correlations between strategies and technology transfer success imply that particular strategies cause success, it is certainly worth examining the strategies' relationship with effectiveness measures. The respondents evaluated the degree of success of each of the strategies listed below:[16]

—On-site seminars and conferences [STRAT-SEMINAR]

—Fliers, newsletters, or other mailed correspondence [STRAT-MAIL]

—Person-to-person contacts of our scientific and technical personnel with persons in technology-recipient organizations [STRAT-CONTACTS]

—Presentations at scientific meetings sponsored by professional organizations [STRAT-PROFCONF]

—Presentations at scientific meetings sponsored by government organizations [STRAT-GOVCONF]

Table 11.6

Kendall's Tau Correlation between Technology Transfer Effectiveness Indicators and Technology Transfer Strategies

	T-DOOR	T-MARKET	LICENSE	PROFITSCI	PROFITLAB
STRAT-SEMINAR	.197**	.151*	-.058	.094	-.045
STRAT-MAIL	.012	.083	-.011	4.045	.102
STRAT-CONTACTS	.186**	.138*	.075	.058	------
STRAT-PROFCON	.163*	.111	.094	.081	.081
STRAT-GOVCON	.155*	.076	.023	.032	-.025
STRAT-CONSORT	.207**	.225**	.247**	.178*	.101
STRAT-OFFICE	.091	.131	.159	.183*	.071
STRAT-VISITS	.204**	.148*	.040	-.003	.075
STRAT-COOP	.270^	.186*	.099	.082	.095
STRAT-CONTRACT	.247**	.129	.137	.004	.047
STRAT-EQUIP	.028	.131	-.010	-.012	.163*
STRAT-LICEN	.226**	.358^^	.341^^	.473^^	.245**

Notes: *p < .05; **p < .01; ^p < .001; ^^p < .0001.

—Membership in research consortia, university, or government centers [STRAT-CONSORT]

—A central office with responsibility for technology transfer [STRAT-OFFICE]

—Encouraging informal on-site visits [STRAT-VISITS]

—Personnel exchanges [STRAT-EXCHANGE]

—Cooperative R&D (as a technology transfer strategy, rather than other possible purposes) [STRAT-COOP]

—Contractual relations for direct R&D funding between our lab and the organization receiving the technology [STRAT-CONTRACT]

—Permitting persons from other organizations access to our laboratory's equipment and facilities [STRAT-EQUIP]

—Sales or gifts of patents, copyrights, or licenses [STRAT-LICEN]

As Table 11.6 shows, strategy does make a difference. In light of the finding reported above about research centers, it is important to note that as a strategy, as well as a motive, membership in research centers seems to have considerable payoff in terms of technology transfer success. Four of the five effectiveness indicators are significantly and positively associated with this strategy. Similarly, cooperative R&D as a strategy also seems to produce positive outcomes for technology transfer success, at least in getting the technology out the door and reaping some market success.

The sale of patents and licenses (STRAT-LICENSE) is positively associated with each of the effectiveness indicators. This is perhaps not surprising, since this particular strategy may be a good reflection of the earnestness of the laboratory in its commercial technology transfer activities.

The use of a central office for technology transfer doesn't seem to make much difference, but the single significant relationship is worth noting. The strategy of having a central office for technology transfer seems to have the effect of providing pecuniary benefits to the lab's scientists and engineers, perhaps providing the administrative support needed for these part-time entrepreneurs to realize economic benefit from their work.

Another single correlation worth noting is that between STRAT-EQUIP and pecuniary benefit to the lab. Perhaps this is simply a matter of user fees coming to the laboratory, but in many instances the economic value of equipment access may be realized by the lab in more indirect ways.

Finally, it is obviously the case that the type of technology transfer that is the most strategy-sensitive is out-the-door success. Nine of the various strategies are significantly and positively related to T-DOOR. This may be because it is the least stringent success criterion. By contrast, the number of licenses issued seems to be largely independent of strategy. This is not simply a matter of its dependence on size, as a per capita measure of licenses (number of licenses divided by number of scientific and professional employees) was found to be even less strongly related to the various strategy indicators. This further underscores the importance of the findings about the relationship between research centers' strategy and licensing success—it is one of the few strategies that seems to work.

CONCLUSION

The findings presented here do not provide a definitive judgment of Erich Bloch's (1991) assertion about the ineffectiveness of government laboratories' technology transfer strategy. There is some evidence of the successes that Argonne National Laboratory director Alan Schriesheim (1990) anticipates, but it seems that success is concentrated in relatively few laboratories.

According to market impact and simple out-the-door measures of technology transfer effectiveness, lab directors report a wide range of experience, with most reporting moderate success. In terms of the more tangible criterion of number of technologies licensed, the average number of licenses (1.5) is somewhat deceptive, because there is a trimodal distribution. About half the laboratories report no licensed technologies, another group reports less than ten, and a handful of labs report much greater success with licenses, from twenty to several hundred per year. To the extent that patents are an input to licenses, the low number of licenses is understandable, as the median number of patents reported was only one. Regarding the pecuniary benefits received from technology transfer activity, a very small minority reports significant benefits either to the laboratory or to individual scientists and engineers working in the lab.

From a theoretical standpoint, the explanation of determinants of technology transfer effectiveness is advanced somewhat, but not through the structure of the contingency model. There is no support for the assumption of sequential causation that is implicit in the contingency model.[17] While the contingency model seems useful for identifying important determinants of technology transfer effectiveness, various effectiveness criteria are not sensitive to those determinants.

From an instrumental standpoint, the most interesting aspect of these data is in their clues, albeit somewhat conjectural ones, as to what works. Provisionally, we can make the following assertions about what works and what doesn't work for technology transfer effectiveness.

Among the technology transfer strategies examined here, the most effective seems to be participation in a research center. Closely behind are the strategies of emphasizing sales of patents, copyrights, and licenses and the use of cooperative R&D for technology transfer. The strategy of using a central office for technology transfer doesn't have much effect, except to enhance the likelihood of pecuniary benefit to the lab's scientists and engineers. Similarly, equipment access is not a significant strategy except for providing pecuniary benefits for the laboratory. Regarding labs' motivation for technology transfer, an emphasis on economic development is clearly the most closely tied to success (indeed, to each indicator of success). Having a legislative mandate or statutory requirement as the chief motivation for technology transfer does seem to inhibit effectiveness.

Some laboratory missions complement technology transfer success, and others don't. Specifically, a focus on applied research—either commercial or precommercial—is salutary. Involvement in technical assistance is related to technology transfer effectiveness, but negatively if the target of assistance is the parent agency, positively if the target is industry. There is only a modest relationship between the way work is organized (department, principal investigator, and so forth) and technology transfer success, but labs with a variety of organizational schemes appear to be more successful. One of the strongest correlates of success in licensing is simply the size of the laboratory, whether measured in total personnel or size of budget.

In considering the correlates of success, it is important to remember that the various success measures did not all correlate strongly with one another. There are at least two dimensions to effectiveness—perhaps more—and effectiveness in one realm does not guarantee effectiveness in another.

Without time series data, it is difficult to make inferences about the possible relationships among changes in public policy, laboratory activities, and technology transfer success. However, the fact that a comparison of 1987 (Rahm, Bozeman, & Crow, 1988) and 1990 (Bozeman & Coker, 1992) data shows that government laboratories' technology transfer activity has increased more than 40 percent is evidence of considerably enhanced government laboratory technology transfer activity in a relatively brief amount of time.

What do these early results indicate for the contribution of the cooperative technology development paradigm to United States competitiveness? The policies of the new paradigm are many and varied, and this study examines only one set: technology transfer from government laboratories. However, this set of policies, embodied in the Stevenson-Wydler, Bayh-Dole, and Federal Technology Transfer acts and seeking to make the federal government a partner in commercialization of technology, is perhaps the acid test of the ability of the United States to move from its traditional reliance on the free market for development of civilian technology.

One clear implication is that the policies have broken through the conservative, "business as usual" government laboratory culture criticized in the Packard Report (White House Science Council, 1983). Technology transfer from government laboratories to industry, an activity barely even conceptualized just a few years ago, now pervades the government laboratory system. Laboratories of every ilk—small, large, science-based, technology-based, federal, and state—are involved in technology transfer. Whether labs are working at the frontiers of high-energy physics or developing new techniques to treat potato blight, they are likely to have at least some concern with technology transfer to industry. The policy message has been delivered loud and clear, the laboratories have responded, and this early systematic assessment suggests a variety of levels, types, and intensities of success. The next step is to document successful strategies so that they may be widely recognized and replicated.

NOTES

The author gratefully acknowledges Karen Coker's assistance with legislative analysis, and the comments of Maria Papadakis and Michael Crow.

1. Agencies contributing research support for the NCRDP include the National Science Foundation, the U.S. Department of Commerce, the U.S. Department of Energy, Syracuse University, and the Institute for Physical Research and Technology of Iowa State University. The author gratefully acknowledges this support.

2. Based on survey data and 30 in-depth case studies, Phase I—the prototype phase—began as a study of research and development performance in more than 250 United States energy laboratories (Bozeman & Crow, 1987). Phase II set as its goal developing a profile of the structures, behaviors, and environments of a representative sample (n = 935) of U.S. R&D laboratories (Bozeman & Crow, 1988; 1990).

3. The sampling criteria specified that laboratories should be involved chiefly in research in the physical sciences or engineering, not in the social or behavioral sciences or in clinical medicine, and should actually perform research rather than being an administrative unit for an agency funding or otherwise supporting research. Laboratories reporting fewer than 25 total personnel were not included.

4. The population was defined from all laboratories listed in at least one of the following standard research directories: *Research Centers Directory* (1987), *Government Research Centers Directory* (1987), and *Industrial Research Laboratories in the U.S.* (1987). For the population of government laboratories in Phase III, the source was *Government Research Centers Directory* (1990). The research center directories were used as a starting point because of the lack of a general enumeration of R&D laboratories.

According to Camille Killens, Senior Assistant Editor, Gale Research (personal communication, September 2, 1988), the Gale Research directories use Bacon's Clipping Service to identify all new laboratories and centers in the United States and collect data annually and cross-validate entries using standard references. According to Rea Christofferson of Bowkers, Inc. (personal communication, September 9, 1988), Bowker's directories collect data via mailed questionnaire and follow-up phone calls. Bowkers has developed models estimating that more than 90 percent of all industrial laboratories are included in their directories.

To verify correct addresses and directors' names, the research team telephoned each of the 1,500 laboratories included in the original Phase II sample. This procedure reduced the effective sample to 1,341 eligible laboratories (i.e., those meeting sampling criteria of size and chiefly scientific or engineering, rather than social science, research).

5. Not all of the 189 government laboratories are examined here, as 39 reported no involvement in technology transfer.

6. Measuring technology transfer effectiveness from a survey presents problems, as does measuring effectiveness from case studies or from aggregate technological indicators. Case studies permit analysts to make inferences that are based on detailed, rich, qualitative data but have the disadvantage of presenting limited prospects for statistical analysis and generalization. Using aggregate statistics (such as national patent indicators) provides a broader scope analysis and hard data but gives little feel for local context and nuance. Surveys provide an "in between" method of studying effectiveness, permitting statistical analysis and generalization but at the same time enabling analysis of detail, albeit aggregated detail. Despite their benefits, surveys are plagued by the facts that (1) the data are based on self-reports (sometimes but not always a problem), (2) likelihood of response is not often random and, thus, response bias confounds analysis, and (3) instrumentation presents difficulties. Clearly, each of the major approaches to evaluating effectiveness presents problems, but this may be another way of saying that different insights can be gleaned from each approach.

7. Two of the models developed by Bozeman and Fellows (1988) are not tested here because of the difficulty of using survey or aggregate data for these models. Their political model assumes that technology transfer is in part a political game, where the payoffs are indirect. That is, the government actors involved in technology transfer are less interested in the social good or market impact of the transfer activity than in any political currency that can be garnered by having their organization seem more responsive.

The "opportunity cost model" focuses on the alternative uses of technology transfer resources, not only funds but human resources and time as well. The assumption is that the effects of technology transfer activity on the organization are not neutral. When more attention is devoted to technology transfer, it is likely that less will be devoted to other core missions of the laboratory (e.g. basic research, precommercial applied research, technical assistance, testing).

8. Defined as "the transfer of physical devices, processes, 'know how' or proprietary information from your laboratory, to either business or government, either U.S. or foreign."

9. Directors were asked: "During calendar year 1989, about how many technologies, if any, were licensed by your lab or lab employees?"

10. Item: "From the standpoint of 'getting technology out the door' (getting others interested in using your lab's technology), how would you evaluate the lab's success during the past three years? Please rate on a 0–10 scale where 10 is excellent, 5 is average, and 0 is totally ineffective."

11. Item: "From the standpoint of commercial impact on the organizations receiving the technology, how would you evaluate your lab's technology transfer success during the past three years?" Scale specified was same as in note 10.)

12. Using a Likert scale: "No Benefit," "Minor Benefit," "Major Benefit," "Single Most Important Benefit."

13. A simple ordinal scale was used: "Not a Factor," "Of Little Importance," "Somewhat Important," "Very Important."

14. Response categories included: "Not a Mission," "Mission of Little Importance," "Somewhat Important Mission," "Important Mission," or "Single Most Important Mission."

15. Specifically, respondents were asked: How many administrative levels are there between (but not including) the level of the most senior bench-level scientists and the engineers and the laboratory director?

16. Rating categories included: "Not a Strategy We Use" [treated as missing data], "No Success as a Strategy," "Little Success as a Strategy," "Somewhat Successful Strategy," and "Very Successful Strategy."

17. An initial plan to perform a path analysis test of the model was abandoned after examining the results of the regression analysis. It seems clear from the results that the sequential model presented here is not supported by the data.

CHAPTER 12

Policy Toward
Civil-Military Integration

LINDA BRANDT

THE CHANGING ENVIRONMENT

The world has changed. The Cold War ended, and in 1992 a Democratic administration was sworn into office. The Department of Defense (DoD) has struggled to cope with various aspects of these and other profound changes. Under the Reagan and Bush administrations, the DoD spent billions of dollars for the research and development of a wide range of advanced weapons systems. While vast sums of money flowed into the *nation's* technology and industrial bases, most of the fruits of that development stayed within the *defense* technology and industrial bases. In most cases, the rules of acquisition, as well as policy and custom, neither facilitated nor encouraged the transfer of technology to the commercial side of the economy. In addition, given the magnitude of the funding and the size of the dedicated defense industrial base, there was neither the need nor the desire to incorporate a great deal of commercial technology into the weapon systems produced by that defense industrial base.

With the rapid and dramatic cuts experienced in the defense budget, especially in the procurement accounts, thanks to the end of the Cold War, and a Democratic administration joining a then Democratic congressional majority, two new little-used terms found their way into the DoD lexicon: ''dual-use technologies'' and ''industrial conversion.'' Even before the change in administration (from the Bush administration to the Clinton administration), a Democratic Congress had jumped into the arena, earmarking some $1.3 billion in the 1993 defense authorization and appropriation acts for funding defense conversion programs aimed at remaking the defense industrial base into a national technology and industrial base with a high degree of civil-military integration and emphasizing a dual-use approach to research and development (R&D). The Defense Advanced Research Projects Agency (DARPA), the DoD's high-tech development agency, was given significant responsibility for the implementation of this legislation, and at the same time lost the "D" ("Defense") from its title, signifying the hoped-for civil and military integration. (The agency since has reverted back to its original name.)

There were military, civilian, and political ramifications to the implementation of conversion policies. For the military, the policies provided a chance to influence the outcome of the inevitable shrinking of the defense industrial base. Whatever its condition, the Department of Defense would have to rely on some combination of civilian and defense industrial bases to produce the weapons systems of the 1990s and beyond. The DoD bottom line was to have an industrial base, preferably an integrated civilian/defense base capable of supporting national security needs within the constraints of a smaller budget and a rapidly changing technological environment. For the civilian sector, conversion promised the capacity to soften the impacts of drastic declines in defense budgets with the promise of jobs at the same or similar companies catering to a new set of customers. For the political sector it was a chance to provide funding and visible programs designed to save jobs in an otherwise sluggish economy. At the same time, the Defense Department budget provided a perfect source of funding for those programs, funding that would be almost impossible to initiate by any other means. Finally, such programs might both strengthen the economic competitiveness of certain manufacturers and also keep them available in the defense marketplace.

CONVERSION AND DUAL USE

The Department of Defense Conversion Commission, chartered to assess the impact of the defense drawdown, defined conversion as "the process by which the people, skills, technology, equipment, and facilities in defense are shifted into alternative economic applications" (Defense Conversion Commission, 1992). The commission, using the terms "conversion" and "transition" interchangeably, focused on conversion as a process of economic change. The reason for such widespread concern over conversion becomes clear when the decline of the defense budget and the related loss of jobs are examined.

Dual-use technology was often used as an adjunct to the process of defense conversion. In its simplest definition, "dual-use" technology can be defined as "technology that has both military and commercial applications" (Alic et al., 1992). Both spin-off and spin-on are aspects of dual-use technology. The Defense Department has spent and is likely to continue to spend vast amounts of money to research, develop, and produce defense weapon systems. A large part of that process involves the development of leading-edge technology. Computers, semiconductors, numerically controlled machine tools, jet engines, and aircraft all owe their successful commercial applications to the investment of federal research and development dollars through the Defense Department.

These are examples of spin-off, or the use of defense technology for nondefense, commercially viable products or processes.

Spin-on is the use of existing nondefense, commercially viable technologies in defense systems. Spin-on is usually thought of as a way of incorporating leading-edge commercial technology that is not now available to defense systems because of either commercial or governmental barriers to their incorporation. For example, commercial computer chips often are more capable than stringently specified military chips. Because military chips are produced in small quantities, the production facilities producing low-volume defense and those producing the high-volume civilian chips are often very different, with the commercial plants incorporating the most modern product and process technology. Companies such as IBM, Motorola, Boeing, Hewlett-Packard, Digital Equipment Corporation (DEC), and Intel operate strikingly different defense and commercial facilities.

Changes in the security environment already have had profound influences on the nation's Defense Industrial Base (DIB). The DIB is the combination of people, institutions, technology, and facilities used to design, develop, manufacture, and maintain the weapon systems and equipment needed to meet national security objectives (U.S. Congress, Office of Technology Assessment, 1991). This base, made up of research, development, production, and maintenance components, largely supported the U.S. government in its reaction to the Cold War Soviet threat. With the collapse of that threat and in the face of severe domestic budget deficit problems, the decline of the defense budget has become a reality. Indeed, the U.S. defense budget declined approximately 40 percent (after inflation) between Fiscal Year (FY) 1985, the Cold War peak, and the president's budget authorization request of $242.6 billion in FY 1997 (Johnson & Blaker, 1996). Both congressional and executive planning figures show a leveling out of the Cold War budget decline, with the budget remaining at about the FY 1997 level, in constant dollars, through FY 2001. Given the state of competing budget demands, that figure may or may not hold as a bottom for the defense budget drawdown. The Electronic Industries Association (EIA) has prepared a ten-year forecast suggesting that the defense budget could fall to $215 billion by the year 2000. Others, including members of Congress, have suggested defense budgets below $180 billion.

Acquisition budgets have declined more sharply than the total DoD budget. Combined outlays for procurement and Research Development Test & Evaluation (RDT&E), the defense budget categories with the greatest impact on defense contractors, are projected to drop from a peak of $142 billion in 1987 to $86 billion in 1997 (in constant 1993 dollars), a fall of nearly 40 percent (Logistics Management Institute, 1993). When only procurement dollars are compared, the drop is over 70 percent from peak spending levels. A decline of this magnitude has caused real stress for defense market participants, particularly in a market based on one-customer purchasing under a rigid set of rules and guidelines. Corporations that are already partially diversified are choosing whether to consolidate or to exit the defense business. Others, already heavily reliant on the defense market, are choosing whether to acquire additional defense mass or to devise other survival mechanisms.

While the consequences of such a drawdown would be noticeable even in a booming economy, the impacts were magnified in the early 1990s by slow economic recovery and the need to preserve well-paid jobs in the face of commercial industrial restructuring. The defense industrial base was then a relatively small but visible portion of the nation's industrial base. Defense-related manufacturing accounted for about 9 percent of manufacturing employment in 1990. While manufacturing's share of the gross domestic product (GDP) had remained stable at between 20 percent and 23 percent of GDP for the last 30 years, manufacturing employment had declined as a share of the nation's employment, and the number of people employed in manufacturing had fluctuated between 17 and 20 million workers. The Defense Conversion Commission estimated that approximately 960,000 jobs (mostly in manufacturing) would be lost from 1991 through 1997 because of reduced DoD purchasing (Defense Conversion Commission, 1992). While private-sector job losses overshadow public-sector cuts, the DoD is the largest direct government purchaser of research, technology, and manufacturing output.

POLICY RESPONSES

Cutting defense budgets has always been a painful activity. During times of slow economic growth, policymakers responded to the cuts with a series of programs designed to ease the pain, while at the same time "civilizing" the sophisticated technology and production capability of the defense industrial base. This process predates the Clinton administration, and Congress expressed concern over the health of the industrial base during the Reagan and Bush administrations. These concerns were escalated at the end of the Bush administration, when it became clear that real-dollar cuts in the DoD budget meant real job cuts in congressional districts, affecting real voters.

The FY 1993 National Defense Authorization Act and the Department of Defense Appropriation Act authorized $1.512 billion in support of defense conversion. Of this, $575 million was earmarked for defense industry- and technology-base programs. Another $300 million of existing high-technology programs were categorized as conversion assistance in the appropriation act. In addition, as a signal of intent to push conversion into the civilian economy, Congress changed the Defense Advanced Research Projects Agency (DARPA) to the Advanced Research Projects Agency (ARPA), by dropping "Defense." This popular agency, already well regarded in Congress for its flexible approach to advanced technology research,[1] was to act in the vanguard of civilian-military integration. Indeed, the logo for the Defense Technology Conversion, Reinvestment, and Transition Assistance Project highlighted dual-use technologies and economic growth along with the normal (for the DoD) slogan of national security. This signaled a very strong change of direction within the DoD.

President Clinton made conversion a key part of his domestic economic policies. In March 1993, the president made a speech at Westinghouse Electronic Corporation, in Baltimore, Maryland. Westinghouse, a major defense contractor, was embarking on the type of projects the president had in mind: the development of electric cars and the use of sophisticated defense electronic equipment in civilian law enforcement and transportation applications. In the speech, he announced a plan to spend $19.5 billion on defense reinvestment and transition assistance between FY 1993 and FY 1997. The administration emphasized that the president would request $3.3 billion in FY 1994 for defense transition and assistance programs, including $1.7 billion for programs in the Department of Defense. Of that amount, $964 million would go to DoD dual-use technology programs. An additional $1.6 billion would be spent in FY 1994 through other agencies, including $1.2 billion for new federal high-technology investments. The Clinton administration planned to spend a total of $4.7 billion on dual-use technology development and $9.7 billion on new high-technology investments (Bitzinger, 1993).

ACQUISITION PRACTICES AND CONVERSION

A mixture of government laws, regulations, and culture is often blamed for causing a deep rift between civilian and military producers. Some of these barriers include unique accounting and audit requirements, military specifications and standards, government claims on technical data rights, and unique contract requirements. These requirements are far more restrictive than those applicable in civilian business practices. Many of these practices are founded in law, but the DoD often implements these laws in a more stringent manner than may be required by those laws. Under these circumstances, therefore, companies with defense and commercial divisions find it difficult, if not impossible, to transfer technologies between those divisions. Government also finds it difficult to buy civilian, off-the-shelf technology, even though such technologies might be appropriate, readily available, and affordable.

There is also a strong cultural bias against changing the way the Department of Defense does business. Many of these laws and regulations are designed to protect the public's funds and the interests of the users of the goods acquired. Severe public and congressional disapproval in the face of perceived or real failures in the acquisition process makes the defense community feel extremely cautious about changes in business practices that might make the acquisition system more open to failure. Congress adds to this difficulty by legislating additional requirements in the aftermath of acquisition ''scandals.'' In many respects, the DoD rules are designed, by both Congress and the DoD, to ensure equity, access, and fiscal control. Efficiency, while highly desirable, is not a likely outcome of the process.

Even before the sharp downturn in the defense budget, some in the acquisition community were trying to institute commercial buying practices to facilitate the purchase of off-the-shelf commercial technologies. The rigid and defined military specifications (milspecs) and military standards, imposed on the product as well as on the processes of production, often yield products that cost significantly more than their commercial counterparts. These milspecs and standards are often vital in the production of the specialized, leading-edge products needed by the DoD, but they impose product design and production methods and products that are slower and more costly than can be borne by the commercial marketplace. They also prevent the inclusion of commercially developed technology that might be appropriate yet does not meet military specifications. Changes in these processes are difficult to accomplish because of the built-in conservatism and the inertia of the acquisition system. The military also keeps certain products in production (for logistical or other reasons) long after they have lost their commercial viability.

The Clinton administration brought strong proponents for acquisition reform into the Pentagon. The late Les Aspin, former Secretary of Defense and Chairman of the House Armed Services Committee (HASC), and Secretary William Perry had both been active in the field of acquisition reform. Perry, in particular, served on a 1990 Carnegie Commission report that called for:

—The replacement of military specifications with commercial standards;

—Program managers to justify the use of milspecs rather than needing to justify commercial specs; and

—Integration of the defense and commercial bases into a national technology base. (Carnegie Commission Report on Science, Technology, and Government, 1990)

Some of William Perry's first public pronouncements dealt with the issue of milspecs and military standards, hinting strongly at a policy close to the ones articulated in the Carnegie report. Milspecs, though cumbersome, do ensure appropriate, working products. Commercial specs provide no such assurances, and if failures occur the careers of those managers might be at risk. Because of the potential public "failures" of the system, risk avoidance and aversion have become major characteristics of the system. Without a sweeping cultural change—one that not only tolerates failures but also encourages risks—the current system will be very difficult to change. Without change in this and other procurement practices, true dual-technology usage is not likely to be achieved. Dual use is incompatible with the existing milspecs and standards system. Although there was resistance from within the Pentagon (program managers and attorneys opposed the plan because it would shift an unacceptable burden of risks onto existing programs ["Milspec Reform Stirs Resistance," 1993]), milspec reform was enacted by Secretary Perry in 1995. The changes in milspec and standard regulations enacted within the Pentagon ensured that the more difficult process of cultural change would begin.

While resistance exists, there are also reasons, both budgetary and operational, that the DoD will be forced to deal with the processes of industry restructuring and dual-use technology. Aside from acting as a source of funding for conversion programs, the DoD must find mechanisms for coping with profound changes in both budgets and operations. While the U.S. military has always depended on superior weapon technology as part of its military doctrine, the Reagan and Bush administrations had little interest in programs that smacked of "industrial policy" or planning. The superior weaponry developed and deployed in the 1970s, 1980s, and 1990s depended on a strong defense technology and industrial base. The strength of the technology base was assured by ample research and development funding. In 1992, 60 percent of federal R&D funding went to the DoD, with another 11 percent going to space. Since the federal government funded 44 percent of the nation's total R&D expenditures, a redirection of R&D funding would have a significant impact on the technology base available to the DoD in the future.

The strength of the industrial base was assured by a steady stream of contracts that supported a first-tier prime-contractor base and in turn fed thousands of subcontractors and vendors. With both research and development and procurement dollars drying up, the ability of the DoD to sustain the kind of technological base it needs for current and future systems may be threatened. It is clear that the DoD needs to rely more heavily on the general, commercial industrial base for its needs. It was initially hoped that conversion would help certain defense contractors remain in the base, providing opportunities in the commercial markets that allow them to continue to be available to the department, if needed.

Dual-use technology was of greater interest to the DoD. As the world reaped advantages made possible by a rapid explosion of technology, as well as shorter cycle times needed to develop each succeeding generation of new products, the department finds itself in an explosion of new technology, yet with fewer resources to develop and produce that technology. In addition, the shorter product cycle time makes it difficult to take advantage of commercially developed technology in weapon systems that have an extremely long development and production cycle. Commercial products often are developed and in the market within three to four years, and good manufacturers are concentrating great effort to cut their development-to-market cycle time. The DoD, on the other hand, can take as long as fifteen years or more to develop and field products. This often produces a product with technology older than commercial technology on the market. The production cycle mismatch is another challenge that the military must solve as it attempts to integrate defense and nondefense firms. Perhaps of greater importance is the attempt to buy and integrate leading-edge commercially developed technology into existing and new defense systems.

INDUSTRY RESPONSES

In an often-quoted remark about defense conversion, Norman Augustine, then Chairman and Chief Executive Officer of Martin Marietta Corporation, said that: "[our] industry's record at defense conversion is unblemished by success. . . . Why is it rocket scientists can't sell toothpaste? Because we don't know the market, or how to research, or how to market the product. Other than that, we're in good shape" (Mintz, 1993). The defense industry faced formidable challenges in the conversion process and made choices about how to face the challenges of a shrinking defense budget. Most of these choices were made by the companies themselves, with tacit support from the DoD; and the final shape of the defense industrial base will be determined more by market forces than by federal policies.

There have always been a variety of barriers that companies must overcome before they can either convert to commercial work or convert to a company that can handle dual-use technologies profitably. Indeed, any number of military technologies might be appropriate for dual-use conversion. Several companies already have embarked upon efforts to reorient their defense technology toward a civilian market. Westinghouse Electronic Systems, Martin Marietta, Lockheed Electronics, and others already are using information, data processing, and remote sensing technologies of military origin for air and highway control systems, electronic vehicles, drug interdiction, and law enforcement purposes. All of those companies have been more profoundly affected by the rush toward mergers and acquisitions in the field than any success in commercial dual-use technology.

Sales, however, were small in comparison to their defense contracts, because companies, for the most part, have concentrated on marketing core technologies for other government entities. To increase the market share, these companies would have to reach out to the commercial market. Spokesmen for a variety of defense contractors cite the disastrous conversion attempts of the 1960s and 1970s for their hesitation on branching out to new and totally commercial markets. For example, from 1983 to 1985, Grumman lost $15 million in its non-aerospace commercial ventures. In 1983, McDonnell Douglas purchased Computer Sharing Services for $69 million. After losing $333 million in 1989, the company reduced the size of its commercial information systems division. Even Boeing, the most successful builder of commercial jet airliners, reported a cumulative loss in its nonaerospace, nongovernment sales over the 1981–1988 time frame. It also fared poorly when it entered the mass transit business in the 1970s, as an attempt to offset declines in the defense market. At its peak, Boeing's transit production employed about 150 engineers and 400 factory workers, compared to about 9,000 employees laid off by its helicopter divisions (Weidenbaum, 1992). These failures serve as a potent reminder of what can happen to defense contractors that are used to dealing with one customer when they attempt to switch their focus from the military to the commercial market.

Barriers to the commercial market are as much based in corporate culture as in technological or engineering difficulties. During the Cold War, most large, diversified defense contractors separated their defense divisions from other portions of the organization. Some companies also withdrew almost entirely from the commercial marketplace. Very few companies have maintained integrated defense and commercial operations. There are a number of reasons for this segregation. Defense contractors produce small numbers of very complex, high-value weapons systems or subsystems, while meeting stringent technical and performance requirements. By contrast, commercial manufacturers generally produce a high volume of goods to meet market demands, taking into consideration the reliability and affordability of the products. The manufacturing processes that produce a high volume of product are often very different from those employed in defense production. The successful commercial manufacturers are the ones that continue to shorten the product development-to-market cycle time. The defense cycle usually is long, often spanning fifteen years and sometimes even longer as systems are stretched out for budgetary reasons. One of the techniques commercial companies use to shorten cycle time is to design the product and the process at the same time. This is at variance with current defense budget realities, as the DoD defers new production on all but a few major new procurements.[2]

A study on integrating civilian and military technologies declared government regulations as counterproductive, because they force contractors like Boeing and Motorola to:

—implement elaborate and expensive cost-accounting systems and staff;

—make radical revisions in commercial procurement practices and long-term supplier relationships;

—release highly confidential information to competitors;

—make changes in the transportation of goods and materials;

—overturn existing compensation and fringe-benefit practices;

—revise production techniques; and

—risk closure of the entire facility in the event of reporting errors or other perceived legal or regulatory abuses. (Center for Strategic and International Studies Steering Committee on Security and Technology, 1991)

It is not surprising, therefore, that military contractors stringently wall off commercial and military divisions, preventing the diffusion of technology across divisions. This wall makes both spin-off and spin-on extremely difficult.

Many defense contractors have very little experience with commercial marketing and distribution systems. Prime contractors deal with few customers, most of them different DoD or government agencies. Government rules, regulations, and requirements are so specialized that marketing and even management and technical specialists know only a limited part of their operation. Many will not want to move from their comfortable market niches to a high-risk marketplace. While the acquisition budget is down, it will still provide annual outlays of over $80 billion well into the 1990s. In addition, the maintenance and modification of existing systems will likely remain a long-term, lucrative market for the prime contractors who initially developed and produced those systems, as long as the move toward privatization and outsourcing of logistics continues.

HOW THE MARKET IS OPERATING

Rather than conversion, the solution that the majority of the defense industry is following involves consolidations, divestitures, and other merger and acquisition strategies. According to a report by Paine Webber Incorporated, given the declining defense budget, defense contractors can choose from a number of strategies for the 1990s. They can:

—Exit the defense market by selling or shutting down operations;

—Selectively divest;

—Diversify into commercial business;

—Invest and grow the defense business, competing aggressively to gain market share;

—Make selective niche acquisitions;

—Make major acquisitions in defense;

—Shrink the business; or

—Merge with an equal competitor. (Koonce, 1993)

The major defense contractors have already chosen from among these strategies, even without the overt encouragement of government policies or consideration of government conversion programs. The industry can respond to the declining defense market by selecting one of the above options, by means of either consolidation or diversification. This is not an unusual or even new reaction to changes in the marketplace. In 1945, there were twenty manufacturers of U.S. military aircraft in the industrial base. By 1955, there were sixteen; in 1965, fourteen; in 1975, twelve; and in 1990, nine. Most of the reductions were achieved through consolidations and mergers. The French and English aircraft industries have shown even more dramatic consolidations (Koonce, 1993).

Table 12.1 shows that a significant concentration has already occurred in the top ten defense contractors over the past fourteen years. The list of companies that comprise the top ten companies in the aerospace/defense sector in terms of revenues is essentially the same in 1980 and 1994. The total sales of the top ten, however, have grown almost 268 percent, from $53 billion to approximately $142 billion, indicative of the consolidation and in some cases growth of the sector (Bear Stearns, 1995). Companies with a high degree of commercial and military diversity have divested defense operations, and companies with a low

Table 12.1
Consolidation in the Defense Industry

Rank	Name (1980)	Sales (a)	Rank	Name (1985)	Sales (a)
1	United Technologies	$9.1	1	United Technologies	$16.3
2	Boeing	8.1	2	Boeing	10.4
3	Rockwell	6.5	3	McDonnell Douglas	9.7
4	McDonnell Douglas	5.7	4	Rockwell	9.3
5	Signal Companies	4.2	5	Lockheed	8.1
6	Litton Industries	4.1	6	General Dynamics	7.8
7	Lockheed	4.1	7	Raytheon	6.1
8	General Dynamics	4.1	8	Signal Companies	6.0
9	Raytheon	3.7	9	Litton Industries	5.0
10	Textron	3.4	10	Martin Marietta	4.4
	Total	$53.0		Total	$83.0

Rank	Name (1990)	Sales (a)	Rank	Name (1994)	Sales (a)
1	Boeing	$20.3	1	Lockheed Martin	$23.2 (b)
2	United Technologies	19.8	2	Boeing	21.9
3	McDonnell Douglas	15.0	3	United Technologies	21.2
4	Rockwell	12.6	4	McDonnell Douglas	13.2
5	Allied-Signal	12.0	5	Allied-Signal	12.8
6	General Dynamics	10.1	6	Raytheon	12.0 (d)
7	Lockheed	9.9	7	Rockwell	10.8 (c)
8	Raytheon	8.8	8	Textron	9.7
9	Textron	7.4	9	TRW	9.1
10	Martin Marietta	5.8	10	Northrop Grumman	6.7
	Total	$121.7		Total	$142.3

Source: Bear Sterns, the Evolving Structure of the Defense Industry, unpublished briefing.

[a] Data represent total sales in billions. *Source*: Fortune magazine's Fortune 500
[b] Pro forma for the merger; data available for the latest twelve months ended September 1994.
[c] Pro forma for the acquisition of Reliance Electric.
[d] Pro forma for the acquisition of E-Systems, Inc.

degree of diversity have acquired and consolidated. This table, using 1994 data, shows how much activity has already occurred. If 1995 data were included, it would show the sale of Westinghouse Defense Electronics to Northrop Grumman for $3 billion, and Lockheed Martin's purchase of most of Loral for $9.1 billion. The push to consolidate signals the desire of the surviving companies to remain solidly in the defense marketplace, where they enjoy near-monopolies owing to their understanding of both the business and the customer.

Even when defense firms have tried to diversify, they have taken relatively small steps. Martin Marietta, a firm whose top executives have expressed caution about defense conversion, (prior to the merger with Lockheed) entered into some commercial ventures using military technology. One included the refining of equipment for the Arbitron Company, to be used in estimating the size of television audiences. The product would use technology developed to scan the oceans for submarines to pick up signals emitted in TV transmissions. This is the type of project that the Clinton administration seemed to be looking for under its dual-use technology programs. Yet it will be a long time before this type of project can replace the gaps left by defense contracts. Martin Marietta, prior to the merger with Lockheed, laid off over 14,000 workers but converted only ten part-time engineers to the Arbitron project (Mintz, 1993). While attempting small steps, many largely defense firms will continue to stick to their core business, pursuing military sales here and abroad.

WHAT MIGHT LIE AHEAD?

The federal government will continue to implement a variety of industrial and dual-use technology programs. Some will be promulgated by Congress, concerned about the shrinking job base, and others will find support within the Clinton administration, inside the Pentagon, or by the defense contractor community. The effectiveness of these programs will be tested in the marketplace as they are implemented.

In the end, the structure of the remaining, dedicated, defense industrial base will be more dependent on market forces and on the number of major defense contracts available than on specific conversion programs. The government simply cannot appropriate enough money to help the entire DIB convert. Indeed, there are those who ask about the appropriateness of the government aiding this group of businesses over others who have been hurt badly by recession or global competition.

The base that remains will be smaller and more consolidated and made up of contractors actively wanting to stay in the defense market. The DoD will always need contractors producing systems and subsystems that have only a military utility. Tanks and nuclear submarines have limited civilian applicability. The dedicated contractors will include aerospace contractors who are consolidating around core competencies (e.g., Lockheed Martin), and others who have been structured specifically to meet the needs of the defense market. Alliant Tech

Systems, Inc., is one such example. All the remaining companies will continue to "right size," the current euphemism for reductions in forces, or divest defense capability.

Major contractors have taken advantage of relatively modest programs that are funded. The Defense Technology Conversion Reinvestment and Transition Program administered by ARPA provided close to $600 million in dual-use grants and contracts. The amount may well draw a response from those contractors consolidating and planning to stay in the defense market. That is so because nondefense contractors may find it difficult to respond to the complicated government requirements and because Congress has required a 50 percent match from respondents. Large firms will find it easiest to meet this requirement. While many of these contractors are skeptical of defense conversion programs, they will respond to the Request for Proposal now on the street. The program has been likened to "red meat on the street" for hungry contractors (Mintz, 1993). It has, however, come under attack from a Republican Congress, which does not find these type of "industrial policy" programs as appealing as did their Democratic predecessors.

Any successful program will be dependent on regulatory and cultural changes within the Department of Defense, Congress, and industry. Regulatory changes will streamline the existing process, allowing easier use of commercial specs and standards. Accounting procedures, auditing, and other processes that preclude the creation and utilization of a broad technology and industrial base must be and are being addressed. Some of the regulatory changes, as with milspec reform, can be made inside the department. Others are dependent on Congress. Congress, too, has acted on acquisition reform, passing streamlining legislation in 1994 and 1995.

These changes must be made in conjunction with broad cultural changes that allow risk-taking and innovation in the acquisition system. This, too, cannot be done alone. People will be loath to change processes as long as failures mean public humiliations, ruined careers, or even criminal prosecutions. Congress has become part of this cultural reform process, as have the political and military leadership in the department; but changing a system with such deep legal, bureaucratic and cultural roots is proving to be a difficult challenge.

Contractors need to reform business practices that stand in the way of conversion or integration. Successful defense contractors may complain about the defense market, but they have become reflections of their government customer's way of doing business. If the government is cumbersome, so are the contractors who work with them. Past failures in conversion have made many contractors skeptical of conversion schemes. Most have downsized, consolidated, or purchased other defense divisions and plan on staying largely defense contractors. Regardless of any conversion processes and despite budget drawdowns, a significant amount of funding still will go toward acquisition. Whatever reforms take place, the defense market will remain significantly different from the commercial marketplace.

Conversion programs may help incrementally, but the real challenge for all involved is to define new ways of doing business that will allow the department to take advantage of fast-moving technological advances available in a broad technology base that encompasses both the defense and commercial sectors. Without this capability, the department will have difficulty keeping up with the state of the art within the constraints of smaller budgets and fewer systems.

NOTES

1. A previous director, Craig Fields, was removed during the Bush administration for a perceived push toward "industrial policy," a forbidden policy area under the Bush and Reagan administrations but of great interest to many in Congress.

2. Since procurement accounts have dropped 70 percent, far more than the top-line reduction of the total DoD budget, the DoD has, in effect, taken a pause in modernizations. During this pause, very few weapon systems have been started. The department plans to increase the funding in procurement accounts, peaking at $60 billion in 2001. This is the figure that many feel is needed to recapitalize and modernize the military services.

CHAPTER 13

Emerging Sources of Technology and Technical Information

J. DAVID ROESSNER AND ANNE WISE

INTRODUCTION AND BACKGROUND

A number of competitive pressures are influencing industrial research in the United States today: Customers are demanding higher quality and greater product diversity, technological change is occurring more rapidly, and foreign firms are increasingly effective in competing against domestic companies. These factors have led to a restructuring in many industries. In rapidly changing fields, cooperative research efforts are on the increase in an effort to develop and commercialize products in a shorter time frame (Hamilton & Singh, 1992). Such collaboration is one consequence of growth in the corporate search for external sources of knowledge and technology. Environmental scanning can also yield complementary knowledge from competitors that, when effectively utilized, can speed a product to market faster than relying completely upon internal resources (Hamilton & Singh, 1992) and can sometimes lead to ideas for entirely new products.

As technologies grow in complexity, companies often target their internal research resources on core competencies and utilize outside sources for supporting knowledge or technology (Sen & Rubenstein, 1990). Single firms are finding it difficult, if not impossible, to keep up-to-date on the growing quantity and diversity of innovations in technological fields undergoing rapid change. Therefore, firms in many emerging fields are evolving a mixture of internal and external research assets (Pavitt, 1984). A major challenge for the firm is finding the proper balance between building new capabilities and identifying and utilizing existing ones outside the company (Hamilton & Singh, 1992). Two primary responses to this balancing act are a growth in conglomerate firms, which conduct research in a broader range of distinctive competencies within the firm, and external scanning for knowledge and technology (Granstrand & Sjaalander, 1990). This chapter focuses primarily on the latter, emphasizing the role of recent public policies intended to strengthen linkages between industry and publicly funded research and development (R&D)–performing institutions.

Participation in research consortia, strategic alliances, and other forms of R&D partnering are on the increase (Sen & Rubenstein, 1990). Many researchers have found that firms with competent internal R&D capabilities are better able to exploit such collaborative external efforts (e.g., Mowery & Rosenberg, 1989). Rosenberg (1990) has found that in-house capability must be in a field related to the external effort. Cohen & Levinthal (1990) argue for an ''absorptive capacity'' that is dependent not only on the type of internal research conducted but also on the communication mechanisms in use in the R&D culture of the organization. Growth of this ability to absorb external knowledge efficiently is one reason firms engage in R&D; the other is the generation of new knowledge. There is general agreement that the amount of relevant external research is growing. With this growth comes the need for industry to be able to utilize this knowledge. For efficient use of this information, the organization's absorptive capacity must grow, leading to increased reliance on internal R&D (Cohen & Levinthal, 1990). In other words, external knowledge generation is a complement, rather than a supplement, to internal corporate R&D.

Further evidence of the importance to American industries of external knowledge and technology is provided by Edwin Mansfield's work comparing the United States to Japan in industrial innovation (Mansfield, 1988). His data, gathered from 50 Japanese firms and 75 American firms in 1985, showed that Japanese cost and time advantages may be confined to innovations based on external technology. Mansfield's data demonstrate no significant differences in cost or time to production when the innovations are based on internally developed technology. Japanese firms commercialize technology in 10 percent less time and use 50 percent less money when the innovation is based on external, rather than internal, knowledge.

SOURCES OF EXTERNAL KNOWLEDGE AND TECHNOLOGY

If the trend toward searching externally for knowledge is increasing, the next question is where firms turn to find such resources. There is evidence that universities are often the subject of industry attention. Feller (1990) notes that new alliances between universities and industry are growing in importance to many company-level R&D programs. Structural changes in United States industries and the use of high technology for production have stimulated the need for knowledge-based products. The growing importance of knowledge leads to increasing cooperation between industries and universities (Rees & Debbage, 1992). One way industry demonstrates the importance of this avenue of external knowledge is through its funding of university research. In 1970, industry funded $61 million in university research. By 1985, $485 million of industry money was being spent in university research, a threefold increase in constant dollars (Business–Higher Education Forum, 1988). Many universities themselves are reaching out to industry, by encouraging faculty to patent and license relevant research efforts. A survey of 89 research universities found that 844 patents were issued to these academies between 1986 and 1989. During the same period approximately 500 licenses were granted, generating $11 million for these universities (Goldstein & Luger, 1990). However, industry usually does not enter into funded or cooperative research with universities to seek patentable technology. A recent government survey of member firms of the Engineering Research Centers, for example, found that developing patentable products was the least frequently stated reason among the fifteen mentioned (General Accounting Office, 1988).

Other sources of knowledge external to the firm also exist. Customers, suppliers, and competitors are commonly cited sources. Beyond individual firms and universities, however, there are other possible origins for knowledge and technology. For over a decade, the U.S. government has been encouraging technology transfer from government to industry. Two recent legislative acts intended to foster private-sector access to government-funded research build upon the Stevenson-Wydler Act of 1980, which required federal R&D agencies to create Offices of Research and Technology Applications in the federal laboratories and to devote half of 1 percent of their R&D budgets to technology transfer. The Federal Technology Transfer Act of 1986 permitted some federal laboratories to participate in Cooperative Research and Development Agreements (CRADAs) with industry and other nonfederal partners. It also established the Federal Laboratory Consortium to assist in connecting private-sector organizations with complementary researchers in the federal labs. Three years later, the National Competitiveness Technology Transfer Act of 1989 permitted the large, contractor-operated, multiprogram Department of Energy laboratories to participate in CRADAs. Cooperative research conducted under CRADAs permits companies, singularly or in groups, to pool resources and share risks with federal laboratories in developing technologies. CRADAs can create new teams for solving complex industrial problems and can leverage R&D efforts (Pearman, 1993).

1992 INDUSTRY SURVEY

A 1992 survey supported by the Department of Energy and the Industrial Research Institute (IRI) produced information about the patterns of industry interaction with the federal laboratories (Roessner & Wise, 1993). This vehicle provided an opportunity to explore the significance of federal laboratories in relation to other external sources available to large, research-intensive firms representing a variety of industries. The survey built upon the results of a similar survey conducted in 1988. Results of the 1988 survey are summarized in Roessner and Bean (1991) and detailed in Roessner and Bean (1990). The 1988 data reflected company experiences shortly after passage of the Federal Technology Transfer Act of 1986. Respondents for the 1992 survey were 68 chief technical officers (CTOs) of IRI member firms and 101 of these firms' laboratory or division directors. The more recent survey was conducted by the Georgia Institute of Technology in collaboration with the Center for Innovation Management Studies at Lehigh University. The survey results were supplemented by discussions with representatives of IRI-member companies obtained in several seminar settings.[1]

IRI membership consists of approximately 270 large, research-intensive companies. Most are American-owned, but a small number of foreign firms are members. IRI-member companies account for 85 percent of industrially performed R&D in the United States. Included are the ten companies with the largest 1991 R&D budgets in the United States: General Motors, IBM, Ford, Digital Equipment, General Electric, Hewlett-Packard, AT&T, Eastman Kodak, Boeing, and du Pont. Membership is diverse by industry and is not necessarily representative of any larger population of firms. The 68 firms that responded to the survey were reasonably representative of IRI membership by industrial category: in very broad terms, about one-third were in chemicals and pharmaceuticals; about 20 percent in aerospace, transportation, and electrical/electronics; about 10 percent in energy; and the rest were in "other" (primary industries, food, machinery, fabricated materials).

The respondents were asked how significant for their company (or division/laboratory) is each item of a list of potential external sources of knowledge and new technology. The seven sources listed were universities, United States-based companies, foreign-based companies, federal laboratories, government data bases, private data bases, and R&D consortia. All but two of these sources (federal laboratories and R&D consortia) were also included in a similar question on the 1988 survey. Respondents were given a five-point Likert scale, with answers ranging from "not at all" to "crucial" for each of the potential external sources.

RESEARCH RESULTS

Figure 13.1 shows a comparison of the 1988 and the 1992 survey responses. United States-based companies ranked first and universities second, both being regarded as, on average, between "moderately" and "very" significant. Foreign-based companies and private data bases are considered "moderately" significant, while federal laboratories and government data bases are only "somewhat" significant. CTOs and division directors gave similar responses, although CTOs considered federal labs to be a more significant source of external technology and knowledge than did the division directors. A comparison with results of the 1988 survey (Figure 13.1) shows that the significance of most sources of external information has increased over the last four years, especially in the case of the sources rated as most important: other companies and uni-

Figure 13.1
Significance of External Sources of Knowledge and New Technology

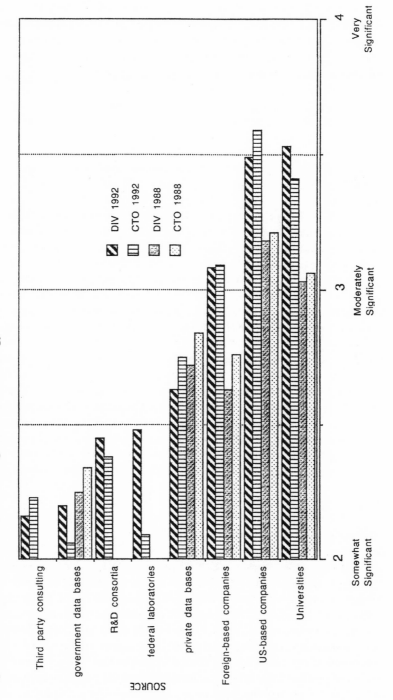

Table 13.1
Mean Significance Rating for Each External Source, by Size of Company R&D Budget

	Over $500 Million (n=14)	$100 Million to $500 Million (n=18)	$26 Million to $99 Million (n=17)	Under $25 Million (n=18)
Universities	4.07*	3.33	3.35	3.06
U.S.-based firms	3.93	3.39	3.71	3.39
Foreign-based firms	3.64*	2.72	3.06	3.00
Private data bases	2.64	2.33	3.06	2.88
R&D consortia	2.50	2.38	2.56	2.00
Federal labs	2.43	2.17	2.25	1.61
Gov't data bases	2.07	2.11	2.00	2.00

versities. A laboratory manager in a large petroleum company put it this way: "As internal R&D support decreased, there has been increased reliance on outside sources, including federal labs. There has also been a trend in both our labs and in outside labs towards more short term, applied research."

Both the firm and the division-level data were broken down by size of R&D budget. The results are shown in Tables 13.1 and 13.2. In general, both show that larger firms and divisions (that is, those with larger R&D budgets) ascribe greater significance to external sources than do smaller ones. The exceptions are government and private data bases, which maintain their significance for smaller firms and divisions. Companies spending over $500 million in R&D consider universities and foreign firms "very" significant, while other firms viewed them as "moderately" significant, sources. Differences in reported significance of external sources between the largest firms ($500 million and higher in R&D) and all other firms combined is statistically significant at the .05 level in the case of universities and foreign firms, but not for United States-based firms. The largest companies rank universities first, followed by United States-based firms, and then by foreign firms. Other firms rank United States-based firms first and universities second, but the differences are not large (Table 13.1).

The results at the division or laboratory level are less clear. Only in the case of universities does size of division make a statistically significant difference: Divisions or labs with budgets of over $50 million consider universities to be more important than do smaller divisions. However, universities also top the list of sources for all but divisions with R&D budgets below $10 million (see Table 13.2). As was the case with CTOs, universities, United States-based firms, and foreign-based firms are again universally considered by division directors to be the three most significant external sources for knowledge and new technology.

Next, the survey data were analyzed by industrial sector: chemical and pharmaceutical; aerospace, transportation, and electrical; energy; and "other," which includes primary metals, textile mills, and paper products (see Figures 13.2 and 13.3). Three of the four industry groupings reflect the overall preferences: United States-based firms, universities, and foreign firms. The eight energy firms in the

Table 13.2
Mean Significance Rating for External Sources by Size of Division/Laboratory R&D Budget

	Over $50 Million (n=22)	$26 Million to $50 Million (n=21)	$10 Million to $25 Million (n=27)	Under $10 Million (n=28)
Universities	3.95*	3.52	3.74	2.96
U.S.-based firms	3.55	3.48	3.52	3.46
Foreign-based firms	3.36	2.90	3.19	2.86
Federal labs	2.64	2.48	2.48	2.36
Gov't data bases	2.18	1.95	2.33	2.29
Private data bases	2.68	2.25	2.59	2.85
R&D consortia	2.77	2.45	2.46	2.23

survey, which include several large petroleum companies, rated R&D consortia equal to United States-based firms as the most significant sources of external knowledge and new technology. While these results cannot be pushed too far with such a small sample size, it is interesting to note that the sixteen divisions conducting primarily energy R&D also ranked R&D consortia higher than the other three sectors (see Figure 13.3). The aerospace, transportation, and electronics sector ranked government data bases as more significant both in absolute means and relative rankings than did the other three sectors, perhaps reflecting these industries' greater reliance on and experience with federal R&D contracts.

To sum up, when preferences for external knowledge sources are analyzed by R&D budget and by industry, United States-based firms, universities, and foreign firms generally retain their status as the three most significant external sources. The least significant source was generally government data bases. Federal laboratories seemed to be viewed more favorably by division directors than by CTOs, and R&D consortia were relatively highly rated by firms in the energy sector.

COMPARISON WITH OTHER RESEARCH RESULTS

How do these results compare with those of others who have looked at the external technology and knowledge sources of United States companies? In a recent survey of 216 firms (Rees & Debbage, 1992), vice presidents of production or engineering were asked to rate the importance of various sources of technical knowledge in the "development of new products and production processes." Industries participating in the survey were metalworking machinery, office and computing machinery, electronic components and accessories, and aircraft and parts. The sources of knowledge were split into two rating groups: important or not important. Rees and Debbage's data show the percentages of respondents who rated each source as "important," as summarized in Table 13.3.

While these categories are not the same as those used in the IRI survey, there

Figure 13.2
Significance of External Sources of Technology and Information, by Industry, CTO Responses: 1992

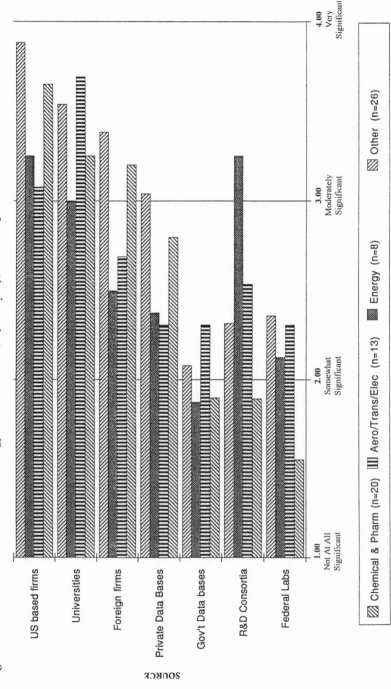

Figure 13.3
Significance of External Sources of Technology and Information, by Industry, Division Director Responses: 1992

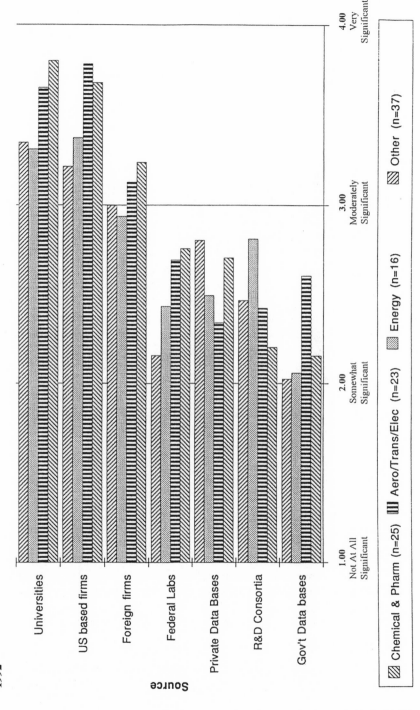

Table 13.3
Sources of Technical Knowledge in the Development of New Products and Production Processes

Source	%	Rated Important (n)
in-house R&D	86	(184)
trade or scientific publications	82	(176)
customers	81	(173)
competitors	61	(131)
suppliers	55	(118)
consultants	44	(94)
university institutions	37	(79)
licensed technologies	32	(69)
government agencies	21	(46)
parent company R&D	15	(33)

Source: Rees & Debbage, 1992.

appears to be a major difference in the perception of universities between these two surveys (compare Tables 13.3 and 13.4). This may be explained by the different industrial sectors represented or, more likely, by the considerable difference in the size of the responding firms. Firms in the Rees and Debbage survey (1992) had a median annual sales figure of $12.6 million, whereas the IRI firms whose responses are discussed in this chapter were many times larger (the median R&D budget was between $51 and $99 million). Rees and Debbage also noted a large effect of firm size, and Link and Bauer (1989) found in their 1986 telephone/mail survey of R&D consortia members that firm size had a similar effect. These results, supported by the analysis offered by Mowery and Rosenberg (1989), suggest that large, research-intensive firms are the natural industrial "partners" of both universities and federal laboratories. Additionally, if Rees and Debbage's category of "trade or scientific publications" is combined with "university institutions," the rating of what might be interpreted as "university-generated knowledge" increases considerably, more closely matching the results of the IRI survey.

Finally, a poll of readers[2] was recently conducted in the newsletter *Focus*, published by the National Center for Manufacturing Sciences (NCMS) ("Technology Acquisition," 1993). Readers were asked to rate "how useful the following sources of collaboratively developed technology are in meeting your needs." Of the 376 respondents, 13 percent said universities were highly useful, while 12 percent said consortia (NCMS or other), and 11 percent said foreign technology. Government labs were regarded as highly useful by 8 percent of the respondents.

CONCLUSIONS AND IMPLICATIONS

As a result of increased competitive pressures, tighter company budgets, and the globalization of competition, United States firms increasingly are seeking

Table 13.4
Percentage of Respondents Rating Each Source as Moderately and Very Significant, IRI Survey, CTO Responses

Source	% at least moderately significant	% at least very significant
Universities	82.4	45.6
U.S.-based companies	92.6	54.4
Foreign-based firms	69.2	32.4
Federal laboratories	27.9	4.4
Government data bases	25.0	1.5
Private data bases	48.5	29.4
R&D consortia	36.7	17.6

new technology and technical information outside their organizations. Federal laboratories represent one among many possible sources of technical information, expertise, and access to specialized equipment. The survey of IRI member companies showed that the significance of most sources of external information has increased over the last four years, especially in the case of the sources rated by IRI member companies as most important: other companies and universities. Although federal labs have become more visible, they are still relatively unimportant compared to competitors, suppliers, customer firms, and universities as sources of external technology and knowledge, at least in the case of large, research-intensive companies. Even among IRI-member companies, it is the larger firms that tend to interact more frequently and productively with federal labs.

Survey results suggest that the legislative initiatives intended to promote interaction between industry and federal laboratories have worked in the sense that companies are increasingly and significantly tapping the knowledge, expertise, and facilities available in government labs. Competitive pressures and financial stringencies also have brought a more traditional alliance—large companies and universities—into even closer collaboration. Public initiatives, such as the National Science Foundation's Centers programs, have further stimulated these linkages. Added to these is the increased appearance of R&D consortia, also stimulated by federal legislation—in this case the Cooperative Research and Development Act of 1984.

If the limited data available to date are any guide, legislative stimuli seeking to strengthen the linkages from research universities and government sources of R&D and expertise to U.S. industry have influenced primarily the largest firms. For such firms, universities are now virtually on a par with other firms as valued sources of external technology and technical information, and federal laboratories are at least in the running. However, improving small- and medium-sized firms' access to sources of technology and expertise remains a significant public policy problem for the United States. It remains to be seen whether the Clinton administration's initiatives in areas such as manufacturing extension will fill the gap.

NOTES

1. National Conference on the Advancement of Research (NCAR-046), Ruidoso, NM, September 20–23, 1992; Session on "Technology Transfer from National Laboratories to Industry: Promise and Reality," annual meeting of the American Association for the Advancement of Science, Boston, MA, February 13, 1993; "Industry Interaction with Federal Labs," symposium sponsored by the Industrial Research Institute, Washington, DC, March 15, 1993.

2. As the poll was not conducted as a sample survey, the significance of the results for any particular population of firms cannot be determined.

CHAPTER 14

Conclusion: Lessons Learned

YONG S. LEE

In conclusion, this chapter lists significant observations and insights discussed in each preceding chapter. The listing should be useful for policy and management discourse. As much of policy dynamics, I believe, is elusive, nonlinear, and essentially unpredictable, each new situation would require yet another fresh appraisal of "here and now." In this relentless process of appraisal and reappraisal, the lessons learned and insights gained from past experience, including systematic studies, should have a role to play. The observations and insights included in the list may not all be in agreement with one another, because of the different perspectives and different data these authors bring to bear on their respective studies. Collectively, though, as the listing will show, the studies evince a remarkable consensus on what works and what does not, what is important and what is not, what is simple and what is complex, and where the United States and the rest of the world are headed in the global economy with respect to technology transfer and collaboration.

I. INTRODUCTION

1.1 The issues of economic growth and competitiveness in the global economy require a shift of mind in perspective—from local to global, from sequential to parallel, from competition to collaboration, from linearity to nonlinearity, from order to chaos.

1.2 Whereas economic development and competitiveness in the global economy are determined not by the factors of natural endowment but by the rate of technological innovation, the rate of innovation is determined not only by the amount of R&D invested to create technology but also by the capacity to pool and transfer the scientific and technological resources that are historically compartmentalized in the arbitrary social and international division of labor.

1.3   Increasingly, the needed S&T resources reside "out there" in other boundaries: other firms, other sectors, and other nations.

1.4   Technology transfer covers a wide spectrum of activities incorporating the ideas of diffusion, knowledge, know-how, technology transfer, and R&D collaboration on technology development.

1.5   Technology transfer is very much like a "body-contact sport" in that conversations, consultations, and coaching are far more important than publishing and circulating papers.

1.6   The purpose (and rationale) of technology transfer policy is to create an infrastructure in which various components in the national innovation system can be linked and allowed to interact, exchange, and cooperate in pursuit of innovation.

1.7   The major players in the U.S. technology transfer regime are the federal government, research universities, federally funded R&D centers, and private firms and labs. In 1996, the total R&D expenditure ($184.3 billion) in the United States represented 2.48 percent of its GDP. This amount represented 44 percent of the R&D total of the OECD countries.

1.8   In 1995, the federal government provided 35.5 percent ($60.7 billion) of the total national R&D expenditures ($171 billion). Of this, it spent $20.3 billion (33.4%) for industry, $13 billion (21.4%) for universities, $8 billion (13.2%) for FFRDCs, $0.9 billion (1.6%) for nonprofit R&D institutions, and $16.7 billion (27.5%) for its own intramural research.

1.9   The basic rationale for the federal technology transfer policy is based on the assumption that U.S. industrial competitiveness is slipping in spite of the fact that the nation's research universities and federal laboratories are world-class R&D institutions with almost unlimited R&D resources.

1.10   During the 1980s, Congress constructed a rudimentary structure for the cooperative technology paradigm.

1.11   The National Cooperative Research Act relaxed the antitrust laws to make it easier for firms to collaborate on precompetitive, joint R&D ventures. While encouraging joint R&D ventures, it eliminated the treble damage standard and replaced it with actual damages and attorney fees.

II. CROSS-NATIONAL CASE STUDIES

2.1   Technology and science are commonly accepted in the leading world trading countries as being major contributors to economic and social progress.

2.2   The U.S. R&D system and organization are at the pluralistic, less centralized, and market-oriented end of the spectrum. By comparison, the French system and organization are at the more centralized, planned, and strategically targeted end of the spectrum. The United Kingdom, Germany, and Japan are somewhere in between. In each of the other countries, there is greater emphasis than in the United States on focusing or strategically targeting national S&T efforts.

2.3   As the United Kingdom, Germany, Japan, France, the European Union, and the United States are all *strategically* targeting national efforts on electronics, computers, informatics, biotechnology, materials, robotics, and manufacturing technologies, overcapacity could result that would make recoupment of public and private investment difficult and could put further strains on international technological competition.

2.4   While each country is looking at the policies and strategies of other countries to see what can be learned and possibly applied, the other countries are doing the same. As a result, there is likely to be a convergence in policies and strategies of the countries.

2.5   Should the United States move toward greater centralization or coordination of government S&T activities and needs? There is no good evidence from other countries that would support the thesis that the centralized system is more efficient than the pluralistic system.

2.6   While the U.S. reliance on pluralistic, shorter-term project support contributes to greater flexibility, mobility, and market orientation, such an approach results in less stability, less proportionate investment in infrastructure, and less general support for graduate students than exist in other countries. Such advantages and disadvantages tend to be reversed in most of the other countries.

3.1   Contrary to perspectives that the United States has always been a laissez-faire, totally market-based economy, the federal government has long been involved with aiding businesses and, more recently, with technology-based industrial policy.

3.2   Since the founding of this nation, the states (or at least some states) have been more innovative in most areas of industrial technology policy than the federal government.

3.3   Because the term ''industrial policy'' has become laden with such negative connotations relative to the American myth of a free-market approach to technology development and technology transfer, policymakers often underplay the extent of federal and state involvement in market intervention. Yet, the United States is moving toward a comprehensive industrial technology policy to position its key industries relative to international competitors.

4.1   Technology transfer is a major determinant in the efforts of newly industrialized countries to foster economic development.

4.2   For a newly industrializing state, fostering technology transfer is a balancing act. Technology importation can help industries accumulate technology in a short period of time, but, by the same measure, these industries can expose themselves to foreign dominance in key industrial sectors.

4.3   Technology transfer is also a balancing act for those states seeking to share technology with newly industrialized states. Transfer strategies can encourage the development of foreign markets, integrated development processes, and trade alliances. By transferring technology, however, the state runs the risk of giving away valuable resources, creating new competitors, and risking loss of position in the global market.

4.4   Without the ability to exert influence over domestic markets and capital, the capacity of the state to guide technology acquisition is limited. In those states with relatively strong government institutions, such as Korea, there have been coordinated policy initiatives aimed at technology transfer.

4.5   While the capacity of the state to absorb new technologies depends on several factors, including natural resources, infrastructure networks, social institutions, and human resources, it also depends on the state to influence absorption prospects through policy initiatives.

4.6   South Korea has been able to influence the course of technology transfer through a mix of policy instruments that have been applied to realize economic, industrial, and technology policy aims. In particular, the regulation of foreign direct investment and technology licensing has been especially useful in shaping the flow of technology from advanced countries, most notably the United States and Japan.

5.1   The successful international technology transfer of improved technology is largely responsible for many of the success stories in agriculture development throughout sub-Saharan Africa.

5.2   Agricultural technology transfer in sub-Saharan Africa is essentially a political process. The process becomes particularly political when governmental or nongovernmental agencies seek to work through village groups, who have high stakes in the distribution of benefits. To promote successful technology transfer it is of foremost importance to build a sound relationship between farmers, extension workers, and researchers and to delineate the interests of various actors— both within villages and between villages and government development agencies.

5.3   Whereas agricultural technology transfer involves many approaches, capacity transfer is key to its success or sustainability. The idea of capacity transfer goes beyond the diffusion of ideas and the craft of agricultural science; it must assure commensurate consideration for local, indigenous scientific knowledge with that circulating in international arenas.

5.4   Hierarchically organized agencies with well-defined roles and patterns of responsibility do actually impede agricultural technology transfer; these bureaucratic agencies display inertia and a defensive mentality and prefer to offer oversimplified versions of problems and deal with only those problems for which there is a ready solution.

5.5   Agricultural technology transfer in sub-Saharan Africa requires new partnerships for rural development and new collaborative institutional frameworks beginning with a bottom-up identification of issues and problems and the establishment of politically powerful farm or rural organizations. Government agencies must assume more responsibility for nurturing these organizations, yet have the capability to step back and move aside.

III. AMERICAN UNIVERSITY–INDUSTRY INTERACTION

6.1   As universities step aggressively into the marketplace, trying to make money through aggressive commercialization of their intellectual property, conflict of interest problems are likely to arise. It is important that, from the beginning, appropriate mechanisms be put in place to avoid conflict of interest or the perception of conflict of interest.

6.2   General policies expressing the university's support of technology transfer and explaining how this support fits with the institutional mission should be formulated and adopted formally by the board of trustees after a process involving extensive consultation with faculty.

6.3 Traditionally, universities, particularly public and land-grant universities, are not supposed to make money from the knowledge they produce. Although this principle steadily is being modified, many members of the general public (including university alumni), government officials, and faculty members still believe in it. The public justification for university technology transfer activity, therefore, must emphasize the good that such efforts are likely to bring to society and place the benefits to the university treasury in a secondary position.

6.4 Many universities have run into difficulties because of a poor choice of partners in technology development. Universities can protect themselves to some extent, however, by establishing standard procedures and criteria to evaluate the background, reputation, and capabilities of potential partners (both individuals and organizations).

6.5 In developing technology transfer initiatives, universities should seek the early involvement of external groups to assure that university programs mesh with and support related efforts, rather than compete with them.

7.1 Scientific advances made in academic research, even where research has been conducted with applications in mind, represent the very early stage of technological innovation, containing a high risk for commercial exploitation. Unless the risk is otherwise reduced significantly, firms are not likely to invest their fortunes to commercialize them.

7.2 Focused applied research is a means to "de-risk" academic discoveries, but it requires large R&D expenditures. This is the money that universities do not have and that firms are unwilling to invest. This "funding gap" is a major challenge to the transformation of academic research to technological innovation.

7.3 Typically, focused applied research is protracted research, which often leads to many more technological spin-offs and inventions, which also require additional focused applied research.

7.4 The process of transforming academic discoveries to technologies is anything but a simple linear process. It zigs and zags, often haltingly, and repeats itself in response to a multitude of forces: an unexpected increase in cost of research, a technical snag, pressures from market competition, university politics, legislative vicissitudes, and luck.

7.5 Whereas technology-push theory argues that innovation is driven (or "pushed") by scientific research, market-pull theory counters that innovation is rather driven (or "pulled") by market forces. In reality, even within the university setting, the two models run in parallel in almost every stage with extensive market interaction.

7.6 The key to successful technology transfer from university to firms is the development of a collaborative research team whose members would meet frequently and interact extensively.

7.7 Intellectual property negotiation is always very complicated. Negotiation is particularly troublesome when the firm has contributed original ideas to the project and partially defrayed the R&D expenses. In this case, the firm would demand the ownership or at least co-ownership of the patent resulting from the project. From the university perspective, this demand creates a dilemma because such transfer of ownership is tantamount to "privatization of university research." Moreover, the university would be deprived of an opportunity to collect rent needed to reinvest in basic research, and the faculty inventor would be deprived of his or her reward for invention.

8.1   University researchers who participate in technology transfer activities differ from their nonparticipating, university-bound colleagues in several ways. They tend to come from departments and universities that provide firm-friendly curricular offerings and to affiliate with research centers; are more likely to be cross-disciplinary; are prone to apply for or have been granted a patent; and are apt to take the initiative personally to approach a firm regarding their research expertise.

8.2   Despite the university norm of openness, a majority of spanning (participating) researchers find that firms, in an attempt to protect the secrecy of a potential commercial product, place restrictions on their sharing information regarding R&D breakthroughs with colleagues. This restriction creates a feeling of conflict for researchers between loyalty to the firm and the university value of open knowledge.

9.1   The last fifteen years (the 1980s and 1990s) in the United States has seen a significant growth in university-industry collaboration on technology transfer, which is evidenced by a large number of university-industry research centers established within universities, the breadth of interaction taking place between university faculty and industry scientists, and an increased number of university patents licensed to industry followed by a dramatic increase in royalty income.

9.2   Notwithstanding, controversy continues over what the proper relationship should be between university and industry in technology transfer collaboration.

9.3   Although, on the surface, American academics in general appear to be favorably disposed to university-industry collaboration, their views vary substantially and systematically from issue to issue.

9.4   While academics are quite favorably disposed to a close university-industry collaboration—insofar as such collaboration is structured to contribute to public welfare or economic development—their views are negative, or split at best, when the collaboration is viewed as a move toward privatization of university research, narrowly benefiting individual firms.

9.5   Given the R&D environment of declining budget but tough competition, American faculty appear to be troubled by the collision of two powerful but not necessarily complementary motives: the instrumental need for external funding for research and the intrinsic need to preserve academic freedom and intellectual autonomy. While the need for research funding forces academics to become more realistic ("not to be too picky") about their search for external sources—even if the conditions for funding are not entirely compatible with their fundamental research mission—the intrinsic need for academic freedom emphasizes the potential dangers of being "side-tracked" from fundamental research.

9.6   In spite of continuing debate over whether academics should or should not perform application-oriented research, there is a general consensus among science and engineering faculty that application-oriented research (or user-oriented research) per se is not really an important point of debate. The consensus is that faculty members should be left free to get involved in application-oriented, precompetitive research as long as they do their "academic chores" of teaching and publication.

IV. FEDERAL LAB–INDUSTRY INTERACTION

10.1   Whereas it has been argued that large firms are primary beneficiaries of CRADAs (Cooperative Research & Development Agreements between federal laboratories and firms), analysis shows that participation by small firms in CRADAs is widespread (43%).

10.2   Most CRADAs involve firms in high-technology industries with extensive R&D programs.

10.3   Outcomes of CRADA research are varied and generally involve (1) applications of federal technology to problems of industrial manufacturing, (2) assistance in the development of commercial products, (3) access to test equipment in federal laboratories, and (4) research results.

10.4   The most significant barrier in CRADA negotiation involves legal issues. While CRADA negotiations with no legal complications normally take about two to four months, they would otherwise last from four to six months or, in some instances, twelve to eighteen months, when legal complications arise. Among the frequently noted complications are (1) U.S. manufacturing preference laws, (2) product liability and indemnification, (3) fair access, (4) intellectual property rights, and (5) future pricing clauses.

10.5   Federal laboratories are slow to implement technology transfer legislation and directives because they are not provided with additional personnel and funds for marketing their resources to industry and their new technology transfer mission is not given priority by their parent agencies.

10.6   Federal in-kind support for CRADAs is an important determinant of research collaboration between federal labs and industry.

10.7   Industry is generally unaware of the capabilities of federal labs.

11.1   Economic decline has a way of encouraging reexamination of fundamental values, including the bedrock faith in the private sector and the characteristic hands-off approach—the "market-failure paradigm." A number of policy initiatives undertaken by the federal government during the 1980s challenged the preeminence of the market-failure paradigm for technology policy with a new one, "cooperative technology."

11.2   Technology transfer activity is ubiquitous in government laboratories, and about half the labs view it as an important mission.

11.3   Measuring the success (or effectiveness) of technology transfer in terms of technology licensing and commercial impact, the federal labs' technology transfer performance is quite variable. A few laboratories have most of the licenses, and nearly 60 percent have no licenses. The level of perceived benefits, either for the labs themselves or for their client firms, is modest.

11.4   Successful technology transfer at federal labs is promoted by three specific motives: (1) emphasis on economic development, (2) outgrowth of cooperative R&D

or a research consortium, and (3) scientists' and engineers' interest in entrepreneurship and personal wealth.

11.5　It makes little difference to the success of technology transfer whether the lab is oriented to basic research or to applied research and technology development. Nor does it make any difference whether the lab is centrally and hierarchically structured or not, large or small in terms of total personnel, or has simple or complex schemes for organizing research.

11.6　Technology transfer strategies employed by federal labs appear to make a difference in the transfer results. The most effective seems to be participation in a research center, and closely behind are the strategies of emphasizing sales of patents, copyrights, and licenses and the use of cooperative R&D for technology transfer.

12.1　With the collapse of the Cold War, acquisition budgets have declined sharply, which causes real stress for the defense industrial base, a relatively small but visible portion of the nation's industrial base in the past.

12.2　Post–Cold War U.S. policy is aimed at remaking the defense industrial base into a national technology and industrial base with a high degree of civil-military integration, emphasizing a dual-use approach to research and development.

12.3　A mixture of government laws (e.g., unique accounting and audit requirements), military regulations (e.g., military specifications and standards), and culture is causing a deep rift between civilian and military producers. While companies with defense and commercial divisions find it difficult to transfer technologies between those divisions, government also finds it difficult to buy civilian, off-the-shelf technology, even though such technologies are appropriate, readily available, and affordable.

12.4　Milspecs and standards are often vital in the production of the specialized, leading-edge products needed by the Department of Defense, but they impose product design and production methods that are slower and more costly than can be borne by the commercial market.

12.5　Dual use is incompatible with the existing milspecs and standards system, particularly because of the production cycle mismatch.

12.6　Facing formidable challenges in the conversion process, with no reform in milspecs and standards on the horizon, some companies in the military industrial base exit the defense market altogether, and others divest selectively, merge with competitors, or consolidate in order to gain market share. The base that remains will be smaller, more consolidated, and made up of contractors actively wanting to stay in the defense market.

12.7　Dual use and civil-military integration are elusive concepts unless accompanied with regulatory changes, including milspecs and standards, and accounting and audit procedures.

13.1　As technologies grow in complexity, companies often target their internal resources on core competencies and utilize outside sources for supporting knowledge or technology. Single firms are finding it difficult, if not impossible, to keep up-to-date on the growing quantity and diversity of innovations in technological fields undergoing rapid change.

13.2 Firms with competent internal R&D capabilities are better able to exploit collaborative external efforts. Equally important are the communication mechanisms in use in the R&D culture of the organization.

13.3 While no significant differences in cost or time to production exist between Japanese and U.S. firms when the innovations are based on internally developed technology, Japanese firms commercialize technology in 10 percent less time and use 50 percent less money when the innovation is based on external, rather than internal, knowledge.

13.4 Potential external sources of knowledge and new technology for firms include universities, United States-based companies, foreign-based companies, federal laboratories, government data bases, private data bases, and R&D consortia.

13.5 Significant external sources of knowledge and technical information to large U.S. companies (IRI members) are United States-based firms and universities, followed by foreign-based companies and private data bases. Federal laboratories and government data bases are rated only a ''somewhat'' significant source.

13.6 Although federal labs have become more visible, they are relatively unimportant compared to competitors, suppliers, customer firms, and universities as sources of external technology and knowledge.

13.7 It appears that legislative stimuli seeking to strengthen the linkages from research universities and government sources of R&D and expertise to U.S. industry have influenced primarily the largest firms. For such firms, universities are now virtually on a par with other firms as valued sources of external technology and technical information.

13.8 Improving small and medium-sized firms' access to sources of technology and expertise remains a significant public policy problem.

APPENDIX A

The Stevenson-Wydler Technology Innovation Act of 1980 (P. L. 96–480) as Amended

CHAPTER 63--TECHNOLOGY INNOVATION

§   **3701. Findings**

The Congress finds and declares that:

(1) Technology and industrial innovation are central to the economic, environmental, and social well-being of citizens of the United States.

(2) Technology and industrial innovation offer and improved standard of living, increased public and private sector productivity, creation of new industries and employment opportunities, improved public services and enhanced competitiveness of United States products in world markets.

(3) Many new discoveries and advances in science occur in universities and Federal laboratories, while the application of this new knowledge to commercial and useful public purposes depends largely upon actions by business and labor. Corporation among academia, Federal laboratories, labor, and industry, in such forms as technology transfer, personnel exchange, joint research projects, and others, should be renewed, expanded, and strengthened.

(4) Small businesses have performed an important role in advancing industrial and technological innovation.

(5) Industrial and technological innovation in the United States may be lagging when compared to historical patterns and other industrialized nations.

(6) Increased industrial and technological innovation would reduce trade deficits, stabilize the dollar, increase productivity gains, increase employment, and stabilize prices.

(7) Government antitrust, economic, trade, patent, procurement, regulatory, research and development, and tax policies have significant impacts upon industrial innovation and development of technology, but there is insufficient knowledge of their effects in particular sectors of the economy.

(8) No comprehensive national policy exists to enhance technological innovation for commercial and public purposes. There is a need for such a policy, including a strong national policy supporting domestic technology transfer and utilization of the science and technology resources of the Federal Government.

(9) It is in the national interest to promote the adaptation of technological innovations to State and local government uses. Technological innovations can improve services, reduce their costs, and increase productivity in State and local governments.

(10) The Federal laboratories and other performers of federally funded research and development frequently provide scientific and technological developments of potential use to State and local governments and private industry. These developments, which include inventions, computer software, and training technologies, should be made accessible to those governments and industry. There is a need to provide means of access and to give adequate personnel and funding support to these means.

(11) The Nation should give fuller recognition to individuals and companies which have made outstanding contributions to the promotion of technology or technological manpower for the improvement of the economic, environmental, or social well-being of the United States.

(Pub. L. 96-480, §2, Oct. 21, 1980, 94 Stat. 2311; Pub. L. 99-502, § 9(f)(1), Oct. 20, 1986, 100 Stat. 1797.)

§ 3702. Purpose

It is the purpose of this chapter to improve the economic, environmental, and social well-being of the United States by--

(1) establishing organizations in the executive branch to study and stimulate technology;
(2) promoting technology development through the establishment of cooperative research centers;
(3) stimulating improved utilization of federally funded technology developments, including inventions, software, and training technologies, by State and local governments and the private sector;
(4) providing encouragement for the development of technology through the recognition of individuals and companies which have made outstanding contributions in technology; and
(5) encouraging the exchange of scientific and technical personnel among academia, industry, and Federal laboratories.

(Pub. L. 96-480, § 3. Oct. 21, 1980, 94 Stat. 2312; Pub. L. 99-502, § 9(b)(1),

(f)(2), Oct. 20, 1986, 100 Stat. 1795, 1797.)

§ 3704. Commerce and technological innovation

(a) Establishment

There is established in the Department of Commerce a Technology Administration, which shall operate in accordance with the provisions, findings, and purposes of this chapter. The Technology Administration shall include--

(1) the National Institute of Standards and Technology;
(2) the National Technical Information Service; and
(3) a policy analysis office, which shall be known as the Office of Technology Policy.

(b) Under Secretary and Assistant Secretary

The President shall appoint, by and with the advice and consent of the Senate, to the extent provided for in appropriations Acts--

(1) Under Secretary of Commerce for Technology, who shall be compensated at the rate provided for level III of the Executive Schedule in section 5314 of title 5; and
(2) an Assistant Secretary of Commerce for Technology Policy, who shall serve as policy analyst for the Under Secretary.

(c) Duties

(d) Japanese technical literature

(Pub. L. 96-480, § 5, Oct. 21, 1980, 94 Stat. 2312; Pub. L. 99-382, § 2, Aug.

14, 1986, 100 Stat. 811; Pub. L. 99-
502, § 9(b)(3)-(5), (e)(2)(A), Oct. 20,
1986, 100 Stat. 1795, 1797; Pub. L.
100-519, title II, § 201(a)-(c), (d)(2),
Oct. 24, 1988, 102 Stat. 2593, 2594;
Pub. L. 102-245, title III, § 306, Feb.
14, 1992, 106 Stat. 20.)

§   **3704a. Clearinghouse for State
     and Local Initiatives on
     Productivity, Technology, and
     Innovation**

(a) Establishment

There is established within the
Office of Productivity, Technology,
and Innovation a Clearinghouse for
State and Local Initiatives on
Productivity, Technology, and
Innovation. The Clearinghouse shall
serve as a central repository of
information on initiatives by State and
local governments to enhance the
competitiveness of American business
through the stimulation of productivity,
technology, and innovation
and Federal efforts to assist State and
local governments to enhance
competitiveness.

(b) Responsibilities

The Clearinghouse may--
(1) establish relationships with
    State and local governments,
    and regional and multistate
    organizations of such
    governments, which carry out
    such initiatives;
(2) collect information on the
    nature, extent, and effects of
    such initiatives, particularly
    information useful to the
    Congress, Federal agencies,
    State and local governments,
    regional and multistate
    organizations of such

governments, business, and
the public throughout the
United States;
(3) disseminate information
    collected under paragraph (2)
    through reports, directories,
    handbooks, conferences, and
    seminars;
(4) provide technical assistance
    and advice to such
    governments with respect to
    such initiatives, including
    assistance in determining
    sources of assistance from
    Federal agencies which may
    be available to support such
    initiatives;
(5) study ways in which Federal
    agencies, including Federal
    laboratories, are able to use
    their existing policies and
    programs to assist State and
    local governments, and
    regional and multistate
    organizations of such
    governments, to enhance the
    competitiveness of American
    business;
(6) make periodic
    recommendations to the
    Secretary, and to other
    Federal agencies upon their
    request, concerning
    modifications in Federal
    policies and programs which
    would improve Federal
    assistance to State and local
    technology and business
    assistance programs;
(7) develop methodologies to
    evaluate State and local
    programs, and, when
    requested, advise State and
    local governments, and
    regional and multistate
    organizations of such
    governments, as to which
    programs are most effective

in enhancing the competitiveness of American business through the stimulation of productivity, technology, and innovation; and

(8) make use of, and disseminate, the nationwide study of State industrial extension programs conducted by the Secretary.

(c) Contracts

(Pub. L. 96-480, § 6, as added Pub. L. 100-418, title V, § 5122(a)(2), Aug. 23, 1988, 102 Stat. 1438.)

§ 3704b. National Technical Information Service

(a) Powers

(1) The Secretary of Commerce, acting through the Director of the National Technical Information Service (hereafter in this section referred to as the "Director") is authorized to do the following:

(A) Enter into such contracts, cooperative agreements, joint ventures, and other transactions, in accordance with all relevant provisions of Federal law applicable to such contracts and agreements, and under reasonable terms and conditions, as may be necessary in the conduct of the business of the National Technical Information Service (hereafter in this section referred to as the "Service").

(B) In addition to the authority regarding fees contained in section 2 of the Act entitled "An Act to provide for the dissemination of technological, scientific, and engineering information to American business and industry, and for other purposes" enacted September 9, 1950 (15 U.S.C. 1152), retain and, subject to appropriations Acts, utilize its net revenues to the extent necessary to implement the plan submitted under subsection (f)(3)(D) of this section.

(C) Enter into contracts for the performance of part or all the functions performed by the Promotion Division of the Service prior to October 24, 1988. The details of any such contract, and a statement of its effect on the operations and personnel of the Service, shall be provided to the appropriate committees of the Congress 30 days in advance of the execution of such contract.

(D) Employ such personnel as may be necessary to conduct the business of the Service.

(E) For the period of October1, 1991 through September 30, 1992, only, retain and use all earned and unearned monies heretofore or hereafter received, including receipts, revenues, and advanced payments and deposits, to fund all obligations and expenses, including inventories and capital equipment.

An increase or decrease in the personnel of the Service shall not affect or be affected by any ceilings on the number or grade of personnel.

(2) The functions and activities of the Service specified in subsection (e)(1) through (6) of this section are permanent Federal functions to be carried out by the Secretary through the Service and its employees, and shall not be transferred from the Service, by contract or otherwise, to the private sector on a permanent or temporary basis without express approval of the Congress. Functions or activities--

(A) for the procurement of supplies, materials, and equipment by the Service;

(B) referred to in paragraph (1)(c); or

(C) to be performed through joint ventures or cooperative agreements which do not result in a reduction in the Federal workforce of the affected programs of the Service,

shall not be considered functions or activities for purposes of this paragraph.

(3) For the purposes of this subsection, the term "net revenues" means the excess of revenues and receipts from any source, other than royalties and other income described in section 3710c(a)(4) of this title, over operating expenses.

(4) Omitted.

(b) Director of the Service

(c) Advisory Board

(d) Audits

(e) Functions

(f) Notification of Congress

(Pub. L. 100-519, title II, § 212, Oct. 24, 1988, 102 Stat. 2594; Pub. L. 102-140, title II, Oct. 28, 1991, 105 Stat. 804; Pub. L. 102-245, title V, § 506(c), Feb. 14, 1992, 106 Stat. 27.)

§   **3704b-2. Transfer of Federal scientific and technical information**

(a) Transfer

The head of each Federal executive department or agency shall transfer in a timely manner to the National Technical Information Service unclassified scientific, technical, and engineering information which results from federally funded research and development activities for dissemination to the private sector, academia, State and local governments, and Federal agencies. Only information which would otherwise be available for public dissemination shall be transferred under this subsection. Such information shall include technical reports and information, computer software, application assessments generated pursuant to section 3710(c) of this title, and information regarding training technology and other federally owned or originated technologies. The Secretary shall issue regulations within one year after February 14, 1992, outlining procedures for the ongoing transfer of such information to the National Technical Information Service.

(b) Annual report to Congress

(Pub. L. 102-245, title I, § 108, Feb. 14, 1992, 106 Stat. 13.)

§   3705. Cooperative Research Centers

(a) Establishment

The Secretary shall provide assistance for the establishment of Cooperative Research Centers. Such Centers shall be affiliated with any university, or other nonprofit institution, or group thereof, that applies for and is awarded a grant or enters into a cooperative agreement under this section. The objective of the Centers is to enhance technological innovation through--

(1) the participation of individuals from industry and universities in cooperative technological innovation activities;

(2) the development of the generic research base, important for technological advance and innovative activity, in which firms have little incentive to invest, but which may have significant economic or strategic importance, such as manufacturing technology;

(3) the education and training of individuals in the technological innovation process;

(4) the improvement of mechanisms for the dissemination of scientific, engineering, and technical information among universities and industry;

(5) the utilization of the capability and expertise, where appropriate, that exists in Federal laboratories; and

(6) the development of continuing financial support from other mission agencies, from State and local government, and from industry and universities through, among other means, fees, licenses, and royalties.

(b) Activities

The activities of the Centers shall include, but need not be limited to--

(1) research supportive of technological and industrial innovation including cooperative industry-university research;

(2) assistance to individuals and small businesses in the generation, evaluation, and development of technological ideas supportive of industrial innovation and new business ventures;

(3) technical assistance and advisory services to industry, particularly small businesses; and

(4) curriculum development, training, and instruction in

invention, entrepreneurship, and industrial innovation.

Each Center need not undertake all of the activities under this subsection.

(c) Requirements

Prior to establishing a Center, the Secretary shall find that--
(1) consideration has been given to the potential contribution of the activities proposed under the Center to productivity, employment, and economic competitiveness of the United States;
(2) a high likelihood exists of continuing participation, advice, financial support, and other contributions from the private sector;
(3) the host university or other nonprofit institution has a plan for the management and evaluation of the activities proposed within the particular Center, including:
> (A) the agreement between the parties as to the allocation of patent rights on a nonexclusive, partially exclusive, or exclusive license basis to and inventions conceived or made under the auspices of the Center; and
> (B) the consideration of means to place the Center, to the maximum extent feasible, on a self-sustaining basis;
(4) suitable consideration has been given to the university's or other nonprofit

institution's capabilities and geographical location; and
(5) consideration has been given to any effects upon competition of the activities proposed under the Center.

(d) Planning grants

The Secretary is authorized to make available nonrenewable planning grants to universities or nonprofit institutions for the purpose of developing a plan required under subsection (c)(3) of this section.

(e) Research and development utilization

In the promotion of technology from research and development efforts by Centers under this section, chapter 18 of title 35 shall apply to the extent not inconsistent with this section.

(Pub. L. 96-480, § 7, formerly § 6, Oct 21, 1980, 94 Stat. 2313; Pub. L. 99-502, § 9(b)(6)-(10), Oct. 20, 1986, 100 Stat. 1796; renumbered § 7, Pub. L. 100-418, title V, § 5122(a)(1), Aug. 23, 1988, 102 Stat. 1438.)

§   **3706. Grants and cooperative**

(a) In general

The Secretary may make grants and enter into cooperative agreements according to the provisions of this section in order to assist any activity consistent with this chapter, including activities performed by individuals. The total amount of any such grant or cooperative agreement may not exceed 75 percent of the total cost of the program.

(b) Eligibility and procedure

Any person or institution may apply to the Secretary for a grant or cooperative agreement available under this section. Application shall be made in such form and manner, and with such content and other submissions, as the Assistant Secretary shall prescribe. The Secretary shall act upon each such application within 90 days after the date on which all required information is received.

(c) Terms and conditions

(1) Any grant made, or cooperative agreement entered into, under this section shall be subject to the limitations and provisions set forth in paragraph (2) of this subsection, and to such other terms, conditions, and requirements as the Secretary deems necessary or appropriate.

(2) Any person who receives or utilizes any proceeds of any grant made or cooperative agreement entered into under this section shall keep such records as the Secretary shall by regulation prescribe as being necessary and appropriate to facilitate effective audit and evaluation, including records which fully disclose the amount and disposition by such recipient of such proceeds, the total cost of the program or project in connection with which such proceeds were used, and the amount, if any, of such costs which was provided through other sources.

(Pub. L. 96-480, § 8, formerly § 7, Oct 21, 1980, 94 Stat. 2315; renumbered § 8 and amended Pub. L. 100-418, title V, §§ 5115(b)(1), 5122(a)(1), Aug. 23, 1988, 102 Stat. 1433, 1438.)

§ 3707. National Science Foundation Cooperative Research Centers

(a) Establishment and provisions

The National Science Foundation shall provide assistance for the establishment of Cooperative Research Centers. Such Centers shall be affiliated with a university, or other nonprofit institution, or a group thereof. The objective of the Centers is to enhance technological innovation as provided in section 3705(a) of this title through the conduct of activities as provided in section 3705(b) of this title.

(b) Planning grants

The National Science Foundation is authorized to make available nonrenewable planning grants to universities of nonprofit institutions for the purpose of developing the plan, as described under section 3705(c)(3) of this title.

(c) Terms and conditions

Grants, contracts, and cooperative agreements entered into by the National Science Foundation in execution of the powers and duties of the National Science Foundation under this chapter shall be governed by the National Science Foundation Act of 1950 [42 U.S.C. 1861 et seq.] and other pertinent Acts.

(Pub. L. 96-480, § 9, formerly § 8, Oct 21, 1980, 94 Stat. 2316; Pub. L. 99-502, § 9(b)(11), (12), (e)(2)(B), Oct. 20, 1986, 100 Stat. 1796, 1797; renumbered § 9, Pub. L. 100-418, title V, § 5122(a)(1), Aug. 23, 1988, 102 Stat. 1438.)

§ 3708. Administrative
arrangements

(a) Coordination

The Secretary and the National
Science Foundation shall, on a
continuing basis, obtain the advice and
cooperation of departments and
agencies whose missions contribute to
or are affected by the programs
established under this chapter,
including the development of an
agenda for research and policy
experimentation. These departments
and agencies shall include but not be
limited to the Departments of Defense,
Energy, Education, Health and Human
Services, Housing and Urban
Development, the Environmental
Protection Agency, National
Aeronautics and Space Administration,
Small Business Administration,
Council on Environmental Quality, and
Office of Science and Technology
Policy.

(b) Cooperation

It is the sense of the Congress that
departments and agencies, including
the Federal laboratories, whose
missions are affected by, or could
contribute to, the programs established
under this chapter, should, within the
limits of budgetary authorizations and
appropriations, support or participate
in activities or projects authorized by
this chapter.

(c) Administrative authorization

(Pub. L. 96-480, § 10, formerly § 9,
Oct 21, 1980, 94 Stat. 2316; Pub. L.
99-502, § 9(e)(2)(c), Oct. 20, 1986,
100 Stat. 1797; Pub. L. 100-107, §
3(b), Aug. 20, 1987, 101 Stat. 727;
renumbered § 10 and amended Pub. L.

100-418, title V, § 5122(a)(1), (c),
Aug. 23, 1988, 102 Stat. 1438, 1439;
Pub. L. 102-240, title VI, § 6019, Dec.
18, 1991, 105 Stat. 2183.)

§ 3709. Repealed. Pub. L. 99-502,
§ 9(a), Oct. 20, 1986, 100 Stat.
1795

§ 3710. Utilization of Federal
technology

(a) Policy

(1) It is the continuing
responsibility of the Federal
Government to ensure the full
use of the results of the
Nation's Federal investment in
research and development. To
this end the Federal
Government shall strive where
appropriate to transfer federally
owned or originated technology
to State and local governments
and to the private sector.

(2) Technology transfer, consistent
with mission responsibilities, is
a responsibility of each
laboratory science and
engineering professional.

(3) Each laboratory director shall
ensure that efforts to transfer
technology are considered
positively in laboratory job
descriptions, employee
promotion policies, and
evaluation of the job
performance of scientists and
engineers in the laboratory.

(b) Establishment of Research and
Technology Applications
Offices

Each Federal laboratory shall
establish an Office of Research and
Technology Applications. Laboratories

having existing organizational structures which perform the functions of this section may elect to combine the Office of Research and Technology Applications within the existing organization. The staffing and funding levels for these offices shall be determined between each Federal laboratory and the Federal agency operating or directing the laboratory, except that (1) each laboratory having 200 or more full-time equivalent scientific, engineering, and related technical positions shall provide one or more full-time equivalent positions as staff for its Office of Research and Technology Applications, and (2) each Federal agency which operate or directs one or more Federal laboratories shall make available sufficient funding, either as a separate line item or from the agency's research and development budget, to support the technology transfer function at the agency and at its laboratories, including support of the Office of Research and Technology Applications. Furthermore, individuals filling positions in an Office of Research and Technology Applications shall be included in the overall laboratory/agency management development program so as to ensure that highly competent technical managers are full participants in the technology transfer process. The agency head shall submit to Congress at the time the President submits the budget to Congress an explanation of the agency's technology transfer program for the preceding year and the agency's plans for conducting its technology transfer function for the upcoming year, including plans for securing intellectual property rights in laboratory innovations with commercial promise and plans for managing such innovations so as to benefit the competitiveness of United States industry.

(c) Functions of Research and Technology Applications

It shall be the function of each Office of Research and Technology Applications--

(1) to prepare application assessments for selected research and development projects in which that laboratory is engaged and which in the opinion of the laboratory may have potential commercial applications;

(2) to provide and disseminate information on federally owned or originated products, processes, and services having potential application to State and local governments and to private industry;

(3) to cooperate with and assist the National Technical Information Service, the Federal Laboratory Consortium for Technology Transfer, and other organizations which link the research and development resources of that laboratory and the Federal Government as a whole to potential users in State and local government and private industry;

(4) to provide technical assistance to State and local government officials; and

(5) to participate, where feasible, in regional, State, and local programs designed to facilitate or stimulate the transfer of technology for the benefit of the region, State, or local jurisdiction in which the Federal laboratory is located.

Agencies which have established organizational structures outside their Federal laboratories which have as their principal purpose the transfer of federally owned or originated technology to State and local government and to the private sector may elect to perform the functions of this subsection in such organizational structures. No Office of Research and Technology Applications or other organizational structures performing the functions of this subsection shall substantially compete with similar services available in the private sector.

(d) Dissemination of technical information

(e) Establishment of Federal Laboratory Consortium for Technology Transfer

(1) There is hereby established the Federal Laboratory Consortium for Technology Transfer (hereinafter referred to as the "Consortium") which, in cooperation with Federal Laboratories and the private sector, shall--

    (A) develop and (with the consent of the Federal laboratory concerned) administer techniques, training courses, and materials concerning technology transfer to increase the awareness of Federal laboratory employees regarding the commercial potential of laboratory technology and innovations;

    (B) furnish advice and assistance requested by Federal agencies and laboratories for use in their technology transfer programs (including the planning of seminars for small business and other industry);

    (C) provide a clearinghouse for requests, received at the laboratory level, for technical assistance from States and units of local governments, businesses, industrial development organizations, not-for-profit organizations including universities, Federal agencies and laboratories, and other persons, and--

      (i) to the extent that such requests can be responded to win published information available to the National Technical Information Service, refer such requests to that Service, and

      (ii) otherwise refer these requests to the appropriate Federal Laboratories and agencies;

    (D) facilitate communication and coordination between Office of Research and Technology Applications of Federal laboratories;

    (E) utilize (with the consent of the agency involved) the expertise and services of the National Science

Foundation, the Department of Commerce, the National Aeronautics and Space Administration, and other Federal agencies, as necessary;

(F) with the consent of any Federal laboratory, facilitate the use by such laboratory of appropriate technology transfer mechanisms such as personnel exchanges and computer-based systems;

(G) with the consent of any Federal laboratory, assist such laboratory to establish programs using technical volunteers to provide technical assistance to communities related to such laboratory;

(H) facilitate communication and cooperation between Office of Research and Technology Applications of Federal laboratories and regional, State, and local technology transfer organizations;

(I) when requested, assist colleges or universities, businesses, nonprofit organizations, State or local governments, or regional organizations to establish programs to stimulate research and to encourage technology transfer in such areas as technology program development, curriculum design, long-term research planning, personnel needs projections, and productivity assessments; and

(J) seek advice in each Federal laboratory consortium region from representatives of State and local governments, large and small business, universities, and other appropriate persons on the effectiveness of the program (and any such advice shall be provided at no expense to the Government).

(2) The membership of the Consortium shall consist of the Federal laboratories described in clause (1) of subsection (b) of this section and such other laboratories as may choose to join the Consortium. The representatives to the Consortium shall include a senior staff member of each Federal laboratory which is a member of the Consortium and a senior representative appointed from each Federal agency with one or more member laboratories.

(3) The representatives to the Consortium shall elect a Chairman of the Consortium.

(4) The Director of the National Institute of Standards and Technology shall provide the Consortium, on a reimbursable basis, with administrative services, such as office space, personnel, and support services

of the Institute, as requested by the Consortium and approved by such Director.

(5) Each Federal laboratory or agency shall transfer technology directly to users or representatives of users, and shall not transfer technology directly to the Consortium. Each Federal laboratory shall conduct and transfer technology only in accordance with the practices and policies of the Federal agency which owns, leases, or otherwise uses such Federal laboratory.

(6) Not later than one year after October 20, 1986, and every year thereafter, the Chairman of the Consortium shall submit a report to the President, to the appropriate authorization and appropriation committees of both Houses of the Congress, and to each agency with respect to which a transfer of funding is made (for the fiscal year or years involved) under paragraph

(7) concerning the activities of the Consortium and the expenditures made by it under this subsection during the year for which the report is made. Such report shall include an annual independent audit of the financial statements of the Consortium, conducted in accordance with generally accepted accounting principles.

(A) Subject to subparagraph (B), an amount equal to 0.008 percent of the budget of each Federal agency from any Federal source, including related overhead, that is to be utilized by or on behalf of the

laboratories of such agency for a fiscal year referred to in subparagraph (B)(ii) shall be transferred by such agency to the National Institute of Standards and Technology at the beginning of the fiscal year involved. Amounts so transferred shall be provided by the Institute to the Consortium for the purpose of carrying out activities of the Consortium under this subsection.

(B) A transfer shall be made by any Federal agency under subparagraph (A), for any fiscal year, only if •
• •

(f) Agency reporting

(g) Functions of Secretary

(h) Repealed. Pub. L. 100-519, title II, § 212(a)(4), Oct. 24, 1988, 102 Stat. 2595

(i) Research equipment

(Pub. L. 96-480, § 11, Oct 21, 1980, 94 Stat. 2318; renumbered § 10 and amended Pub. L. 99-502, § § 3-5, 9(e)(1), Oct. 20, 1986, 100 Stat. 1787, 1789, 1791, 1797; renumbered § 11 and amended Pub. L. 100-418, title V, § § 5115(b)(2), 5122(a)(1), 5162(b), 5163(c)(1), (3), Aug. 23, 1988, 102 Stat. 1433, 1438, 1450, 1451; Pub. L. 100-519, title II, § § 201(d)(3), 212(a)(4), Oct. 24, 1988, 102 Stat. 2594, 2595; Pub. L. 100-189, div. C, title XXXI, § 3133(e), Nov. 29, 1989,

103 Stat. 1679; Pub. L. 102-245, title III, §§ 301, 303, Feb. 14, 1992, 106 Stat. 19, 20.)

§ 3710a. Cooperative research and development agreements

(a) General authority

Each Federal agency may permit the director of any of its Government-operated Federal laboratories, and to the extent provided in an agency-approved joint work statement, the director of any of its Government-owned, contractor-operated laboratories--

(1) to enter into cooperative research and development agreements on behalf of such agency (subject to subsection (c) of this section) with other Federal agencies; units of State or local government; industrial organizations (including corporations, partnerships, and limited partnerships, and industrial development organizations); public and private foundations; nonprofit organizations (including universities); or other persons (including licensees of inventions owned by the Federal agency); and

(2) to negotiate licensing agreements under section 207 of title 35, or under other authorities (in the case of a Government-owned, contractor-operated laboratory, subject to subsection (c) of this section) for inventions made or other intellectual property developed at the laboratory and other inventions or other intellectual property that may be voluntarily assigned to the Government.

(b) Enumerated authority

Under agreements entered into pursuant to subsection (a)(1) of this section, a Government-operated Federal laboratory, and, to the extent provided in an agency-approved joint work statement, a Government-owned, contractor-operated laboratory, may (subject to subsection (c) of this section)--

(1) accept, retain, and use funds, personnel, services, and property from collaborating parties and provide personnel, services, and property to collaborating parties;

(2) grant or agree to grant in advance, to a collaborating party, patent licenses or assignments, or options thereto, in any invention made in whole or in part by a laboratory employee under the agreement, retaining a nonexclusive, nontransferrable, irrevocable, paid-up license to practice the invention or have the invention practiced throughout the world by or on behalf of the Government and such other rights as the Federal laboratory deems appropriate;

(3) waive, subject to reservation by the Government of a nonexclusive, irrevocable, paid-up license to practice the invention or have the invention practiced throughout the world by or on behalf of the Government, in advance, in whole or in part, any right of ownership which the Federal Government may have to any subject invention made under the agreement by a collaborating party or employee of a collaborating party;

(4) determine rights in other intellectual property developed under an agreement entered into under subsection (a)(1) of this section; and

(5) to the extent consistent with any applicable agency requirements and standards of conduct, permit employees or former employees of the laboratory to participate in efforts to commercialize inventions they made while in the service of the United States.

A Government-owned, contractor-operated laboratory that enters into a cooperative research and development agreement under subsection (a)(1) of this section may use or obligate royalties or other income accruing to such laboratory under such agreement with respect to any invention only (i) for payments to inventors; (ii) for the purposes described in section 3710c(a)(1)(B)(i), (ii), and (iv) of this title; and (iii) for scientific research and development consistent with the research and development mission and objectives of the laboratory.

(c) Contract considerations

(1) A Federal agency may issue regulations on suitable procedures for implementing the provisions of this section; however, implementation of this section shall not be delayed until issuance of such regulations.

(2) The agency in permitting a Federal laboratory to enter into agreements under this section shall be guided by the purposes of this chapter.

    (3)(A) Any agency using the authority given it under subsection (a) of this section shall review standards of conduct for its employees for resolving potential conflicts of interest to make sure they adequately establish guidelines for situations likely to arise through the use of this authority, including but not limited to cases where present or former employees or their partners negotiate licenses or assignments of title to inventions or negotiate cooperative research and development agreements with Federal agencies (including the agency with which the employee involved is or was formerly employed).

    (B) If, in implementing subparagraph (A), an agency is unable to resolve potential conflicts of interest within its current statutory framework, it shall propose necessary statutory changes to be forwarded to its authorizing committees in Congress.

(4) The laboratory director in deciding what cooperative research and development agreements to enter into shall--

    (A) give special consideration to small business firms, and consortia involving small business firms; and

(B) give preference to business units located in the United States which agree that products embodying inventions made under the cooperative research and development agreement or produced through the use of such inventions will be manufactured substantially in the United States and, in the case of any industrial organization or other person subject to the control of a foreign company or government, as appropriate, take into consideration whether or not such foreign government permits United States agencies, organizations, or other persons to enter into cooperative research and development agreements and licensing agreements.

(5)(A) If the head of the agency or his designee desires an opportunity to disapprove or require the modification of any such agreement presented by the director of a Government-operated laboratory, the agreement shall provide a 30-days period within which such action must be taken beginning on the date the agreement is presented to him or her by the head of the laboratory concerned.

(B) In any case in which the head of an agency or his designee disapproves or requires the modification of an agreement presented by the director of a Government-operated laboratory under this section, the head of the agency or such designee shall transmit a written explanation of such disapproval or modification to the head of the laboratory concerned.

(C)(i) Except as provided in subparagraph (D), any agency which has contracted with a non-Federal entity to operate a laboratory shall review and approve, request specific modifications to, or disapprove a joint work statement that is submitted by the director of such laboratory within 90 days after such submission. In any case where an agency has requested specific modifications to a joint work statement, the agency shall approve or disapprove any resubmission of such joint work statement within 30 days after such resubmission, or 90days after the original submission, whichever occurs later. No agreement may be entered into by a Government-owned, contractor-operated laboratory under this section before both approval of the agreement under clause (iv) and approval under this clause of a joint work statement.

(ii) In any case in which an agency which has contracted with a non-Federal entity to operate a laboratory disapproves or requests the modification of a joint work statement submitted under this section, the agency shall promptly transmit a written explanation of such disapproval or modification to the director of the laboratory concerned.

(iii) Ant agency which has contracted with a non-Federal entity to operate a laboratory or laboratories shall develop and provide to such laboratory or laboratories one or more model cooperative research and development agreements, for the purposes of standardizing practices and procedures, resolving common legal issues, and enabling review of cooperative research and development agreements to be carried out in a routine and prompt manner.

(iv) An agency which has contracted with a non-Federal entity to operate a laboratory shall review each agreement under this section. Within 30 days after the presentation, by the director of the laboratory, of such agreement, the agency shall, on the basis of such review, approve or request specific modification to such agreement. Such agreement shall not take effect before approval under this clause.

(v) If an agency fails to complete a review under clause (iv) within the 30-day period specified therein, the agency shall submit to the Congress, within 10days after the end of that 30-day period, a report on the reasons for such failure. The agency shall, at the end of each successive 30-day period thereafter during which such failure continues, submit to the

Congress another report on the reasons for the continuing failure. Nothing in this clause relieves the agency of the requirement to complete a review under clause (iv).

(vi) In any case in which an agency which has contracted with a non-Federal entity to operate a laboratory requests the modification of an agreement presented under this section, the agency shall promptly transmit a written explanation of such modification to the director of the laboratory concerned.

(D)(i) Any non-Federal entity that operates a laboratory pursuant to a contract with a Federal agency shall submit to the agency any cooperative research and development agreement that the entity proposes to enter into with a small business firm and the joint work statement required with respect to that agreement.

(ii) A Federal agency that receives a proposed agreement and joint work statement under clause (i) shall review and approve, request specific modifications to, or disapprove the proposed agreement and joint work statement within 30days after such submission. No agreement may be entered into by a Government-owned, contractor-operated laboratory under this section before both approval of the agreement and approval of a joint work statement under this clause.

(iii) In any case in which an agency which has contracted with an entity referred to in clause (i) disapproves or requests the modification of a cooperative research and development agreement or joint work statement submitted under that clause, the agency shall transmit a written explanation of such disapproval or modification to the head of the laboratory concerned.

(6) Each agency shall maintain a record of all agreements entered into under this section.

(7)(A) No trade secrets or commercial or financial information that is privileged or confidential, under the meaning of section 552(b)(4) of title 5, which is obtained in the conduct of research or as a result of activities under this chapter from a non-Federal party participating in a cooperative research and development agreement shall be disclosed.

(B) The director, or in the case of a contractor-operated laboratory, the agency, for a period of up to 5 years after development of information that results from research and development activities conducted under this chapter and that would be a trade secret or commercial or financial information that is privileged or confidential if the information had been obtained from a non-Federal party participating in a cooperative research and development agreement, may provide appropriate protections against the dissemination of such information, including exemption from subchapter II of chapter 5 of title 5.

(d) Definitions

(e) Determination of laboratory missions

(f) Relationship to other laws

(g) Principles

In implementing this section, each agency which has contracted with a non-Federal entity to operate a laboratory shall be guided by the following principles:

(1) The implementation shall advance program missions at the laboratory, including any national security mission.

(2) Classified information and unclassified sensitive information protected by law, regulation, or Executive order shall be appropriately safeguarded.

(Pub. L. 96-480, § 12, as added and renumbered § 11, Pub. L. 99-502, §§ 2, 9(e)(1), Oct. 20, 1986, 100 Stat. 1785, 1797; renumbered § 12, Pub. L. 100-418, title V, § 5122(a)(1), Aug. 23, 1988, 102 Stat. 1438; amended Pub. L. 100-519, title III, § 301, Oct. 24, 1988, 102 Stat. 2597; Pub. L. 101-189, div. C, title XXXI, § 3133(a), (b), Nov. 29, 1989, 103 Stat. 1675, 1677; Pub. L. 102-25, title VII, § 705(g), Apr. 6, 1991, 105 Stat. 121; Pub. L. 102-245, title III, § 302(a), Feb. 14, 1992, 106 Stat. 20; Pub. L. 102-484, div. C, title XXXI, § 3135(a), Oct. 23, 1992, 106 Stat. 2640; Pub. L. 103-160, div. C, title XXXI, § 3160, Nov. 30, 1993, 107 Stat. 1957.)

§   3710b. Rewards for scientific, engineering, and technical personnel of Federal agencies

The head of each Federal agency that is making expenditures at a rate of more than $50,000,000 per fiscal year for research and development in its Government-operated laboratories shall use the appropriate statutory authority to develop and implement a cash awards program to reward its scientific, engineering, and technical personnel for--

(1) inventions, innovations, computer software, or other outstanding scientific or technological contributions of value to the United States due to commercial application or due to contributions to missions of the Federal agency or the Federal government, or

(2) exemplary activities that promote the domestic transfer of science and technology development within the Federal Government and result in utilization of such science and technology by American industry or business, universities, State or local governments, or other non-Federal parties.

(Pub. L. 96-480, § 13, as added and renumbered § 12, Pub. L. 99-502, §§ 6, 9(e)(1), Oct. 20, 1986, 100 Stat. 1792, 1797; renumbered § 13, Pub. L. 100-418, title V, § 5122(a)(1), Aug. 23, 1988, 102 Stat. 1438; amended Pub. L. 100-519, title III, § 302, Oct. 24, 1988, 102 Stat. 2597.)

§ 3710c. Distribution of royalties received by Federal agencies

(a) In general

(1) Except as provided in paragraphs (2) and (4), any royalties or other income received by a Federal agency from the licensing or assignments of inventions under agreements entered into by Government-operated Federal laboratories under section 3710a of this title, and inventions of Government-operated Federal laboratories licensed under section 207 of title 35, or under any other provision of law, shall be retained by the agency whose laboratory produced the invention and shall be disposed of as follows:

(A)(i) The head of the agency or his designee shall pay at least 15 percent of the royalties or other income the agency receives on account of any invention to the inventor (or co-inventors) if the inventor (or each such co-inventor) has assigned his or her rights in the invention to the United States. This clause shall take effect on October 20, 1986, unless the agency publishes a notice in the Federal Register within 90 days of October 20, 1986, indicating its election to file a Notice of Proposed Rulemaking pursuant to clause (ii).

(ii) An agency may promulgate, in accordance with section 553 of title 5, regulations providing for an alternative programs for sharing royalties with inventors under clause (i). Such regulations must--

(I) guarantee a fixed minimum payment to each

such inventor, each year that the agency receives royalties from that inventor's invention;

(II) provide a percentage royalty share to each such inventor, each year that the agency receives royalties from that inventor's invention in excess of a threshold amount;

(III) provide that total payments to all such inventor shall exceed 15 percent of total agency royalties in any given fiscal year; and

(IV) provide appropriate incentives from royalties for those laboratory employees who contribute substantially to the technical development of a licensed invention between the time of the filing of the patent application and the licensing of the invention.

(iii) An agency that has published its invention to promulgate regulations under clause (ii) may elect not to pay inventors under clause (i) until the expiration of two years after October 20, 1986, or until the date of the promulgation of such regulations, whichever is earlier. If an agency makes such an election and after two years the regulations have not been promulgated, the agency shall make payments (in accordance with clause (i)) of at least 15 percent of the royalties involved, retroactive to October 20, 1986. If promulgation of the regulations occurs within two years after October 20, 1986, payments shall be made in accordance with such regulations, retroactive to October 20, 1986. The agency shall retain its royalties until the inventor's portion is paid under either clause (i) or (ii). Such royalties shall not be transferred to the agency's Government-operated laboratories under subparagraph (B) and shall not revert to the Treasury pursuant to paragraph (2) as a result of any delay caused by rulemaking under this subparagraph.

(B) The balance of the royalties or other income shall be transferred by the agency to its Government-operated laboratories, with the majority share of the royalties or other income from any invention going to the laboratory where the invention occurred; and the funds so transferred to any such laboratory may be used or obligated by that laboratory during the fiscal year in which they are received or during the succeeding fiscal year--

    (i) for payment of expenses incidental to the administration and licensing of inventions by that laboratory or by the agency with respect to inventions which occurred at that laboratory, including the fees or other costs for the services of other agencies, persons, or organizations for invention management and licensing services;

    (ii) to reward scientific, engineering, and technical employees of that laboratory, including payments to inventors and developers of sensitive or classified technology, regardless of whether the technology has commercial applications;

    (iii) to further scientific exchange among the Government-operated laboratories of the agency; or

    (iv) for education and training of employees consistent with the research and development mission and objectives of the agency, and for other activities that increase the licensing potential for transfer of the technology of the laboratories of the agency.

And of such funds not so used or obligated by the end of the fiscal year succeeding the fiscal year in which they are received shall be paid into the Treasury of the United States.

    (2) If, after payments to inventors under paragraph (1), the royalties received by an agency in any fiscal year exceed 5 percent of the budget of the Government-operated laboratories of the agency for that year, 75 percent of such excess shall be paid to the Treasury of the United States and the remaining 25 percent may be used or obligated for the purposes described in clauses (i) through (iv) of paragraph (1)(B) during that fiscal year or the succeeding fiscal year. Any funds not so used or obligated shall be paid into the Treasury of the United States.

(3) Any payment made to an employee under this section shall be in addition to the regular pay of the employee and to any other awards made to the employee, and shall not affect the entitlement of the employee to any regular pay, annuity, or award to which he is otherwise entitled or for which he is otherwise eligible or limit the amount thereof. Any payment made to an inventor as such shall continue after the inventor leaves the laboratory or agency. Payments made under this section shall not exceed $100,000 per year to any one person, unless the President approves a larger award (with the excess over $100,000 being treated as a Presidential award under section 4504 of title 5).

(4) A Federal agency receiving royalties or other income as a result of invention management services performed for another Federal agency or laboratory under section 207 of title 35, may retain such royalties or income to the extent required to offset the payment of royalties to inventor under clause (i) of paragraph (1)(A), costs and expenses incurred under clause (i) of paragraph (1)(B), and the cost of foreign patenting and maintenance for any invention of the other agency. All royalties and other income remaining after payment of the royalties, costs, and expenses described in the preceding sentence shall be transferred to the agency for which the services were performed, for distribution in accordance with clauses (i) through (iv) of paragraph (1)(B).

(b) Certain assignments

If the invention involved was one assigned to the Federal agency--

(1) by a contractor, grantee, or participant in a cooperative agreement with the agency, or

(2) by an employee of the agency who was not working in the laboratory at the time the invention was made,

the agency unit that was involved in such assignment shall be considered to be a laboratory for purposes of this section.

(c) Reports

(Pub. L. 96-480, § 14, as added, renumbered § 13, and amended Pub. L. 99-502, §§ 7, 9(e)(1), (3), Oct. 20, 1986, 100 Stat. 1792, 1797; renumbered § 14 and amended Pub. L. 100-418, title V, §§ 5122(a)(1), 5162(a), Aug. 23, 1988, 102 Stat. 1438, 1450; Pub. L. 100-519, title III, § 303(a), Oct. 24, 1988, 102 Stat. 2597; Pub. L. 101-189, div. C, title XXXI, § 3133(c), Nov. 29, 1989, 103 Stat. 1677.)

§   3710d. Employee activities

(a) In general

If a Federal agency which has the right of ownership to an invention under this chapter does not intend to file for a patent application or otherwise to promote commercialization of such invention, the agency shall allow the inventor, if the inventor is a Government employee or former employee who made the invention during the course of employment with the Government, to retain title to the invention (subject to reservation by the Government of a nonexclusive, nontransferrable, irrevocable, paid-up license to practice the invention or have the invention practiced throughout the world by or on behalf of the Government). In addition, the agency may condition the inventor's right to title on the timely filing of a patent application in cases when the Government determines that it has or may have a need to practice the invention.

(b) "Special Government employees" defined

For purposes of this section, Federal employees include "special Government employees" as defined in section 202 of title 18.

(c) Relationship to other laws

(Pub. L. 96-480, § 15, as added and renumbered § 14 Pub. L. 99-502, §§ 8, 9(e)(1), Oct. 20, 1986, 100 Stat. 1794, 1797; renumbered § 15. Pub. L. 100-418, title V, § 5122(a)(1), Aug. 23, 1988, 102 Stat. 1438.)

§ 3711. National Technology Medal

(a) Establishment

There is hereby established a National Technology Medal, which shall be of such design and materials and bear such inscriptions as the President, on the basis of recommendations submitted by the Office of Science and Technology policy, may prescribe.

(b) Award

The President shall periodically award the medal, on the basis of recommendations received from the Secretary or on the basis of such other information and evidence as he deems appropriate, to individuals or companies, which in his judgment are deserving of special recognition by reason of their outstanding contribution to the promotion of technology or technological manpower for the improvement of the economic, environmental, social well-being of the United States.

(c) Presentation

(Pub. L. 96-480, § 16, formerly § 12, Oct. 21, 1980, 94 Stat. 2319; renumbered § 16. Pub. L. 99-502, § 2, Oct. 20, 1986, 100 Stat. 1785; renumbered § 15. Pub. L. 99-502, § 9(e)(1), Oct. 20, 1986, 100 Stat. 1797; renumbered § 16, Pub. L. 100-418, title V, § 5122(a)(1), Aug. 23, 1988, 102 Stat. 1438.)

§ 3711a. Malcolm Baldrige National Quality Award

(a) Establishment

There is hereby established the Malcolm Baldrige National Quality Award, which shall be evidenced by a medal bearing the inscriptions "Malcolm Baldrige National Quality Award" and "The Quest for Excellence". The medal shall be of such design and materials and bear such additional inscriptions as the Secretary may prescribe.

(b) Making and presentation of award

(c) Categories in which award may be given

(d) Criteria for qualification

(e) Information and technology transfer program

(f) Funding

(g) Report

(Pub. L. 96-480, § 17, formerly § 16, as added Pub. L. 100-107, § 3(a), Aug. 20, 1987, 101 Stat. 725; renumbered § 17 and amended Pub. L. 100-418, title V, § 5115(b)(2)(A), 5122(a)(1), Aug. 23, 1988, 102 Stat. 1433, 1438; Pub. L. 102-245, title III, § 305, Feb. 14, 1992, 106 Stat. 20.)

§ **3711b. Conference on advanced automotive technologies**

Not later than 180 days after December 18, 1991, the Secretary of Commerce, through the Under Secretary of Commerce for Technology, in consultation with other appropriate officials, shall convene a conference of domestic motor vehicle manufacturers, parts suppliers, Federal laboratories, and motor vehicle users to explore ways in which cooperatively they can improve the competitiveness of the United States motor vehicle industry by developing new technologies which will enhance the safety and energy savings, and lessen the environmental impact of domestic motor vehicles, and the results of such conference shall be published and then submitted to the President and to the Committees on Science, Space, and Technology and Public Works and Transportation of the House of Representatives and the Committee on Commerce, Science, and Transportation of the Senate.

(Pub. L. 96-480, § 18, as added Pub. L. 102-240, title VI, § 6019, Dec. 18, 1991, 105 Stat. 2183.)

§ **3711c. Advanced motor vehicle research award**

(a) Establishment

There is established a National Award for the Advancement of Motor Vehicle Research and Development. The award shall consist of a medal, and a cash prize if funding is available for the prize under subsection (c) of this section. The medal shall be of such design and materials and bear inscriptions as is determined by the Secretary of Transportation.

(b) Making and presenting award

(c) Funding for award

(Pub. L. 96-480, § 19, as added Pub. L. 102-240, title VI, § 6019, Dec. 18, 1991, 105 Stat. 2184.)

§ **3712. Personnel exchanges**

The Secretary and the National Science Foundation, jointly, shall establish a program to foster the exchange of scientific and technical personnel among academia, industry, and Federal laboratories. Such program shall include both (1) federally supported exchanges and (2) efforts to stimulate exchanges without Federal funding.

§ **3713. Authorization of appropriations**

§ **3714. Spending authority**

§ **3715. Use of partnership intermediaries**

(a) Authority

Subject to the approval of the Secretary or head of the affected department or agency, the Director of a Federal laboratory, or in the case of a federally funded research and development center that is not a laboratory (as defined in section 3710a(d)(2) of this title), the Federal employee who is the contract officer, may--

(1) enter into a contract or memorandum of understanding with a partnership intermediary that provides for the partnership intermediary to perform services for the Federal laboratory that increase the likelihood of success in the conduct of cooperative or joint activities of such Federal laboratory with small business firms; and

(2) pay the Federal costs of such contract or memorandum of understanding out of funds available for the support of the technology transfer function pursuant to section 3710(b) of this title.

(b) partnership progress reports

(c) "Partnership intermediary" defined

For purposes of this section, the term "partnership intermediary" means an agency of a State or local government, or a nonprofit entity owned in whole or in part by, chartered by funded in whole or in part by, or operated in whole or in part by or on behalf of a State or local government, that assists, counsels, advises, evaluates, or otherwise cooperates with small business firms that need or can make demonstrably productive use of technology-related assistance from a Federal laboratory, including State programs receiving funds under cooperative agreements entered into under section 5121(b) of the Omnibus Trade and Competitiveness Act of 1988 (15 U.S.C. 278*l* note).

(Pub. L. 96-480, § 23, formerly § 21, as added Pub. L. 101-510, div. A, title VIII, § 827(a), Nov. 5, 1990, 104 Stat. 1606; amended Pub. L. 102-190, div. A, title VIII, § 836, Dec. 5, 1991, 105 Stat. 1448; renumbered § 23, Pub. L. 102-240, title VI, § 6019, Dec. 18, 1991, 105 Stat. 2183.)

§   3716. Critical industries

(a) Identification of industries and development of plan

The Secretary shall--

(1) identify those civilian industries in the United States that are necessary to support a robust manufacturing infrastructure and critical to the economic security of the United States; and

(2) list the major research and development initiatives being undertaken, and the substantial investments being made, by the Federal Government, including its research laboratories, in each of the critical industries identified under paragraph (1).

(b) Initial report

(c) Annual updates

(Pub. L. 102-245, title V, § 504, Feb. 14, 1992, 106 Stat. 24.)

§   **3717. National Quality Council**

(a) Establishment and functions

There is established a National Quality Council (hereafter in this section referred to as the "Council"). The functions of the Council shall be--

  (1) to establish national goals and priorities for Quality performance in business, education, government, and all other sectors of the Nation;

  (2) to encourage and support the voluntary adoption of these goals and priorities by companies, unions, professional and business associations, coalition groups, and units of government, as well as private and nonprofit organizations;

  (3) to arouse and maintain the interest of the people of the United States in Quality performance, and to encourage the adoption and institution of Quality performance methods by all corporations, government agencies, and other organizations; and

  (4) to conduct a White House Conference on Quality Performance in the American Workplace that would bring together in a single forum national leaders in business, labor, education, professional societies, the media, government, and politics to address Quality performance as a means of improving United States competitiveness.

(b) Membership

(c) Terms

(d) Chairman and Vice Chairman

(e) Executive Director and employees

(f) Funding

(g) Contributions

(h) Annual report

(Pub. L. 102-245, title V, § 507, Feb. 14, 1992, 106 Stat. 27.)

APPENDIX B

The Bayh-Dole Act of 1980 (P. L. 96–517) as Amended

CHAPTER 18--PATENT RIGHTS IN INVENTIONS MADE WITH FEDERAL ASSISTANCE

§ 200. Policy and objective

It is the policy and objective of the Congress to use the patent system to promote the utilization of inventions arising from federally supported research or development; to encourage maximum participation of small business firms in federally supported research and development efforts; to promote collaboration between commercial concerns and nonprofit organizations, including universities; to ensure that inventions made by nonprofit organizations and small business firms are used in a manner to promote free competition and enterprises; to promote the commercialization and public availability of inventions made in the United States by United States industry and labor; to ensure that the Government obtains sufficient rights in federally supported inventions to meet the needs of the Government and protect the public against nonuse or unreasonable use of inventions; and to minimize the costs of administering policies in this area.

(Added Pub. L. 96-517, § 6(a), Dec. 12, 1980, 94 Stat. 3018.)

§ 201. Definitions

As used in this chapter--

(a) The term "Federal agency" means any executive agency as defined in section 105 of title 5, United States Code, and the military departments as defined by section 102 of title 5, United States Code.

(b) The term "funding agreement" means any contract, grant, or cooperative agreement entered into between any Federal agency other than the Tennessee Valley Authority, and any contractor for the performance of experimental, developmental, or research work funded in whole or in part by the Federal Government. Such term includes any assignment, substitution of parties, or subcontract of any type entered into for the performance of experimental, developmental, or research work under a funding agreement as herein defined.

(c) The term "contractor" means any person, small business firm, or nonprofit organization that is party to a funding agreement.

(d) The term "invention" means any invention or discovery which is or may be patentable or otherwise protectable under this title or any novel variety of plant which is or may be protectable under the Plant Variety Protection Act (7 U.S.C. 2321 et seq.).

(e) The term "subject invention" means any invention of the contractor conceived or first actually reduced to practice in the performance of work under a funding agreement: *Provided*, That in the case of a variety of plant, the date of determination (as defined in section 41(d) of the Plant Variety Protection Act (7 U.S.C. 2401(d))) must also occur during the period of contract performance.

(f) The term "practical application" means to manufacture in the case of a composition or product, to practice in the case of a process or method, or to operate in the case of a machine or system; and, in each case, under such conditions as to establish that the invention is being utilized and that its benefits are to the extent permitted by law or Government regulations available to the public on reasonable terms.

(g) The term "made" when used in relation to any invention means the conception or first actual reduction to practice of such invention.

(h) The term "small business firm" means a small business concern as defined at section 2 of Public Law 85-536 (15 U.S.C. 632) and implementing regulations of the Administrator of the Small Business Administration.

(i) The term "nonprofit organization" means universities and other institutions of higher education or an organization of the type described in section 501(c)(3) of the Internal Revenue Code of 1986 (26 U.S.C. 501(c)) and exempt from taxation under section 501(a) of the Internal Revenue Code (26 U.S.C. 501(a)) or any nonprofit scientific or educational organization qualified under a State nonprofit organization statute.

(Added Pub. L. 96-517, § 6(a), Dec. 12, 1980, 94 Stat. 3019; amended Pub. L. 98-620, title V, § 501(1), (2), Nov. 8, 1984, 98 Stat. 3364; Pub. L. 99-514, § 2, Oct. 22, 1986, 100 Stat. 2095.)

§   202. Disposition of rights

(a) Each nonprofit organization or small business firm may, within a reasonable time after disclosure as required by paragraph (c)(1) of this section, elect to retain title to any subject invention: *Provided, however,* That a funding agreement may provide otherwise (i) when the contractor is not located in the United States or does not have a place of business located in the United States or is subject to the control of a foreign government, (ii) in exceptional circumstances when it is determined by the agency that restriction or elimination of the right to retain title to any subject invention will better promote the policy and objectives of this chapter (iii) when it

is determined by a Government authority which is authorized by statute or Executive order to conduct foreign intelligence or counter-intelligence activities that the restriction or elimination of the right to retain title to any subject invention is necessary to protect the security of such activities or, (iv) when the funding agreement includes the operation of a Government-owned, contractor-operated facility of the Department of Energy primarily dedicated to that Department's naval nuclear propulsion or weapons related programs and all funding agreement limitations under this subparagraph on the contractor's right to elect title to a subject invention are limited to inventions occurring under the above two programs of the Department of Energy. The rights of the nonprofit organization or small business firm shall be subject to the provisions of paragraph (c) of this section and the other provisions of this chapter.

(b)(1) The rights of the Government under subsection (a) shall not be exercised by a Federal agency unless it first determines that at least one of the conditions identified in clauses (i) through (iv) of subsection (a) exists. Except in the case of Subsection (a)(iii), the agency shall file with the Secretary of Commerce, within thirty days after the award of the applicable funding agreement, a copy of such determination. In the case of a determination under subsection (a)(ii), the statement shall include an analysis justifying the determination. In the case of determinations applicable to funding agreements with small business firms, copies shall also be sent to the Chief Counsel for Advocacy of the Small Business Administration. If the Secretary of Commerce believes that any individual determination or pattern of determinations is contrary to the policies and objectives of this chapter or otherwise not in conformance with this chapter, the Secretary shall so advise the head of the agency concerned and the Administrator of the Office of Federal Procurement Policy, and recommend corrective actions.

(2) Whenever the Administrator of the Office of Federal Procurement Policy has determined that one or more Federal agencies are utilizing the authority of clause (i) or (ii) of subsection (a) of this section in a manner that is contrary to the policies and objectives of this chapter, the Administrator is authorized to issue regulations describing classes of situations in which agencies may not exercise the authorities of those clauses.

(3) At least once every 5 years, the Comptroller General shall transmit a report to the Committees on the Judiciary of the Senate and House of Representatives on the manner in which this chapter is being implemented by the agencies and on such other aspects of Government patent policies and practices with respect to federally funded inventions as the Comptroller General believes appropriate.

(4) If the contractor believes that a determination is contrary to the policies and objectives of this chapter or constitutes an abuse of discretion by the agency, the determination shall be subject to the last paragraph of section 203(2).

(c) Each funding agreement with a small business firm or nonprofit organization shall contain appropriate provisions to effectuate the following:

(1) That the contractor disclose each subject invention to the Federal agency within a reasonable time after it becomes known to contractor personnel responsible for the administration of patent matters, and that the Federal Government may receive title to any subject invention not disclosed to it within such time.

(2) That the contractor make a written election within two years after disclosure to the Federal agency (or such additional time as may be approved by the Federal agency) whether the contractor will retain title to a subject invention: *Provided*, That in any case where publication, on sale, or public use, has initiated the one year statutory period in which valid patent protection can still be obtained in the United States, the period for election may be shortened by the Federal agency to a date that is not more than sixty days prior to the end of the statutory period: *And provided further*, That the Federal Government may receive title to any subject invention in which the contractor does not elect to retain rights or fails to elect rights within such times.

(3) That a contractor electing rights in a subject invention agrees to file a patent application prior to any statutory bar date that may occur under this title due to publication, on sale, or public use, and shall thereafter file corresponding patent applications in other countries in which it wishes to retain title within reasonable times, and that

the Federal Government may receive title to any subject inventions in the Unites State or other countries in which the contractor has not filed patent applications on the subject invention within such times.

(4) With respect to any invention in which the contractor elects rights, the Federal agency shall have a nonexclusive, nontransferrable, irrevocable, paid-up license to practice or have practiced for or on behalf of the United States any subject inventions throughout the world: *Provided*, That the funding agreement may provide for such additional rights, including the right to assign or have assigned foreign patent rights in the subject invention, as are determined by the agency as necessary for meeting the obligations of the United States under any treaty, international agreement, arrangement of cooperation, memorandum of understanding, or similar arrangement, including military agreement relating to weapons development and production.

(5) The right of the Federal agency to require periodic reporting on the utilization or efforts at obtaining utilization that are being made by the contractor or his licensees or assignees: *Provided*, That any such information as well as any information on utilization or efforts at obtaining utilization obtained as part of a proceeding under section 203 of this chapter shall be treated by the Federal agency as commercial and financial information obtained from a person and privileged and confidential and not subject to disclosure under section 552 of title 5 of the United States Code.

(6) An obligation on the part of the contractor, in the event a United States patent application is filed by or on its behalf or by any assignee of the contractor, to include within the specification of such application and any patent issuing thereon, a statement specifying that the invention was made with Government support and that the Government has certain rights in the invention.

(7) In the case of a nonprofit organization, (A) a prohibition upon the assignment of rights to a subject invention in the United States without the approval of the Federal agency, except where such an assignment is made to an organization which has as one of its primary functions the management of inventions (provided that such assignee shall be subject to the same provisions as the contractor); (B) a requirement that the contractor share royalties with the inventor; (C) except with respect to a funding agreement for the operation of a Government-owned-contractor-operated facility, a requirement that the balance of any royalties or income earned by the contractor with

respect to subject inventions, after payment of expenses (including payments to inventors) incidental to the administration of subject inventions, be utilized for the support of scientific research or education; (D) a requirement that, except where it proves infeasible after a reasonable inquiry, in the licensing of subject inventions shall be given to small business firms; and (E) with respect to a funding agreement for the operation of a Government-owned-contractor-operated facility, requirements (i) that after payment of patenting costs, licensing costs, payments to inventors, and other expenses incidental to the administration of subject inventions, 100 percent of the balance of any royalties or income earned and retained by the contractor during any fiscal year up to an amount equal to 5 percent of the annual budget of the facility, shall be used by the contractor for scientific research, development, and education consistent with the research and development mission and objectives of the facility, including activities that increase the licensing potential of other inventions of the facility; provided that if said balance exceeds 5 percent of the annual budget of the facility, that 75 percent of such excess shall be paid to the Treasury of the United States and the remaining 25 percent shall be used for the same purpose as described above in this clause (D); and (ii) that, to the extent it provides the most effective technology transfer, the licensing of subject inventions shall be administered by contractor employees on location at the facility.

(8)   The requirements of sections 203 and 204 of this chapter.

(d) If a contractor does not elect to retain title to a subject invention in cases subject to this section, the Federal agency may consider and after consultation with the contractor grant requests for retention of rights by the inventor subject to the provisions of this Act and regulations promulgated hereunder.

(e) In any case where a Federal employee is a coinventor of any invention made under a funding agreement with a nonprofit organization or small business firm, the Federal agency employing such coinventor is authorized to transfer or assign whatever rights it may acquire in the subject invention from its employee to the contractor subject to the conditions set forth in this chapter.

(f)(1) No funding agreement with a small business firm or nonprofit organization shall contain a provision allowing a Federal agency to require the licensing to third parties of inventions owned by the contractor that are not subject inventions unless such provision has been approved by the head of the agency and a written justification has been signed by the head of the agency. Any such provision shall clearly state whether the licensing may be required in connection with the practice of a subject invention, a specifically identified work object, or both. The head of the agency may not delegate the authority to approve provisions or sign justifications required by this paragraph.

(2) A Federal agency shall not require the licensing of third parties under any such provisions unless the head of the agency determines that the use of the invention by others is necessary for the practice of a subject invention or for the use of a work object of the funding agreement and that such action is necessary to achieve the practical application of the subject invention or work object. Any such determination shall be on the record after an opportunity for an agency hearing. Any action commenced for judicial review of such determination shall be brought within sixty days after notification of such determination.

(Added Pub. L. 96-517, § 6(a), Dec. 12, 1980, 94 Stat. 3020; amended Pub. L. 98-620, title V, § 501(3)-(8), Nov. 8, 1984, 98 Stat. 3364-3366; Pub. L. 102-204, § 10, Dec. 10, 1991, 105 Stat. 1641.)

§   203. March-in rights

(1) With respect to any subject invention in which a small business firm or nonprofit organization has acquires title under this chapter, the Federal agency under whose funding agreement the subject invention was made shall have the right, in accordance with such procedures as are provided in regulations promulgated hereunder to require the contractor, an assignee or exclusive licensee of a subject invention to grant a nonexclusive, partially exclusive, or exclusive license in any field of use to a responsible applicant or applicants, upon terms that are reasonable under the circumstances, and if the contractor, assignee, or exclusive licensee refuses such request, to grant

such a license itself, if the Federal agency determines that such--

(a) action is necessary because the contractor or assignee has not taken, or is not expected to take within a reasonable time, effective steps to achieve practical application of the subject invention in such field of use;

(b) action is necessary to alleviate health or safety needs which are not reasonably satisfied by the contractor, assignee, or their licensees;

(c) action is necessary to meet requirements for public use specified by Federal regulations and such requirements are not reasonably satisfied by the contractor, assignee, or licensee; or

(d) action is necessary because the agreement required by section 204 has not been obtained or waived or because a licensee of the exclusive right to use or sell any subject invention in the United States is in breach of its agreement obtained pursuant to section 204.

(2) A determination pursuant to this section or section 202(b)(4) shall not be subject to the Contract Disputes Act (41 U.S.C. § 601 et seq.). An administrative appeals procedure shall be established by regulations promulgated in accordance with section 206. Additionally, any contractor, inventor, assignee, or exclusive licensee adversely affected by a determination under this section may, at any time within sixty days after the determination is issued, file a petition in the United States Court of Federal Claims, which shall have jurisdiction to determine the appeal on the record and to affirm, reverse, remand or modify, as appropriate, the determination of the Federal agency. In cases described in paragraphs (a) and (c), the agency's determination shall be held in abeyance pending the

exhaustion of appeals or petitions filed under the preceding sentence.

(Added Pub. L. 96-517, § 6(a), Dec. 12, 1980, 94 Stat. 3022; amended Pub. L. 98-620, title V, § 501 (9), Nov. 8, 1984, 98 Stat. 3367; Pub. L. 102-572, title IX, § 902(b)(1), Oct. 29, 1992, 106 Stat. 4516.)

§ 204. Preference for United States Industry

Notwithstanding any other provision of this chapter, no small business firm or nonprofit organization which receives title to any subject invention and no assignee of any such small business firm or nonprofit organization shall grant to any person the exclusive right to use or sell any subject invention in the United States unless such person agrees that any product embodying the subject invention or produced through the use of the subject invention will be manufactured substantially in the United States. However, in individual cases, the requirement for such an agreement may be waived by the Federal agency under whose funding agreement the invention was made upon a showing by the small business firm, nonprofit organization, or assignee that reasonable but unsuccessful efforts have been made to grant licenses on similar terms to potential licensees that would be likely to manufacture substantially in the United States or that under the circumstances domestic manufacture is not commercially feasible.

(Added Pub. L. 96-517, § 6(a), Dec. 12, 1980, 94 Stat. 3023.)

§ 205. Confidentiality

Federal agencies are authorized to withhold from disclosure to the public information disclosing any invention in which the Federal Government owns or may own a right, title, or interest (including a nonexclusive license) for a reasonable time in order for a patent application to be filed. Furthermore, Federal agencies shall not be required to release copies of any document which is part of an application for patent filed with the United States Patent and Trademark Office or with any foreign patent office.

(Added Pub. L. 96-517, § 6(a), Dec. 12, 1980, 94 Stat. 3023.)

§ 206. Uniform clauses and regulations

The Secretary of Commerce may issue regulations which may be made applicable to Federal agencies implementing the provisions of sections 202 through 204 of this chapter and shall establish standard funding agreement provisions required under this chapter. The regulations and the standard funding agreement shall be subject to public comment before their issuance.

(Added Pub. L. 96-517, § 6(a), Dec. 12, 1980, 94 Stat. 3023; amended Pub. L. 98-620, title V, § 501(10), Nov. 8, 1984, 98 Stat. 3367.)

§ 207. Domestic and foreign protection of federally owned inventions

(a) Each Federal agency is authorized to--
   (1) apply for, obtain, and maintain patents or other forms of protection in the United States and in foreign countries on inventions in

which the Federal Government owns a right, title, or interest;

(2) grant nonexclusive, exclusive, or partially exclusive licenses under federally owned patent applications, patents, or other forms of protection obtained, royalty-free or for royalties or other consideration, and on such terms and conditions, including the grant to the licensee of the right of enforcement pursuant to the provisions of chapter 29 of this title as determined appropriate in the public interest;

(3) undertake all other suitable and necessary steps to protect and administer rights to federally owned inventions on behalf of the Federal Government either directly or through contract; and

(4) transfer custody and administration, in whole or in part, to another Federal agency, of the right, title, or interest in any federally owned invention.

(b) For the purpose of assuring the effective management of Government-owned inventions, the Secretary of Commerce is authorized to--

(1) assist Federal agency efforts to promote the licensing and utilization of Government-owned inventions;

(2) assist Federal agencies in seeking protection and maintaining inventions in foreign countries, including the payment of fees and costs connected therewith; and

(3) consult with and advise Federal agencies as to areas of science and technology research and development with potential for commercial utilization.

(Added Pub. L. 96-517, § 6(a), Dec. 12, 1980, 94 Stat. 3023; amended Pub. L. 98-620, title V, § 501(11), Nov. 8, 1984, 98 Stat. 3367.)

§ 208. Regulations governing Federal licensing

The Secretary of Commerce is authorized to promulgate regulations specifying the terms and conditions upon which any federally owned by invention other than inventions owned by the Tennessee Valley Authority, may be licensed on a nonexclusive, partially exclusive, or exclusive basis.

(Added Pub. L. 96-517, § 6(a), Dec. 12, 1980, 94 Stat. 3024; amended Pub. L. 98-620, title V, § 501(12), Nov. 8, 1984, 98 Stat. 3367.)

§ 209. Restrictions on licensing of federally owned inventions

(a) No Federal agency shall grant any license under a patent or patent application on a federally owned invention unless the person requesting the license has supplied the agency with a plan for development and/or marketing of the invention, except that any such plan may be treated by the Federal agency as commercial and financial information obtained from a person and privileged and confidential and not subject to disclosure under section 552 of title 5 of the United States Code.

(b) A Federal agency shall normally grant the right to use or sell any federally owned invention in the

United States only to a licensee that agrees that any products embodying the invention or produced through the use of the invention will be manufactured substantially in the United States.

(c)(1) Each Federal agency may grant exclusive or partially exclusive licenses in any invention covered by a federally owned domestic patent or patent application only if, after public notice and opportunity for filing written objections, it is determined that--

(A) the interests of the Federal Government and the public will best be served by the proposed license, in view of the applicant's intentions, plans, and ability to bring the invention to practical application or otherwise promote the invention's utilization by the public;
(B) the desired practical application has not been achieved, or is not likely expeditiously to be achieved, under any nonexclusive license which has been granted, or which may be granted, on the invention;
(C) exclusive or partially exclusive licensing is a reasonable and necessary incentive to call forth the investment of risk capital and expenditures to bring the invention to practical application or otherwise promote the invention's utilization by the public; and

(D) the proposed terms and scope of exclusivity are not greater than reasonably necessary to provide the incentive for bringing the invention to practical application or otherwise promote the invention's utilization by the public.

(2) A Federal agency shall not grant such exclusive or partially exclusive license under paragraph (1) of this subsection if it determines that the grant of such license will tend substantially to lessen competition or result in undue concentration in any section of the country in any line of commerce to which the technology to be licensed relates, or to create or maintain other situations inconsistent with the antitrust laws.

(3) First preference in the exclusive or partially exclusive licensing of federally owned inventions shall go to small business firms submitting plans that are determined by the agency to be within the capabilities of the firms and equally likely, if executed, to bring the invention to practical application as any plans submitted by applicants that are not small business firms.

(d) After consideration of whether the interests of the Federal Government or United States industry in foreign commerce will be enhanced, any Federal agency may grant exclusive or partially exclusive licenses in any invention covered by a foreign patent application or patent, after public notice and opportunity for filing written objections, except that a Federal agency shall not grant such exclusive or partially exclusive license if it determines that the grant of such license will tend substantially to lessen competition or result in undue concentration in any section of the

United States in any line of commerce to which the technology to be licensed relates, or to create or maintain other situations inconsistent with antitrust laws.

(e) The Federal agency shall maintain a record of determinations to grant exclusive or partially exclusive licenses.

(f) Any grant of a license shall contain such terms and conditions as the Federal agency determines appropriate for the protection of the interest of the Federal Government and the public, including provisions for the following:

> (1) periodic reporting on the utilization or efforts at obtaining utilization that are being made by the licensee with particular reference to the plan submitted: *Provided*, That any such information may be treated by the Federal agency as commercial and financial information obtained from a person and privileged and confidential and not subject to disclosure under section 552 of title 5 of the United States Code;
>
> (2) the right of the Federal agency to terminate such license in whole or in part if it determines that the licensee is not executing the plan submitted with its request for a license and the licensee cannot otherwise demonstrate to the satisfaction of the Federal agency that it has taken or can be expected to take within a reasonable time, effective steps to achieve practical application of the invention;

> (3) the right of the Federal agency to terminate such license in whole or in part if the licensee is in breach of an agreement obtained pursuant to paragraph (b) of this section; and
>
> (4) the right of the Federal agency to terminate the license in whole or in part if the agency determines that such action is necessary to meet requirements for public use specified by Federal regulations issued after the date of the license and such requirements are not reasonably satisfied by the licensee.

(Added Pub. L. 96-517, § 6(a), Dec. 12, 1980, 94 Stat. 3024.)

§   210. Precedence of chapter

The Cooperative Research Act of 1984 (P. L. 96–517) as Amended

CHAPTER 69--COOPERATIVE RESEARCH

§ 4301. Definitions

(a) For purposes of this chapter:

  (1) The term "antitrust laws" has the meaning given it in subsection (a) of section 12 of this title, except that such term includes section 45 of this title to the extent that such section 45 of this title applies to unfair methods of competition.

  (2) The term "Attorney General" means the Attorney General of the United States.

  (3) The term "Commission" means the Federal Trade Commission.

  (4) The term "person" has the meaning given to it in subsection (a) of section 12 of this title.

  (5) The term "State" has the meaning given to it in section 15g(2) of this title.

  (6) The term "joint venture" means any group of activities, including attempting to make, making, or performing a contract, by two or more persons for the purpose of--

    (A) theoretical analysis, experimentation or systematic study of phenomena or observable facts,

    (B) the development or testing of basic engineering techniques,

    (C) the extension of investigative findings or theory of a scientific or technical nature into practical application for experimental and demonstration purposes, including the experimental production and testing of models, prototypes, equipment, materials, and processes,

    (D) the production of a product, process, or service,

    (E) the testing in connection with the production of a product, process, or service by such venture,

    (F) the collection, exchange, and analysis of research or production information, or

    (G) any combination of the purposes specified in subparagraphs (A), (B), (C), (D), (E), and (F),

and may include the establishment and operation of facilities for the conducting of such venture, the conducting of such venture on a protected and proprietary basis, and the prosecuting of applications for patents and the granting of licenses for the results of such venture, but does not include any activity specified in subsection (b) of this section.

(b) The term "joint venture" excludes the following activities involving two or more persons:

(1) exchanging information among competitors relating to costs, sales, profitability, prices, marketing, or distribution of any product, process, or service if such information is not reasonably required to carry out the purpose of such venture,

(2) entering into any agreement or engaging in any other conduct restricting, requiring, or otherwise involving the marketing, distribution, or provision by any person who is a party to such venture of any product, process, or service, other than--

(A) the distribution among the parties to such venture, in accordance with such venture, of a product, process, or service

produced by such venture,

(B) the marketing of proprietary information, such as patents and trade secrets, developed through such venture formed under a written agreement entered into before June 10, 1993, or

(C) the licensing, conveying, or transferring of intellectual property, such as patents and trade secrets, developed through such venture formed under a written agreement entered into on or after June 10, 1993,

(3) entering into any agreement or engaging in any other conduct--

(A) to restrict or require the sale, licensing, or sharing of inventions, developments, products, processes, or services not developed through, or produced by, such venture, or

(B) to restrict or require participation by any person who is a party to such venture in other research and

development
activities,
that is not reasonably
required to prevent
misappropriation of
proprietary information
contributed by any person
who is a party to such
venture or of the results of
such venture,

(4) entering into any
agreement or engaging in
any other conduct
allocating a market with a
competitor,

(5) exchanging information
among competitors
relating to production
(other than production by
such venture) of a
product, process, or
service if such
information is not
reasonably required to
carry out the purpose of
such venture,

(6) entering into any
agreement or engaging in
any other conduct
restricting, requiring, or
otherwise involving the
production (other than the
production by such
venture) of a product,
process, or service,

(7) using existing facilities
for the production of a
product, process, or
service by such venture
unless such use involves
the production of a new
product or technology,
and

(8) except as provided in
paragraphs (2), (3), and
(6), entering into any
agreement or engaging in
an'' other conduct to
re strict or require
participation by any
person who is a party to
such venture, in any
unilateral or joint activity
that is not reasonably
required to carry out the
purpose of such venture.

(Pub. L. 98-462, § 2, Oct. 11,
1984, 98 Stat. 1815; Pub. L. 103-
42, § 3(b), (c), June 10, 1993, 107
Stat. 117, 118.)

COOPERATIVE RESEARCH AND PRODUCTION; CONGRESSIONAL STATEMENT OF FINDINGS AND PURPOSE

Section 2 of Pub. L. 103-42
provided that:
    "(a) **FINDINGS.**--The
Congress finds that--
    "(1) technological innovation
        and its profitable
        commercialization are
        critical components of the
        ability of the United States
        to raise the living
        standards of Americans
        and to compete in world
        markets;
    "(2) cooperative arrangements
        among nonaffiliated
        business in the private
        sector are often essential
        for successful

technological innovation; and

"(3) the antitrust laws may have been mistakenly perceived to inhibit procompetitive cooperation innovation arrangements, and so clarification serves a useful purpose in helping to promote such arrangements.

"(b) **PURPOSE.**--It is the purpose of this Act to promote innovation, facilitate trade, and strengthen the competitiveness of the United States in world markets by clarifying the applicability of the rule of reason standard and establishing a procedure under which businesses may notify the Department of Justice and Federal Trade Commission of their cooperative ventures and thereby qualify for a single-damages limitation on civil antitrust liability."

§   4302. Rule of reason standard

In any action under the antitrust laws, or under any State law similar to the antitrust laws, the conduct of any person in making or performing a contract to carry out a joint venture shall not be deemed illegal per se; such conduct shall be judged on the basis of its reasonableness, taking into account all relevant factors affecting competition including, but not limited to, effects on competition in properly defined,

relevant research, development, product, process, and service markets. For the purpose of determining a properly defined, relevant market, worldwide capacity shall be considered to the extent that it may be appropriate in the circumstances.

(Pub. L. 98-462, § 3, Oct. 11, 1984, 98 Stat. 1816; Pub. L. 103-42, § 3(d), June 10, 1993, 107 Stat. 119.)

§   4303. Limitation on recovery

(a) **Amount recoverable--** Notwithstanding section 15 of this title and in lieu of the relief specified in such section, any person who is entitled to recovery on a claim under such section shall recover the actual damages sustained by such person, interest calculated at the rate specified in section 1961 of title 28 on such actual damages as specified in subsection (d) of this section, and the cost of suit attributable to such claim, including a reasonable attorney's fee pursuant to section 4304 of this title if such claim--

(1) results from conduct that is within the scope of a notification that has been filed under section 4305(a) of this title for a joint venture, and

(2) is filed after such notification becomes effective pursuant to section 4305(c) of this title.

(b) **Recovered by States--**
Notwithstanding section 15c of this title, and in lieu of the relief specified in such section, any State that is entitled to monetary relief on a claim under such section shall recover the total damage sustained as described in subsection (a)(1) of such section, interest calculated at the rate specified in section 1961 of title 28 on such total damage as specified in subsection (d) of this section, and the cost of suit attributable to such claim, including a reasonable attorney's fee pursuant to section 15c of this title if such claim--

(1) results from conduct that is within the scope of a notification that has been filed under section 4305(a) of this title for a joint venture, and

(2) is filed after such notification becomes effective pursuant to section 4305(c) of this title.

(c) **Conduct similar under State law--**Notwithstanding any provision of any State law providing damages for conduct similar to that forbidden by the antitrust laws, any person who is entitled to recovery on a claim under such provision shall not recover in excess of the actual damages sustained by such person, interest calculated at the rate specified in section 1961 of title 28 on such actual damages as specified in subsection (d) of this section, and the cost of suit attributable to such claim,

including a reasonable attorney's fee pursuant to section 4304 of this title if such claim--

(1) results from conduct that is within the scope of a notification that has been filed under section 4305(a) of this title for a joint venture, and

(2) is filed after notification has become effective pursuant to section 4305(c) of this title.

(d) **Interest--**Interest shall be awarded on the damages involved for the period beginning on the earliest date for which injury can be established and ending on the date of judgment, unless the court finds that the award of all or part of such interest is unjust in the circumstances.

(e) **Applicability--**This section shall be applicable only if the challenged conduct of a person defending against a claim is not in violation of any decree or order, entered or issued after October 11, 1984, in any case or proceeding under the antitrust laws or any State law similar to the antitrust laws challenging such conduct as part of a joint venture.

(Pub. L. 98-462, § 4, Oct. 11, 1984, 98 Stat. 1816; Pub. L. 103-42, § 3(e)(1), June 10, 1993, 107 Stat. 119.)

§   **4304. Award of costs, including attorney's fees, to substantially prevailing party; offset**

(Pub. L. 98-462, § 5, Oct. 11, 1984, 98 Stat. 1817; Pub. L. 103-42, § 3(e)(2), June 10, 1993, 107 Stat. 119.)

§   4305. Disclosure of joint venture

(a) **Written notifications; filing**--Any party to a joint venture, acting on such venture's behalf, may, not later than 90 days after entering into a written agreement to form such venture or not later than 90 days after October 11, 1984, whichever is later, file simultaneously with the Attorney General and the Commission a written notification disclosing--

(1) the identities of the parties to such venture,

(2)   the nature and objectives of such venture, and

(3) if a purpose of such venture is the production of a product, process, or service, as referred to in section 4301(a)(6)(D) of this title, the identity and nationality of any person who is a party to such venture, or who controls any party to such venture whether separately or with one or more other persons acting as a group for the purpose of controlling such party.

Any party to such venture, acting on such venture's behalf, may file additional disclosure notifications pursuant to this section as are appropriate to extend the protections of section 4303 of this title, such venture shall, not later than 90 days after a change in its membership, file simultaneously with the Attorney General and the Commission a written notification disclosing such change.

(b) **Publication; Federal Register; notice**--Except as provided in subsection (e) of this section, not later than 30 days after receiving a notification filed under subsection (a) of this section, the Attorney General or the Commission shall publish in the Federal Register a notice with respect to such venture that identifies the parties to such venture and that describes in general terms the area of planned activity of such venture. Prior to its publication, the contents of such notice shall be made available to the parties to such venture.

(c) **Effects of notice**--If with respect to a notification filed under subsection (a) of this section, notice is published in the Federal register, then such notification shall operate to convey the protections of section 4303 of this title as of the earlier of--

(1) the date of publication of notice under subsection (b) of this section, or

(2) if such notice is not so published within the time required by subsection (b) of this section, after the expiration of the 30-day period beginning on the date the Attorney General or the Commission receives the applicable information described in

subsection (a) of this section.

(d) **Exemption; disclosure; information**--Except with respect to the information published pursuant to subsection (b) of this section--

(1) all information and documentary material submitted as part of a notification filed pursuant to this section, and

(2) all other information obtained by the Attorney General or the Commission in the course of any investigation, administrative proceeding, or case, with respect to a potential violation of the antitrust laws by the joint venture with respect to which such notification was filed,

shall be exempt from disclosure under section 552 of title 5, and shall not be made publicly available by any agency of the United States to which such section applies except in a judicial or administrative proceeding in which such information and material is subject to any protective order.

(e) **Withdrawal of notification**

(f) **Judicial review; inapplicable with respect to notifications**

(g) **Admissibility into evidence; disclosure of conduct; publication of notice; supporting or answering claims under antitrust laws**

(Pub. L. 98-462, § 6, Oct. 11, 1984, 98 Stat. 1818; Pub. L. 103-42, § 3(f), June 10, 1993, 107 Stat. 119.)

REPORTS ON JOINT VENTURES AND UNITED STATES COMPETITIVENESS

(a) **Purpose**
(b) **Annual Report By The Attorney General**
(c) **Triennial Report By The Attorney General**
(d) **Review Of Antitrust Treatment Under Foreign Laws**

§ **4306. Application of section 4303 protections to production of products, processes, and services**

Notwithstanding sections 4303 and 4305 of this title the protections of section 4303 of this title shall not apply with respect to a joint venture's production of a product, process, or service, as referred to in section 4301(a)(6)(D) of this title unless--

(1) the principle facilities for such production are located in the United States or its territories, and

(2) each person who controls any party to such venture (including such party itself) is a United States person, or a foreign person from a country whose law accords

antitrust treatment no less
favorable to United States
persons than to such
country's domestic
persons with respect to
participation in joint
ventures for production.

(Pub. L. 98-462, § 7, as added Pub.
L. 403-42, § 3(g), June 10, 1993,
107 Stat. 119.)

Bibliography

CHAPTER 1

Bozeman, B., & Crow, M. (1990). The environment of U.S. R&D laboratories: Political and market influences. *Policy Sciences, 23*, 25–56.

Bozeman, B., Papadakis, M., & Coker, K. (1995). *Industry perspectives on commercial interactions with federal laboratories.* Atlanta: Georgia Institute of Technology, School of Public Policy.

Bush, V. (1945). *Science—The endless frontier.* Washington, DC: U.S. Government Printing Office.

Carnegie Commission. (1992). *Science, technology, and the states in America's third century.* New York: The Carnegie Commission on Science, Technology, and Government.

Cohen, W., Florida, R., & Goe, W. R. (1994). *University industry research centers in the United States.* Unpublished paper, Carnegie Mellon University, Center for Economic Development, H. John Heinz III School of Public Policy and Management.

Council on Competitiveness. (1996). *Endless frontier, limited resources: U.S. R&D policy for competitiveness* [On-line]. Available: http://nii.nist.gov/pubs/coc_rd/rd_cover.html

Fusfeld, H. I. (1994). *Industry's future.* Washington, DC: American Chemical Society, National Science Board.

Lederman, L. (1994). A comparative analysis of civilian technology strategies among some nations: France, the Federal Republic of Germany, Japan, the United Kingdom, and the United States. *Policy Studies Journal, 22* (2), 279–295.

National Science Board. (1996). *Science and engineering indicators—1996.* Washington, DC: U.S. Government Printing Office, 1996 (NSB 96–21).

Paget, K. M. (1990). State government–university cooperation. In J. Schmandt & R.

Wilson (Eds.), *Growth policy in the age of high technology* (pp. 344–380). Boston: Unwin Hyman.

Phelps, P. B., & Brockman, P. R. (1992). *Science and technology programs in the states.* Alexandria, VA: Advanced Development Distribution.

Porter, M. E. (1990). *The competitive advantage of nations.* New York: The Free Press.

Senge, P. M. (1990). *The fifth discipline: The art and practice of the learning organization.* New York: Doubleday.

U.S. Congress. (1980a). Patent and Trademark Laws, Legislative History PL 96–517. *United States Code, Congressional, and Administrative News: 96th Congress—Second Session* (West 1980).

U.S. Congress. (1980b). Stevenson-Wydler Technology Innovation Act of 1980, Legislative History PL 96–480. *United States Code, Congressional, and Administrative News: 96th Congress—Second Session* (West 1980).

U.S. Congress. (1984). National Cooperative Research Act of 1984, Legislative History PL 98–462. *United States Code, Congressional, and Administrative News: 98th Congress—Second Session* (West 1984).

CHAPTER 2

Agency of Industrial Science and Technology, Ministry of International Trade and Industry. (1988). *White paper on science and technology, 1991.* Tokyo: Author.

Anderson, A. M. (1984). *Science and technology in Japan.* London: Longman Group.

Bundesministerium fur Forschung und Technologie. (1988, February). *Statistische informationen.* Bonn: Author.

Cabinet Office. (Series). *Annual review of government funded R&D.* London: Her Majesty's Stationery Office.

Cabinet Office Advisory Council for Applied Research and Development. (1986, May). *Exploitable areas of science.* London: Her Majesty's Stationery Office.

Central Office of Information. (1989). *The promotion of science and technology in Britain.* London: Author.

Commission of the European Communities. (1987). *The European community of research and technology.* Luxembourg: Author.

Commission of the European Communities. (1988). *The first report on the state of science and technology in Europe.* Luxembourg: Author.

Embassy of France (Washington, DC), Science and Technology Office. (1989, especially Summer). *French advances in science and technology* [newsletter].

Federal Ministry for Research and Technology (Federal Republic of Germany). (1988). *Report of the federal government on research* (abridged version). Bonn: Author.

Gamota, G., & Frieman, W. (1988). *Gaining ground: Japan's strides in science and technology.* Cambridge, MA: Ballinger.

Innovation, using technology. (1988, January). In *DTI—The department for enterprise* (White Paper) (pp. 33–37). London: Her Majesty's Stationery Office.

Institute for Future Technology. (1988). *Future technology in Japan: Forecast to the year 2015.* Tokyo: Author.

Lederman, L. L. (1985, June). Science and technology in Europe: A survey. *Science and Public Policy, 12* (3), 131–143.

Lederman, L. L. (1987, September). Science and technology policies and priorities: A comparative analysis. *Science, 237,* 1125–1133.

Lederman, L. L. (1989). U.S. research and development policy and priorities and comparisons with selected countries: Canada, France, the Federal Republic of Germany, Japan, Sweden, the United Kingdom and the United States. In B. Abu-Laban (Ed.), *University research and the future of Canada* (pp. 475–505). Ottawa: University of Ottawa Press.

Lederman, L. L., Lehming, R., & Bond, J. (1986, April). Research policies and strategies in six countries: A comparative analysis. *Science and Public Policy, 13* (2), 67–76.

Martin, B., & Irvine, J. (1989). *Research foresight, creating the future*. London: Pinter Publishers.

McLoughlin, G. J. (1989, March). *The Europe 1992 plan: Science and technology issues*. Washington, DC: Congressional Research Service, Library of Congress.

Ministere de la Recherche et de la Technologie. (1986). *Recherche et developpement dans les entreprises*. Paris: Author.

Ministere de la Recherche et de la Technologie. (1988). *Rapport arnexe sur l'etat de la recherche et du developpement technologique: Activities en 1987 et 1988 et perspectives 1989*. Paris: Author.

National Science Foundation, Division of Science Resources Studies. (1986). *The science and technology resources of West Germany: A comparison with the United States* (NSF 86–310). Washington, DC: Author.

National Science Foundation, Division of Science Resources Studies. (1988a). *The science and technology resources of Japan: A comparison with the United States* (NSF 88–318). Washington, DC: Author.

National Science Foundation, National Science Board. (1988b). *Science and engineering indicators—1987* (biennial). Washington, DC: Author.

National Science Foundation, Directorate for Scientific, Technology and International Affairs, Division of Science Resources Studies. (1991). *International science and technology data update* (annual). Washington, DC: Author.

National Technical Information Service. (1989). *Directory of Japanese technical resources in the U.S.* (#PB 89–158869). Springfield, VA: Author.

Organization for Economic Cooperation and Development. (1988). *Science and technology policy outlook, 1985*. Paris: Author.

Research and development in the United Kingdom in 1986. (1988, August). *Economic Trends*, pp. 82–88.

Science and technology in Europe. (1988, December). *Science and Public Policy, 15* (6), 366–430.

Science in Europe. (1989, April 27). *Nature, 338*, 717–736.

CHAPTER 3

Andrews, E. (1993, February 24). Clinton's technology plan would redirect billions from military research. *New York Times*, p. A8.

Baily, M., & Chakrabarti, A. (1988). *Innovation and the productivity crisis*. Washington, DC: Brookings Institution.

Branscomb, L. (1992). The factory of the future. *Minnesota Technology*, p. 7.

Clinton, W. J., & Gore, A., Jr. (1993). *Technology for America's economic growth: A new direction to build economic strength*. Washington, DC: Executive Office of the President.

Clinton, W. J., & Gore, A., Jr. (1994). *Science in the national interest*. Washington, DC: Executive Office of the President.

Coburn, C. (Ed.). (1995). *Partnerships: A compendium of state and federal cooperative technology programs: 1995*. Columbus, OH: Batelle Press.

Cohen, S., & Zysman, J. (1987). *Manufacturing matters: The myth of the post-industrial economy*. New York: Basic Books.

Competitiveness Policy Council. (1992). *First annual report to the president and congress: Building a competitive America*. Washington, DC: U.S. Government Printing Office.

Council on Competitiveness. (1991). *Gaining new ground: Technology priorities for America's future*. Washington, DC: Author.

DiFilippo, A. (1990). *From industry to arms: The political economy of high technology*. Westport, CT: Greenwood Press.

Eisinger, P. (1988). *The rise of the entrepreneurial state: State and local economic development policy in the United States*. Madison: University of Wisconsin Press.

Ergas, H. (1987). Does technology policy matter? In B. Guile & H. Brooks (Eds.), *Technology and global competition* (pp. 191–245). Washington, DC: National Academy of Engineering.

Feller, I. (1992). American state governments as models for national science policy. *Journal of Policy Analysis and Management, 11*, 288–309.

Flamm, K. (1987). *Targeting the computer: Government support and international competition*. Washington, DC: Brookings Institution.

Fosler, R. S. (1988). *The new economic role of American states*. New York: Oxford University Press.

General Accounting Office. (1988, August). *Engineering Research Centers: NSF program management and industry sponsorship: Report to congressional requesters*. Washington, DC: Author.

Goodrich, G. (1960). *Government promotion of American canals and railroads, 1800–1890*. New York: Basic Books.

The government's guiding hand: An interview with ex-DARPA director Craig Fields. (1991, February/March). *Technology Review*, 35–40.

Graham, O. (1992). *Losing time: The industrial policy debate*. Cambridge: Harvard University Press.

Hafner, K. (1993, November 7). Does industrial policy work? Lessons from Sematech. *New York Times*, p. F5.

Hansen, S. (1990). Industrial policies in the American states: Historical and comparative perspectives. In E. Yanarella & W. Green (Eds.), *The politics of industrial recruitment* (pp. 3–22). Westport, CT: Greenwood Press.

Hayes, R., & Wheelwright, S. (1984). *Restoring our competitive edge: Competing through manufacturing*. New York: Wiley.

Holusha, J. (1993a, February 16). Traveling high-tech agents help update small factories. *New York Times*, p. A1.

Holusha, J. (1993b, June 24). Nurturing technology in Ohio: An education model for federal programs. *New York Times*, p. D1.

Hounshell, D. (1984). *From the American system to mass production: 1800–1932*. Baltimore: Johns Hopkins University Press.

Johnson, C. (1982). *MITI and the Japanese miracle: The growth of industrial policy, 1925–75*. Stanford: Stanford University Press.

Johnson, C. (Ed.). (1984). *The industrial policy debate.* San Francisco, CA: The ICI Press.

Lehne, R. (1993). *Industry and politics: United States in comparative perspective.* Englewood Cliffs, NJ: Prentice-Hall.

Levinson, P. (1982). *The Federal entrepreneur: The nation's implicit industries policy.* Washington, DC: Urban Institute.

Manufacturing Technologies Centers Report. (1992). *Third year review panel.* Washington, DC: Department of Commerce.

McCraw, T. (1984). *Prophets of regulation.* Cambridge, MA: The Belknap Press of Harvard University Press.

Mowery, D., & Rosenberg, N. (1989). *Technology and the pursuit of economic growth.* Cambridge, MA: Cambridge University Press.

National Academy of Sciences, Committee on Science, Engineering and Public Policy. (1992). *The government role in civilian technology: building a new alliance.* Washington, DC: National Academy Press.

National Institute of Standards and Technology. (1992). *1992 report and proposal preparation kit.* Washington DC: U.S. Department of Commerce.

National Institute of Standards and Technology. (1993, January). *1992 annual report of visiting committee on advanced technology.* Washington, DC: Department of Commerce.

National Institute of Standards and Technology. (1996, April 26). *Fiscal Year 1996 Budget History.* Washington, DC: United States Department of Commerce Technology Administration. gopher://potomac.nist.gov:7346/0/.docs/.budget/fy96bdg. hst

National Science Board. (1996). *Science and Engineering Indicators—1996.* Washington, DC: U.S. Government Printing Office, 1996 (NSB 96–21).

North, D. (1990). *Institutions, institutional change and economic performance.* Cambridge, MA: Cambridge University Press.

Norton, R. D. (1986). Industrial policy and American renewal. *Journal of Economic Literature, 24,* 4.

Office of Technology Assessment. (1995). *The effectiveness of research and experimentation tax credits.* Washington, DC: U.S. Government Printing Office (OTA-8P-ITC-174).

Osborne, D. (1988). *Laboratories of democracy.* Boston: Harvard Business School Press.

Ouchi, W. (1981). *Theory Z: How American businesses can meet the Japanese challenge.* Reading, MA: Addison-Wesley.

Scheiber, H. (1987). *State law and industrial policy in American development, 1790–1985.* New York: Rockefeller Institute.

Schmandt, J., & Wilson, R. (1987). *Promoting high-technology industry: Initiatives and policies for state governments.* Boulder, CO: Westview Press.

Shapira, P. (1990). Learning from state initiatives in industrial extension. *Economic Development Quarterly 4,* 186–202.

Smith, B. (1990). *American science policy since World War II.* Washington, DC: Brookings Institution.

Sternberg, E. (1992). *Photonic technology and industrial policy: U.S. responses to technological change.* Albany, NY: State University of New York Press.

Trezise, P. (1983). Industrial policy is not the major reason for Japan's success. *Brookings Review 2,* 13–18.

Uncle Sam's helping hand. (1994, April 2). *The Economist*, pp. 77–79.

Vogel, D. (1989). *Fluctuating fortunes: The political power of business in America*. New York: Basic Books.

Vogel, E. F. (1982). *Japan as number one: Lessons for America*. New York: Harper.

Wilks, S., & Wright, M. (Eds.). (1987). *Comparative government industry relations*. Oxford: Clarendon Press.

Wilson, G. (1990). *Business and politics: A comparative introduction*. 2nd ed. Chatham, NJ: Chatham House.

CHAPTER 4

Amsden, A. H. (1989). *Asia's next giant: South Korea and late industrialization*. New York: Oxford University Press.

Bernard, M., & Ravenhill, J. (1995). Beyond product cycles and flying geese: Regionalization, hierarchy, and the industrialization of East Asia. *World Politics, 47* (January), 171–209.

Chin, H. -S. (1986, November). *Science and technology development strategies: Experience of the Republic of Korea*. Paper presented at the International Workshop on Formulation of Science and Technology Policy, Seoul, Republic of Korea.

Choi, H. (1986). *Technology development in developing countries*. Tokyo: Asian Productivity Organization.

Chou, T. -C. (1988). American and Japanese direct foreign investment in Taiwan: A comparative study. *Hitotsubashi Journal of Economics, 29*, 165–177.

Collins, S. M. (1990). Lessons from Korean economic growth. *American Economic Association Papers and Proceedings, 80*, 113–117.

Deyo, F. C. (Ed.). (1987). *The political economy of new Asian industrialism*. Ithaca, NY: Cornell University Press.

Dunning, J. H. (1988). *Explaining international production*. Boston: Unwin Hyman.

Evans, P. (1979). *Dependent development: The alliance of multinational, state, and local capital in Brazil*. Princeton, NJ: Princeton University Press.

Fallows, J. (1994). *Looking at the sun: The rise of the new East Asian economic and political system*. New York: Vintage.

Graham, O. (1992). *Losing ground: The industrial policy debate*. Cambridge, MA: Harvard University Press.

Haggard, S., & Moon, C.-I. (1990). Institutions and economic policy: Theory and a Korean case study. *World Politics, 42*, 54–73.

Hahm, S. D., & Plein, C. (1994). *The political economy of technology transfer from the U.S. and Japan to Korea: Implications of host country policy strategies*. Working Paper, Georgetown University.

Hahm, S. D., & Plein, C. (1995a). Institutions and technological development in Korea: The role of the president. *Comparative Politics, 28*, 55–77.

Hahm, S. D., & Plein, C. (1995b). Structural and rational foundations of the decline of authoritarian-executive politics in Korea. In Wan-Ki Paik (Chair), *Seeking a new paradigm of public administration in democratic society: Proceedings of 1995 International Symposium of the Korean Association for Public Administration* (pp. 419–448) (Symposium held 24–26 October, 1995, Seoul, Republic of Korea). Seoul: Korean Association for Public Administration.

Hahm, S. D., Plein, C., & Florida, R. (1994). The politics of international technology transfer. *Policy Studies Journal, 22*, 311–321.

Hufbauer, G. C. (1970). The impact of national characteristics and technology on the commodity composition of trade in manufactured goods. In R. Vernon (Ed.), *The technology factor in international trade* (pp. 145–231). New York: Columbia University Press.

Kang, D. C. (1995). South Korean and Taiwanese development and the new institutional economics. *International Organization, 49*, 555–587.

Kim, L., & Dahlman, C. J. (1992). Technology policy for industrialization: An integrative framework and Korea's experience. *Research Policy, 21*, 437–452.

Kim, Y. -W. (1986, November). *Policy for promoting science and technology in Korea.* Paper presented at the International Workshop on Formulation of Science and Technology Policy, Seoul.

Kojima, K. (1973). A macroeconomic approach to foreign direct investment. *Hitotsubashi Journal of Economics, 14*, 1–14.

Kojima, K. (1977). Transfer of technology to developing countries—Japanese types versus American types. *Hitotsubashi Journal of Economics, 18*, 1–14.

Kojima, K. (1985). Japanese and American direct investment in Asia: A comparative analysis. *Hitotsubashi Journal of Economics, 26*, 1–35.

Korean Economic Planning Board. (1985). *Major Statistics of the Korean Economy.* Seoul: Author.

Korean Economic Planning Board. (1993). *The current state of foreign investment.* Seoul: Author.

Korean Ministry of Finance. (1993). *Trends in technology inducement.* Seoul: Author.

Korean Ministry of Science and Technology. (1986). *Science and technology annual.* Seoul: Author.

Krugman, P. (1994). Competitiveness: A dangerous obsession. *Foreign Affairs, 73*, 28–44.

Lall, S. (1993). Understanding technology development. *Development and Change, 24*, 719–753.

Lee, C. H. (1980). United States and Japanese direct investment in Korea: A comparative study. *Hitotsubashi Journal of Economics, 20*, 26–41.

Lee, C. H. (1984). Transfer of technology from Japan and the United States to Korean manufacturing industries: A comparative study. *Hitotsubashi Journal of Economics, 25*, 125–136.

Mardon, R. (1990). The state and the effective control of foreign capital: The case of South Korea. *World Politics, 43*, 111–138.

Mason, E. S., Kim, M. J., Perkins, D. H., Kim, K. S., & Cole, D. C. (1980). *The economic and social modernization of the Republic of Korea.* Cambridge, MA: Harvard University Press.

O'Donnell, G. (1973). *Modernization and bureaucratic authoritarianism: Studies in Latin American politics.* Berkeley: Institute for International Studies, University of California at Berkeley.

Pack, H., & Westphal, L. E. (1986). Industrial strategy and technological change. *Journal of Development Economics, 22*, 87–128.

Wade, R. (1992). East Asia's economic success: Conflicting perspectives, partial insights, shaky evidence. *World Politics, 45*, 270–320.

Westphal, L. E. (1990). Industrial policy in an export-propelled economy: Lessons from
    South Korea's experience. *Journal of Economic Perspective, 4*, 41–59.
Westphal, L. E., Kim, L., & Dahlman, C. J. (1985). Reflections on the Republic of Ko-
    rea's acquisition of technological capability. In N. Rosenberg & C. Frischtak
    (Eds.), *International Technology Transfer* (pp. 167–221). New York: Praeger
    Publishers.
World Bank. (1993). *The East Asian miracle: Economic growth and public policy.* New
    York: Oxford University Press.
Yang, Y. (1972). Foreign investments in developing countries: Korea. In P. Drysdale
    (Ed.), *Direct foreign investment in Asia and the Pacific* (pp. 242–257). Toronto:
    University of Toronto Press.
Young, J. A. (1988). Technology and competitiveness: A key to the economic future of
    the United States. *Science, 241* (July 15), 313–316.
Yu, H. -Y. (1986, November). *Technology transfer policy in Korea.* Paper presented at
    the International Workshop on Formulation of Science and Technology Policy,
    Seoul.

CHAPTER 5

Amanor, K. S. (1994). *The new frontier: Farmers' response to land degradation. A West
    African study.* Geneva and London: UNRISD and Zed Books.
Belloncle, G. (1989). Proposals for a new approach to extension services in Africa. In
    N. Roberts (Ed.), *Agricultural extension in Africa. A World Bank symposium*
    (pp. 37–44). (Symposium held February 1985, Abidjan, Côte d'Ivoire). Washing-
    ton, DC: World Bank.
Biggs, S. D. (1989). *A multiple sources of innovation model of agricultural research and
    technology promotion* (Agricultural Administration [Research and Extension] Net
    work Paper 6). London: Overseas Development Institute.
Bingen, R. J. (1985). *Food production and rural development in the Sahel: Lessons from
    Mali's Operation Riz-Segou.* Boulder, CO: Westview Press.
Bingen, R. J. (1995). *The role of U.S. farmers' organizations in agricultural research*
    (Unpublished report prepared for the Overseas Development Institute [London]).
    East Lansing, MI: Department of Resource Development, Michigan State Uni-
    versity.
Bingen, R. J., Simpson, B., & Berthé, A. (1994). *Analysis of service delivery systems to
    farmers and village associations in the Zone of the Office de la Haute Vallée du
    Niger* (Report). East Lansing, MI: Department of Resource Development, Mich-
    igan State University.
Borlaug, N., & Dowswell, C. R. (1996). Mobilising science and technology to get agri-
    culture moving in Africa. *Development Policy Review, 13*, 115–129.
Brett, E. A. (1993). Voluntary agencies as development organizations: Theorizing the
    problem of efficiency and accountability. *Development and Change, 24*, 269–303.
CIMMYT. (1980). *Planning technologies appropriate to farmers: Concepts and proce-
    dures.* Londres, Mexico: Author.
Cleaver, K. M., & Schreiber, G. A. (1994). *Reversing the spiral: The population, agri-
    culture and environment nexus in sub-Saharan Africa.* Washington, D.C.: The
    World Bank.

Collion, M. H. (1995). *On building a partnership in Mali between farmers and researchers* (Agricultural Administration [Research and Extension] Network Paper 54). London: Overseas Development Institute.

Dowswell, C. R. (1993). Strengthening the institutional foundations for modern agriculture in sub-Saharan Africa. In W. E. Swegle (Ed.), *Developing African agriculture: New initiatives for institutional cooperation* (pp. 99–107) (Conference held 28–30 July, 1993, Cotonou, Benin). Mexico, D. F.: SAA/Global 2000/CASIN.

Eicher, C. K. (1988, March). *An economic perspective on the Sasakawa–Global 2000 initiative to increase food production in sub-Saharan Africa.* Paper presented at the workshop on Reviewing the African Agricultural Projects, The Sasakawa-Global 2000 African Initiative, Nairobi.

Eicher, C. K. (1995). Zimbabwe's maize-based green revolution: Preconditions for replication. *World Development, 23* (5), 805–818.

English, J., Tiffen, M., & Mortimore, M. (1994). *Land resource management in Machakos District, Kenya 1930–1990* (World Bank Environment Paper 5). Washington, D.C.: The World Bank.

Farrington, J. (1995a). Mobilising science and technology or fostering organisational change? A response to Borlaug and Dowswell. *Development Policy Review, 13,* 131–133.

Farrington, J. (1995b). The changing public role in agricultural extension. *Food Policy Review, 20* (6), 537–544.

Ferguson, A. E. (1994). Gendered science: A critique of agricultural development. *American Anthropologist, 96,* 540–552.

Gamser, M. S. (1988). Innovation, technical assistance and development: The importance of technology users. *World Development, 16* (6), 711–721.

Gentil, D. (1989). A few questions on the training and visit method. In N. Roberts (Ed.), *Agricultural extension in Africa: A World Bank symposium* (pp. 25–30) (Symposium held February, 1985, Abidjan, Côte d'Ivoire). Washington, DC: The World Bank.

Gnägi, A. (1991). *Nous avons perdu le respect, mais la pitié n'est pas venus dans nos coeurs: Prozesse des sozialen wandels und soziokulturelle heterogenität im arrondissement Ouéléssébougou, Mali* (Unpublished report). Berne: Institut d'Ethnologie.

Hayami, Y., & Ruttan, V. W. (1985). *Agricultural development: An international perspective* (Rev. ed.). Baltimore, MD: Johns Hopkins University Press.

Hesseling, G., & LeRoy, E. (1990). Le droit et ses pratiques. *Politique Africaine, 40* (Décembre), 2–11.

Hock, D. W. (1995). The chaordic organization: Out of control and into order. *World Business Academy Perspectives, 9* (1), 5–18.

Jiggins, J., Reijntjes, C., & Lightfoot, C. (1996). Mobilising science and technology to get agriculture moving in Africa: A response to Borlaug and Dowswell. *Development Policy Review, 14,* 89–103.

Leisinger, K. M., Schmitt, K., & ISNAR (Eds.). (1995). *Survival in the Sahel: An ecological and developmental challenge.* The Hague: International Service for National Agricultural Research.

Mabogunje, A. L. (1995). The environmental challenges in sub-Saharan Africa. *Environment, 37* (4), 4–35.

Reardon, T. (1995). Sustainability issues for agricultural research strategies in the semi-arid tropics: Focus on the Sahel. *Agricultural Systems, 48,* 345–359.

Reardon, T., & Vosti, S. A. (1995). Links between rural poverty and the environment in developing countries: Asset categories and investment poverty. *World Development, 23* (9), 1495–1506.

Richards, P. (1985). *Indigenous agricultural revolution.* London: Unwin Hyman, Ltd.

Richards, P. (1989). Agriculture as performance. In R. Chambers, A. Pacey, & L. A. Trupp (Eds.), *Farmer first: Farmer innovation and agricultural research* (pp. 39–42). London: Intermediate Technology Publications.

Simpson, B. M. (1994). Gender and the social differentiation of local knowledge. *Indigenous Knowledge and Development Monitor, 2* (3), 21–23.

Simpson, B. M. (1995). *Knowledge, innovation and communication: Contributions of the formal and informal systems to agrarian change in the Office de la Haute Vallée du Niger, Mali.* Unpublished Ph.D. dissertation, Michigan State University, East Lansing, MI.

Tripp, R. (1993). Invisible hands, indigenous knowledge, and inevitable fads. *World Development, 21* (12), 2003–2016.

CHAPTER 6

Best, E. (1987, October 18). U.C. losing millions on inventions. *The San Francisco Examiner,* p. A1.

Gregory, W. D., & Sheahen, T. D. (1991). Technology transfer by spin-off companies versus licensing. In A. M. Brett, D. V. Gibson, & R. W. Smilor (Eds.), *University spin-off companies* (pp. 133–152). Savage, MD: Rowman & Littlefield.

UC's secret stock deals. (1993, June 20). *San Francisco Chronicle/Examiner,* p. E1.

Wilson, M., & Szygenda, S. (1991). Promoting university spin-offs through equity participation. In A. M. Brett, D. V. Gibson, & R. W. Smilor (Eds.), *University spin-off companies* (pp. 153–163). Savage, MD: Rowman & Littlefield.

CHAPTER 7

Brooks, H. (1986). National science policy and technological innovation. In R. Landau & N. Rosenberg (Eds.), *The positive sum strategy: Harnessing technology for economic growth* (pp. 119–167). Washington, DC: National Academy Press.

Bush, V. (1945). *Science—The endless frontier.* Washington, DC: U.S. Government Printing Office.

Campbell, D. T. (1971, April). *Methods for the experimenting society.* Paper presented at the meeting of the Eastern Psychological Association, Washington, DC.

Carnegie Commission on Science, Technology, and Government. (1992). *Science, technology, and the states in America's third century.* New York: Carnegie Commission.

Feller, I. (1990). University-industry R&D relationship. In J. Schmandt & R. Wilson (Eds.), *Growth policy in the age of high technology: The role of regions and states* (pp. 313–343). Boston: Unwin Hyman.

Government-University-Industry Research Roundtable. (1991). *Industrial perspectives on innovation and interactions with universities.* Washington, DC: National Academy Press.

Kline, S. J., & Rosenberg, N. (1986). An overview of innovation. In R. Landau & N. Rosenberg (Eds.), *The positive sum strategy* (pp. 275–305). Washington, DC: National Academy Press.

Lee, Y., Roessner, D., Bozeman, B., & Shapira, P. (1996). Volume 2: case studies. In D. Roessner, Y. Lee, P. Shapira, & B. Bozeman, *Evaluation of Iowa State University's Center for Advanced Technology Development (CATD)* (pp. 1–38). Unpublished manuscript, Georgia Institute of Technology, School of Public Policy.

Mowery, D.C., & Rosenberg, N. (1989). *Technology and the pursuit of economic growth.* Cambridge, MA: Cambridge University Press.

National Academy of Engineering. (1995). *Risk and innovation: The role and importance of small high-tech companies in the U.S. economy.* Washington, DC: National Academy Press.

National Academy of Sciences. (1992). *The government role in civilian technology: Building a new alliance.* Washington, DC: National Academy Press.

Noble, T. (1990). *CATD: A unique technology development and transfer engine at ISU.* Paper delivered at the 15th Annual Meeting of the Technology Transfer Society, Dayton, Ohio.

President's Council of Advisors on Science and Technology. (1992). *Renewing the promise: Research universities and the nation.* Washington, DC: The White House.

Roessner, D., Lee, Y., Shapira, P., & Bozeman, B. (1996). *Evaluation of Iowa State University's Center for Advanced Technology Development (CATD).* Unpublished manuscript, Georgia Institute of Technology, School of Public Policy.

CHAPTER 8

Crow, M. M., & Emmert, M. (1984). Interorganizational management of R&D: University-industry relations and innovation. In B. Bozeman, M. Crow, and A. Link (Eds.), *Strategic management of industrial R&D* (pp. 255–275). Lexington, MA: D.C. Heath and Company.

Frye, A. L. (1985). *From source to use: Bringing university technology to the marketplace.* New York: American Management Association.

Geisler, E., & Rubenstein, A. H. (1989). University-industry relations: A review of major issues. In A. N. Link & G. Tassey (Eds.), *Cooperative research and development: The industry-university-government relationship* (pp. 43–62). Boston: Kluwer Academic Publishers.

Owen, J. V., & Entorf, J. F. (1989). Where factory meets faculty. *Manufacturing Engineering, 102,* 48–71.

Stewart, G. H., & Gibson, D. V. (1990). University and industry linkages: The Austin, Texas, study. In F. Williams & D. V. Gibson (Eds.), *Technology transfer: A communication perspective* (pp. 109–129). Newbury Park, CA: Sage Publications.

CHAPTER 9

Armstrong, J. A. (1991). An industry perspective on the changing university. In D. S. Zinberg (Ed.), *The changing university* (pp. 17–23). London: Kluwer Academic Publishers.

Association of University Technology Managers, Inc. (AUTM). (1995). *AUTM Licensing Survey Fiscal Year 1994.* Cranbury, NJ: The Association of University Managers, Inc.

Bayh-Dole Act of 1980, 35 U.S.C. §200 *et seq.* Washington, DC: U.S. Government Printing Office, 1995.

Blumenthal, D., Cluck, M., Louis, K.-S., Stoto, M. A., & Wise, D. (1986). University-industry research relationships in biotechnology: Implications for the university. *Science, 232,* 1361–1366.

Bok, D. (1991). "Reconciling conflicts: The challenge for the university." In D. S. Zinberg (Ed.), *The changing university* (pp. 15–16). London: Kluwer Academic Publishers.

Bollen, K. A., & Long, J. S. (Eds.). (1993). *Testing structural equation models.* Newbury Park, CA: Sage Publications.

Brooks, H. (1986). National science policy and technological innovation. In R. Landau & N. Rosenberg (Eds.), *The positive-sum strategy: Harnessing technology for economic growth* (pp. 119–167). Washington DC: National Academy Press.

Campbell, T., & Slaughter, S. (1995, February). *Protecting the public's trust: A search for balance among benefits and conflicts in university-industry relations.* Paper presented at the AAAS Conference on University-Industry Cooperation, Atlanta, GA.

Cohen, W., Florida, R., & Goe, W. R. (1994). *University industry research centers in the United States.* Unpublished manuscript, Carnegie Mellon University, Center for Economic Development, H. John Heinz III School of Public Policy and Management.

Cooperative Research Act of 1984, 15 U.S.C. §4301 *et seq.* (U.S. Government Printing Office, 1995).

England, J. M. (1982). *A patron for pure science.* Washington, DC: National Science Foundation.

Feller, I. (1990). Universities as engines of R&D-based economic growth: They think they can. *Research Policy, 19,* 335–348.

Feller, I., & Geiger, R. L. (1993). *The dispersion of academic research during the 1980s.* The Pennsylvania State University, Institute for Policy Research and Evaluation, Graduate School of Public Policy and Administration.

Government-University-Industry Research Roundtable. (1991). *Industrial perspectives on innovation and interactions with universities.* Washington, DC: National Academy Press.

Guston, D. H., & Keniston, K. (1994). The social contract for science. In D. H. Guston & K. Keniston (Eds.), *The fragile contract* (pp. 1–25). Cambridge, MA: MIT Press.

Lee, Y. S. (1995). *The academic climate and technological innovation* (National Science Foundation Report, Research on Science and Technology Program, SBR 9314). Unpublished manuscript, Iowa State University, Department of Political Science.

Lee, Y. S. (1996). "Technology transfer" and the research university: A search for the boundaries of university-industry collaboration. *Research Policy, 25,* 843–863.

Mansfield, E. (1995, February). *Links between academic research and industrial innovation.* Paper presented at the AAAS Conference on University-Industry Cooperation, Atlanta, GA.

Mary Good: A champion for science and technology. (1995, October). *Chemical and Engineering News*, 16–19.

Matkin, G. W. (1994). Technology and public policy: Lessons from a case study. *Policy Studies Journal, 22* (2), 371–383.

Morgan, R. P., Strickland, D. E., Kannankutty, N., & Spelman, C. (1993, June). *Engineering research in U.S. universities: How university-based research directors see it.* Paper presented at ASEE Annual Conference, Washington, DC.

National Academy of Sciences. (1992). *The government role in civilian technology: Building a new alliance.* Washington, DC: National Academy Press.

National Science Board. (1992). *A foundation for the 21st century: A progressive framework for the National Science Foundation.* Washington, DC: National Science Foundation.

Paget, K. M. (1990). State government–university cooperation. In J. Schmandt & R. Wilson (Eds.), *Growth policy in the age of high technology* (pp. 344–380). Boston: Unwin Hyman.

Pressman, L., Guterman, S. K., Abrams, I., Geist, D. E., & Nelson, L. L. (1995). Preproduction investment and jobs induced by MIT exclusive patent licenses: A preliminary model to measure the economic impact of university licensing. *Journal of the Association of University Technology Managers, 7*, 49–81.

Rahm, D. (1995, February). *Factors promoting and inhibiting technology transfer from university to firm.* Paper presented at the AAAS Conference on University-Industry Cooperation, Atlanta, GA.

Rosenberg, N., & Nelson, R. (1994). American universities and technical advance in industry. *Research Policy, 23*, 323–348.

Slaughter, S. (1993). Beyond basic science: Research university presidents' narratives of science policy. *Science, Technology, & Human Values, 18* (3), 278–302.

Smith, B. (1990). *American science policy since World War II.* Washington, DC: The Brookings Institution.

Smith, N. (1993, October). Prospects for technology transfer funding. In Yong S. Lee (Chair), *Technology transfer and public policy symposium: Preparing for the 21st century.* Ames, IA: Iowa State University.

Stevenson-Wydler Technology Innovation Act of 1980, 15 U.S.C. §3701 *et seq.* Washington, DC: U.S. Government Printing Office, 1995.

CHAPTER 10

Andrews, E. (1993, February 16). Swords to plowshares: The bureaucratic snags. *New York Times*, p. C1.

Atlantic Council. (1992). *Technology transfer to industry from the U.S. Department of Energy defense program laboratories.* Washington, DC: Author.

Baron, S. (1990). Overcoming barriers to technology transfer. *Research-Technology Management, 33* (1), 38–43.

Berman, E. (1990). R&D consortia: What impact on competitiveness? *Journal of Technology Transfer, 15* (3), 5–12.

Berman, E. (1992). The politics of federal technology policy: 1980–1988. *Policy Studies Review, 10* (4), 28–41.

Betz, F. (1993). *Strategic technology management.* New York: McGraw-Hill.

Bozeman, B., & Coker, K. (1992). Assessing the effectiveness of technology transfer from U.S. government R&D laboratories: The impact of market orientation. *Technovation, 12* (4), 239–255.

Council on Competitiveness. (1992). *Industry as a customer of the federal laboratories.* Washington, DC: Author.

Energy Advisory Board. (1992). *A report to the secretary on the Department of Energy national laboratories.* Washington, DC: Department of Energy.

Federal Laboratory Consortium. (1992). *Report to Congress and the federal agencies.* Washington, DC: Author.

General Accounting Office. (1989). *Technology transfer: Implementation status of the Federal Technology Transfer Act of 1986.* Washington, DC: U.S. Government Printing Office.

Ham, R., & Mowery, D. (1995). Improving industry-government cooperative R&D. *Issues in Science and Technology, 11* (4), 67–74.

Marshall, W., & Schram, M. (1993). *Mandate for change.* New York: Berkley Books.

National Academy of Sciences. (1992). *The government role in civilian technology: Building a new alliance.* Washington, DC: National Academy Press.

National Institute of Standards and Technology. (1992). *Cooperative research and development agreement with the National Institute of Standards and Technology.* Gaithersburg, MD: Author.

Osborne, D., & Gaebler, T. (1992). *Reinventing government: How the entrepreneurial spirit is transforming the public sector.* Reading, MA: Addison-Wesley.

RD&D Report. (1993, February). *Federal agency CRADA database.* Washington, DC: Technology Publishing Group.

Roessner, D., & Bean, A. (1991). How industry interacts with federal laboratories. *Research-Technology Management, 34* (4), 22–25.

Stewart, C. (1987). Technology transfer versus diffusion: A conceptual clarification. *Journal of Technology Transfer, 12* (4), 71–79.

U.S. Congress. (1992, December 4). *Hearings on obstacles to technology transfer.* U.S. House of Representatives Committee on Small Business, Subcommittee on Regulation, Business Opportunities and Energy. Washington, DC: U.S. Government Printing Office.

U.S. Department of Commerce. (1993). *Technology transfer under the Stevenson-Wydler Technology Innovation Act: The second biennial report.* Washington, DC: Office of the Secretary of Commerce.

U.S. Department of Commerce. (1994, February 16). *Update on CRADAs. Memo of the assistant secretary for technology policy and administration.* Washington, DC: Author.

U.S. Department of Commerce, Office of Technology Policy. (1996). *Effective partnering: A report to Congress on federal technology partnerships.* Washington, DC: Author.

White House. (1993, February 22). *Technology for America's economic growth: A new direction to build economic strength.* Washington, DC: U.S. Government Printing Office.

CHAPTER 11

Blau, P., & Schoenherr, R. (1971). *The structure of organizations.* New York: Basic Books.

Bloch, E. (1991, February). *Toward a U.S. technology strategy.* Washington, DC: National Academy Press.

Bozeman, B., & Coker, K. (1992). Assessing the effectiveness of technology transfer from U.S. R&D laboratories: The impact of market orientation. *Technovation, 12* (4), 239–256.

Bozeman, B., & Crow, M. (1987). R&D laboratories' environmental contexts: Are the government lab–industrial lab stereotypes still valid? *Research Policy, 16* (5), 229-258.

Bozeman, B., & Crow, M. (1988). *U.S. R&D laboratories and their environments: Public and market influence.* Report prepared for the National Science Foundation. Syracuse, NY: Technology and Information Policy Program.

Bozeman, B., & Crow, M. (1990). The environment of U.S. R&D laboratories: Political and market influences. *Policy Sciences, 23* (1), 25–26.

Bozeman, B., & Crow, M. (1991). Technology transfer from U.S. government and university R&D laboratories. *Technovation, 11* (4), 231–246.

Bozeman, B., & Fellows, M. (1988). Technology transfer at the U.S. national laboratories. *Evaluation and Program Planning, 11* (1), 65–75.

Bozeman, B., & Link, A. (1984). Tax incentives for R&D: A critical evaluation. *Research Policy, 13* (1), 21–31.

Bozeman, B., & Link, A. (1985). Public support for private R&D: The case of the joint venture research tax credit. *Journal of Policy Analysis and Management, 4* (3), 370–382.

Bucy, J. F. (1985, Summer). Meeting the competitive challenge: The case for R&D tax credits. *Issues in Science and Technology, 1* (4), 69–78.

Burns, T., & Stalker, G. (1961). *The management of innovation.* London: Tavistock.

Child, J. (1972). Organizational structure, environment, and performance: The role of strategic choice. *Sociology, 6,* 1–22.

Conference Board. (1987). *Getting more out of science and technology.* Research Report No. 904. New York: Author.

Crow, M., & Bozeman, B. (1991). A new typology for R&D laboratories: Implications for policy analysis. *Journal of Policy Analysis and Management, 6* (3), 328–341.

Galbraith, J. (1977). *Organization design.* Reading, MA: Addison-Wesley.

General Accounting Office. (1989). *Technology transfer: Implementation status of the federal technology transfer act of 1986.* Washington, DC: Author.

Government research centers directory. (1987). Detroit: Gale Research Company.

Government research centers directory. (1990). Detroit: Gale Research Company.

Hage, J., & Aiken, M. (1969). Routine technology, social structure and organizational goals. *Administrative Science Quarterly, 14* (3), 366–376.

Hall, R. H. (1968). Professionalization and bureaucratization. *American Sociological Review, 33* (1), 92–104.

Herman, J. (1983). Redefining the federal government's role in technology transfer. *Research Management, 26* (1), 21–24.

Hood, C., & Dunsire, A. (1981). *Bureaumetrics.* University, AL: University of Alabama Press.

Industrial research laboratories in the U.S. (1987). New York: R. R. Bowker Company.

Kearns, D. (1990). Federal labs teem with R&D opportunities. *Chemical Engineering, 97* (4), 131–137.

Krieger, J. H. (1987, April 27). Cooperation key to US technology remaining competitive. *Chemical and Engineering News, 65* (17), 24–28.

Landau, R., & Hannay, N. B. (1981). *Taxation, technology, and the U.S. economy.* New York: Pergamon Press.

Link, A., & Tassey, G. (1987). *Strategies for technology-based competition.* Lexington, MA: Lexington Books.

Magaziner, I., & Reich, R. (1983). *Minding America's business.* New York: Vintage Books.

Massachusetts Institute of Technology Commission on Industrial Productivity. (1989). *Made in America: Regaining the competitive edge.* Cambridge, MA: MIT Press.

Morone, J., & Ivins, R. (1982). Problems and opportunities in technology transfer from the national laboratories to industry. *Research Management, 25* (3), 35–44.

National Academy of Sciences. (1978). *Technology, trade, and the U.S. economy.* Washington, DC: Author.

National Governors' Association. (1987). *The role of science and technology in economic competitiveness.* New York: Author.

O'Keefe, T. G. (1982). Evaluating technology transfer: Some problems and solutions. *Journal of Technology Transfer, 6* (2), 53.

President's Commission on Industrial Competitiveness. (1985). *Global competition: The new reality.* Washington, DC: U.S. Government Printing Office.

Rahm, D., Bozeman, B., & Crow, M. (1988). U.S. competitiveness and technology transfer. *Public Administration Review, 48* (6), 969–978.

Research centers directory. (1987). Detroit: Gale Research Company.

Schriesheim, A. (1990, Winter). Toward a golden age for technology transfer. *Issues in Science and Technology 7* (2), 52–58.

Starbuck, W., & Nystrom, P. (Eds.). (1981). *Handbook of organizational design.* New York: Oxford University Press.

Thompson, J. D. (1967). *Organizations in action.* New York: McGraw-Hill.

U.S. Congress, House of Representatives. (1985, July 15). *Technology transfer and patent policy: DOE and other perspectives.* Hearing before the Subcommittee on Science, Research, and Technology of the Committee on Science and Technology, 99th Cong., 1st Sess. Washington, DC: U.S. Government Printing Office.

Weijo, M. O. (1987). Strategies for promoting technology transfer to the private sector. *Journal of Technology Transfer, 11* (2), 47–52.

Werner, J., & Bremer, J. (1991, Spring). Hard lessons in cooperative research. *Issues in Science and Technology, 7* (3), 44–49.

White House Science Council. (1983). *Report of the federal laboratory review panel.* Washington, DC: U.S. Government Printing Office.

Woodward, J. (1965). *Industrial organization.* London: Oxford University Press.

CHAPTER 12

Alic, J. A., Branscomb, L. M., Brooks, H., Carter, A. B., & Epstein, G. (1992). *Beyond spin-off.* Boston, MA: Harvard Business School Press.

Bear Stearns Brokerage. (1995). *The evolving structure of the defense industry.* Unpublished briefing.

Bitzinger, R. A. (1993). *Adjusting to the drawdown: The transition in the defense industry.* Washington, DC: Defense Budget Project.

Carnegie Commission Report on Science, Technology, and Government. (1990). *New thinking and American defense technology.* New York: Author.

Center for Strategic and International Studies Steering Committee on Security and Technology. (1991). *Integrating commercial and military technologies for national strength: An agenda for change.* Washington, DC: Author.

Defense Conversion Commission. (1992). *Adjusting to the drawdown.* Washington, DC: Department of Defense.

Johnson, S., & Blaker, J. (1996, July). The FY 1997–2001 defense budget. *Strategic Forum, 80*, 1–2.

Koonce, D. M. (1993). *Current trends in the defense industry: A financial overview.* Unpublished briefing.

Logistics Management Institute. (1993). *From war to peace: A history of past conversions.* Washington, DC: Author.

Milspec reform stirs resistance: Program manager, attorneys concerned about risks. (1993, July 15). *Washington Technology*, p. 16.

Mintz, J. (1993, June 27). Is conversion a wash? *Washington Post*, business section, p. 1.

U.S. Congress, Office of Technology Assessment. (1991). *Redesigning defense: Planning the transition to the future U.S. defense industrial base.* Washington, DC: U.S. Government Printing Office.

Weidenbaum, M. (1992). *Small wars, big defense: Paying for the military after the Cold War.* New York: Twentieth Century Fund.

CHAPTER 13

Business–Higher Education Forum. (1988). *Beyond the rhetoric: Evaluating university-industry cooperation in research and technology exchange.* Washington, DC: Author.

Cohen, W., & Levinthal, D. (1989). Innovation and learning: The two faces of R&D. *Economic Journal 99*, 569–596.

Cohen, W., & Levinthal, D. (1990). Absorptive capacity: A new perspective on learning and innovation. *Administrative Science Quarterly, 35*, 128–152.

Feller, I. (1990). University-industry R&D relationships. In J. Schmandt & R. Wilson (Eds.), *Growth policy in the age of high technology: The role of the regions and states* (pp. 313–343). Winchester, MA: Unwin Hyman.

General Accounting Office. (1988, August). *Engineering research centers: NSF program management and industry sponsorship.* Document RCED-88-177. Washington, DC: Author.

Goldstein, H. A., & Luger, M. I. (1990). *Universities as instruments of technology-based economic development policy.* Unpublished paper, University of North Carolina, Chapel Hill.

Granstrand, O., & Sjaalander, S. (1990). Managing innovation in multi-technology corporations. *Research Policy, 19*, 35–36.

Hamilton, W. F., & Singh, H. (1992). The evolution of corporate capabilities in emerging technologies. *Interfaces, 22*, 13–23.

Link, A., & Bauer, L. (1989). *Cooperative research in U.S. manufacturing: Assessing policy initiatives and corporate strategies.* Lexington, MA: Lexington Books.

Mansfield, E. (1988). The speed and cost of industrial innovation in Japan and the United States: External vs. internal technology. *Management Science, 34*, 1157–1168.

Mowery, D., & Rosenberg, N. (1989). *Technology and the pursuit of economic growth.* New York: Cambridge University Press.

Pavitt, K. (1984). Sectoral patterns of technological change: Toward a taxonomy and theory. *Research Policy, 13*, 343–373.

Pearman, D. (1993). Making technology partnerships with government work. In D. O. Thompson & D. E. Chimenti (Eds.), *Review of progress in quantitative nondestructive evaluation, vol. 12* (pp. 31–39). New York: Plenum Press.

Rees, J., & Debbage, K. (1992, Spring). Industry knowledge sources and the role of universities. *Policy Studies Review, 11* (1), 6–25.

Roessner, D. J., & Bean, A. S. (1990, Fall). Federal technology transfer: Industry interactions with federal laboratories. *Journal of Technology Transfer, 15* (4), 5–14.

Roessner, D. J., & Bean, A. S. (1991, July/August). How industry interacts with federal labs. *Research Technology Management, 34* (4), 22–25.

Roessner, D. J., & Wise, A. (1993, May). *Patterns of industry interactions with federal laboratories* (Final report to the U.S. Department of Energy and the Industrial Research Institute). Atlanta: Georgia Institute of Technology, School of Public Policy.

Rosenberg, N. (1990). Why do firms do basic research (with their own money)? *Research Policy, 19*, 165–174.

Sen, F., & Rubenstein, A. H. (1990). An exploration of factors affecting the integration of in-house R&D with external technology acquisition strategies of a firm. *IEEE Transactions on Engineering Management, 37*, 246–258.

Technology acquisition: At a critical junction. (1993, February). *Focus*, p. 8.

Index

About the Contributors

EVAN MICHAEL BERMAN is a faculty member in the Department of Public Administration at the University of Central Florida (Orlando, FL). His research interests are in productivity, technology, quality, organizational behavior, and ethics. He has published widely in these areas, including in such journals as *Public Administration Review*, *Policy Studies Journal*, *Organizational Dynamics*, and *Administration and Society*. He has previously worked as a policy analyst for the National Science Foundation.

R. JAMES BINGEN is an associate professor in the Department of Resource Development at Michigan State University. He has been working on technology transfer and development issues in West Africa for over 25 years, and he is the author of a book and several articles on agriculture and rural development in Mali.

BARRY BOZEMAN is the director of the School of Public Policy and a professor of public policy at the Georgia Institute of Technology. He specializes in science and technology policy and organization theory. Bozeman's most recent book (written with Michael Crow) is *Limited by Design: R&D Laboratories in the National Innovation System*.

LINDA BRANDT is a professor and chair of the Department of Acquisition at the Industrial College of the Armed Forces (ICAF), National Defense University. She directs the Department of Defense's senior acquisitions educational program. Prior to joining ICAF, Brandt served as a senior analyst at the Center for Naval Analyses and also for the Department of the Navy.

RICHARD GAERTNER is the former director of the Center for Advanced Technology and Development in the Institute for Physical Research and Technology, Iowa State University.

SUNG DEUK HAHM is an assistant professor of public policy at Korea University, Seoul. He is also affiliated with the School of Public Policy and Business Administration at Georgetown University. He serves as a managing editor of *Governance*. He has published widely in the areas of international political economy, public budgeting and finance, and science and technology policy.

RENÉE J. JOHNSON is an assistant professor of political science at the University of Florida.

LEONARD L. LEDERMAN is a former senior staff associate and director of the Research on Science and Technology Program, Directorate for Social, Behavioral and Economic Sciences, National Science Foundation.

YONG S. LEE is a professor of political science at Iowa State University and is well known for his contributions to science and technology policy and public administration research. He has written a wide range of articles, book chapters, and monographs dealing with the subject of government-university-industry relations, the academic climate of technological innovation, and new science and public administration. He has also published many articles that integrate constitutional law with public administration theory. His latest book on this topic is *Public Personnel Administration and Constitutional Values*.

GARY W. MATKIN is associate dean of university extension at the University of California, Berkeley. He is chief academic officer for UC Berkeley Extension's program. He has written *Effective Budgeting in Continuing Education*, *Technology Transfer and the University*, and *Using Financial Information in Continuing Education: Accepted Methods and New Approaches*.

CHRISTOPHER PLEIN is an assistant professor of public administration at West Virginia University. He is an expert on agenda setting and issue definition, science and technology policy, and comparative policy and administration. His work has been published in various edited books and journals, including *Comparative Politics*, *Policy Studies Journal*, and *Science, Technology, and Human Values*.

DIANNE RAHM is an associate professor of political science and director of the public administration graduate program at Iowa State University. Rahm specializes in science and technology policy, environmental policy, and information technology. She is the coeditor of *Technology and U.S. Competitiveness: An*

Institutional Focus and has published many articles and book chapters dealing with science, technology, and public policy.

J. DAVID ROESSNER is a professor of public policy at the Georgia Institute of Technology, co-director of the Technology Policy and Assessment Center at Georgia Tech, and currently program manager for Technology Policy at SRI International. Formerly, he was Principal Scientist and Group Manager for Industrial Policy and Planning at the Solar Energy Research Institute in Golden, Colorado, and Policy Analyst for the R&D Assessment Program and Acting Leader of the Working Group on Innovation Processes and Management in the Division of Policy Research and Analysis with the National Science Foundation.

BRENT SIMPSON is a lecturer in Rural Development and convener of the Rural Policy and Project Planning Programme, Institute of Social Studies, The Hague, The Netherlands.

PAUL TESKE is an associate professor of political science at SUNY Stony Brook and is an affiliated research fellow with the Columbia University Institute for TeleInformation.

ANNE WISE is program manager of the Energy Products Division of Motorola Corporation at Lawrenceville, Georgia.

DATE DUE

~~NOV 1 6 1998~~ ~~MAR 1 0 1999~~		
~~APR 0 4 1999~~		
~~JUL 1 6 2001~~		
~~JAN 0 2 2003~~		
		Printed in USA